Also by Peter Greenberg

The Travel Detective: How to Get the Best Service and
the Best Deals from Airlines, Hotels, Cruise Ships,
and Car Rental Agencies

The Travel Detective
Flight Crew Confidential

The Travel Detective
Flight Crew Confidential

People Who Fly for a Living
Reveal Insider Secrets and Hidden
Values in Cities and Airports
Around the World

Peter Greenberg

VILLARD  NEW YORK

Library of Congress Cataloging-in-Publication Data

Greenberg, Peter.
    The travel detective flight crew confidential: people who fly for a living reveal insider secrets and hidden values in cities and airports around the world / Peter Greenberg.
        p.   cm.
    ISBN 0-375-75971-9 (trade paper)
    1. Travel.   I. Title.

G151 .G74   2002
910—dc21   2002024963

Villard Books website address: www.villard.com

Printed in the United States of America

98765432

First Edition

This book is dedicated to the stewards and stewardesses, to the pilots and pursers, to the flight attendants and cockpit crews—and to all of the people who remember the glory of air travel. There was a time when getting there really was half the fun—and this book celebrates the people who still make that possible, not just in the air but, most important, on the ground.

Acknowledgments

The people who helped me with this book are nothing less than air traffic controllers. It's one thing to want to talk to pilots and flight attendants. It's quite another to find them in any one place and at any one time. The biggest challenge is catching up with them long enough to essentially debrief them about their lives—not to mention get them to reveal some of their layover secrets.

My research team didn't sleep much, because with flight crews it's always 7 A.M. *somewhere* in the world. The team networked contacts, interviewed crews, tracked down leads, and fact-checked all the information in this book.

In some cases, they went out to airports themselves and waited for certain flight crews to arrive after a long flight or got out to the airports or hotels at ridiculous hours to hook up with crews leaving for late-night or early-morning flights.

When it came to fact-checking, the same twenty-four-hour clock ruled. The team, led by my dedicated and talented research chief, Cheryl Chaney (who got no sleep at all), networked contacts, transcribed interviews, and did not depend on their computers' spell-check function. They did the detail work the old-fashioned way: they worked the phones. My thanks to Emily Lunz, Penny Marston, Sonja Rabé, and Erin Schelcher, who worked extremely long hours to get, organize, and verify the information in this book. Interns Erin Papworth, Ester Stokman, Susan Snyder, and Gail Strickland also were a big help.

Part of my team consisted of current or former flight crews, including Robin Bowens, a Chicago-based flight attendant for United who helped with domestic crews, and Barbara Hopewell (also from United), who interviewed some of the international crews when she wasn't working the flights herself to Auckland and Sydney. Then there's Liz Friedland, a former Pan Am supervisor whose most recent job was running Delta's Crown Room at La Guardia.

Finally, a big thanks to Aaron Kenedi, who batted in the bottom of the ninth inning with two outs and hit a home run, and to the indefatigable Amy Rennert, my agent, who went above and beyond, and essentially managed the home team. And, of course, to Bruce Tracy, my editor, who continues to believe, as I do, that it's not the product but the process, not just the style but the substance.

It is an understatement to say that this book would not have been possible without these incredible people.

Contents

Introduction

Layover A stop or stay in a place, esp. overnight; a halt, rest, delay. *N. Amer.*

I have been flying constantly—since I was an infant. How do I know this? It says so on the special certificate that hung on my bedroom wall, given to my parents after my first flight.

The document still hangs in my house, now in California:

> At the age of five months and six days, Peter Greenberg became a member of the Sky Cradle Club . . . aboard the American Airlines flagship, flying from New York to Los Angeles.

My mother still has the photo of me, wrapped in an airline blanket, being carried by a flight attendant down the steps of the DC-6 at the old Los Angeles terminal.

So it is not an exaggeration when I tell you that I've been in the capable hands—literally—of flight crews since a very early age.

They have helped me understand the process of travel, from both a passenger and an operational perspective. Air crews and airlines have allowed me, as a journalist, to train as a flight attendant, first with Continental in 1973 and later with United. I've learned the process with airlines ranging from Singapore Airlines to Western Airlines to PSA to Qantas.

I've trained in flight simulators with pilots from Western Airlines on Boeing 727s, and with Royal Jordanian on the old

L-1011s. I've jump-seated during the landing of a fully loaded 747 on the old runway 13 at Hong Kong's Kaitak Airport on Northwest Airlines, and flew the landing myself in the simulator and later with Cathay Pacific.

I've logged, by a rough estimate, thirty million real air miles since. A few years ago, a friend at one airline even had special luggage tags made for me that say "Flight Crew." "You're on the plane more than we are," she said by way of explanation.

But I'm first and foremost a passenger. Last year, there were more than *twenty-two million* flights in the world. That translates into something like twenty-four thousand takeoffs and landings every day in the United States. In an average year, I log close to 450,000 miles. And for as long as I can remember, I've had the utmost respect for the cockpit and cabin crews, who have a very tough job to do—lately, tougher than most people imagine. Every time I board a flight—more than two hundred times last year—I place my trust in these people. We all do.

I also talk to the crew on virtually every flight I take. That's how I learned so much about the process of travel, which I shared in the first *Travel Detective* book. Similarly, that's how I learned so much about the secrets of the great layover cities of the world in this edition.

In travel, the real bonus isn't getting a first-class seat—the ultimate upgrade is information. That's where flight crews come in. They have the best, and the most updated, information on where to go, what to do, whom to speak to, and whom to ignore.

To be sure, this book is a celebration, not only of these people and their work in the air, but of their efficiency and practical use of time on the ground. Flight crews are a living, talking gold mine of information.

Flight crews are the real travel experts when it comes to individual cities. They fly to the same cities often four to five times a month, and have only about twenty-four hours on the ground before their return flight. As a result, who knows better where to find the best deals? The best service? The best prices? Whether it's where to find a cheeseburger at three in the morning in Istanbul or an extra shoelace in São Paolo, flight crews know. Need a great massage in Phoenix? Ask the flight crew. How about skin care? Flight attendants are excellent sources because dehydration from the cabin air is something they fight on a daily basis.

Flight crews have saved me money and, perhaps most important, time. They have taught me that it's not just getting a good deal that makes travel enjoyable, but the *finesse* with which you do so.

They no longer carry me wrapped in a blanket down the stairs after a flight—but they sure know where to find the best-quality blankets, not to mention everything else.

An important note: this book is, in its intention, design, and execution, incomplete. After all, there are 145,000 commercial pilots and 313,000 cabin crew members around the world. This book includes information from more than 300 of them, representing more than thirty different U.S. and world airlines. As you will discover, they provide excellent and detailed suggestions and practical tips.

And since those tips continue to evolve, I offer this to you: if you're a working pilot or flight attendant, I'm open to hearing your city or airport secrets for the next edition of *Flight Crew Confidential*. Please e-mail me at traveldetective@aol.com.

U.S. and Canada

ANCHORAGE

The first time I flew into Anchorage, the flight attendant on Western Airlines gave me some very good advice. When she heard I had rented a car, she warned me, "Don't even go three miles over the speed limit. There's a speed trap right outside the airport, and they nail everyone. We tell all the other crew members to watch out."

I was on assignment for *Newsweek* magazine, in Alaska to interview the notorious head of the Teamsters Union, Jesse Carr. As luck would have it, the plane was late in arriving, and I jumped into my rental car and raced for the appointment. I had driven about three miles from the airport when I heard the siren and saw the lights. Sure enough, I was pulled over by an Anchorage policeman. "And you would be driving thirty miles over the speed limit because . . . ?" he asked as he looked at my driver's license. "Well, I'm here to interview Jesse Carr," I told him. "Oh," he sighed. "Well, that's different!" I then received a police escort to the offices of the Teamsters. Only then did I discover that two days earlier the Teamsters had announced they were representing the Anchorage police. Talk about luck!

But the real point of this story is that I should have listened to the flight attendant's advice. And each time I've arrived since that first flight into Anchorage, I've adhered to the speed limit, thanks to that crew member.

Speaking of crew members, here's a little something about Alaska logistics that may give you some small hint about life in the forty-ninth state: one in fifty-eight Alaskans is a pilot. But don't let that intimidate you—this is your opportunity to make many new friends in Anchorage, just so you can really see the state.

As one flight crew member once told me, Anchorage is the perfect layover. Just about everyone skis, if they don't snowshoe, and at the very least they hike in the Denali. Once in the summer, when it stays light for nearly twenty hours a day here, I was taken to watch a women's late-night softball game—it started at 10 P.M., in broad daylight!

Anchorage is a very young city—the age of the average citizen is just thirty-two years. Many flight attendants—and even more pilots—bid their flights to Anchorage in late August. Why? It's the best time to catch the aurora borealis, or northern lights. Some people will even rent a car the minute they land and drive up the Seward or Glenn Highway to witness the spectacular light show in the sky.

A few flight attendants told me about what they call their summer "suicide run." They don't even check into their hotel. They rent a car, drive 150 miles to the Kenai Peninsula, fish most of the night, and drive back in time to catch their return flight. (Hint: if you see some very tired flight attendants on a southbound flight from Anchorage, be sure to ask how many fish they caught!)

One reason that Anchorage is such a favorite among single female flight crew members is that men outnumber women in the city.

But let me offer one cautionary note: it's not just a matter of dressing warmly. Folks in Anchorage like to joke (and this may be *no* joke to some) that there are only three seasons in the city: last winter, this winter, and *next* winter. Well, it's really not *that* bad. Average temperatures actually get as high as 65 degrees—in July!

CITY TIPS

In downtown Anchorage, Humpy's is the place to go. It's definitely a jeans-and-T-shirt kind of spot. All the servers are surly. It reminds me a lot of the Brick, the bar and grill on the television show *Northern Exposure*. Blackened halibut—don't leave town without having it! It costs about $15. Humpy's is also known for its salmon-spread appetizer. Flight crews box it up, bring it home, and serve a tub of it at dinner parties.

◆ Humpy's, 610 W. 6th Avenue, (907) 276-2337.

We use Anchorage as our fish pit stop. We head directly to 10th & M Seafoods Downtown, a wholesaler that packages and ships fresh salmon and halibut. Or you can pick the frozen seafood you want, and they will pack it in a Styrofoam cooler with an ice pack so you can carry it right on the plane.

◆ 10th & M Seafoods Downtown, 1020 M Street, (907) 272-3474.

Anchorage has a user-friendly path system. There are bike and Rollerblade trails along Cook's Bay, and you can rent bikes or Rollerblades nearby. It's about a twenty-mile round trip, bordering the perimeter of downtown. It's really nice for walking, too—although I don't know that I would walk it alone because the area is rather remote and, once you're on the path, there aren't many places to exit it. However, the bay area is beautiful, and you have a great view of the mountains.

When I'm walking or jogging on the Tony Knowles Coastal Trail during the winter, I nearly always see moose. If you encounter one, stop and get out of its way; do not approach it.

◆ Tony Knowles Coastal Trail, www.mtbreview.com/trails/Alaska/ TonyKnowlesCoastalTrail.html. The northern trailhead is located at 2nd Avenue and H Street, downtown; the southern trailhead is located at Point Campbell (Kincaid Park).

Club Paris is a local hole in the wall and the best place to get a steak in Anchorage. It will probably run you about $25. Club Paris has been around forever, and no one ever leaves there unsatisfied.
◆ Club Paris, 417 W. 5th, (907) 277-6332.

Simon & Seaforth is a restaurant/bar and the best place to watch the sunset. This is a very romantic place, and it serves terrific margaritas.
◆ Simon & Seaforth, 420 L Street, (907) 274-3502.

Darwin's Theory is a smoky, unpretentious bar that has been there for a long time. It is known for the Red Hot, which is a drink concocted from cinnamon schnapps and a couple dashes of Tabasco sauce—great on a cold day. If the owner comes in, he might buy the whole bar a round. Once everyone has a shot, they all say "OOHHHHHHH" and then drink it.
◆ Darwin's Theory, 426 G Street, (907) 277-5332.

The popular drink to order in any bar in Anchorage, especially in the winter, is called a Duck Fart. It's a layered shot with Kahlua, Bailey's Irish Cream, and a float of Crown Royal.

I know it sounds crazy but sometimes flight crew members like to spend layovers in the air. Heidi Russ and her husband have been flying people around Alaska for more than twenty years at Arctic Flyers. This husband-and-wife team have his-and-hers Tailor Craft seaplanes. They offer flying lessons, seaplane ratings, and tours of pristine places that are accessible only by seaplane. For $100 you get approximately an hour of flight instruction.
◆ Arctic Flyers, Lake Hood, (907) 243-3953.

The Crow Creek Pass runs about twenty-six miles, starting in the town of Girdwood. The last thirteen miles of this trail follow along the Eagle River. Some moderate trail climbing is required, but nothing too strenuous. This is a chance to see a lot of wildlife, such as moose, brown and black bears, and eagles. Here's a warning you didn't need to hear: watch out for the bears. They're fearless.

◆ Crow Creek Pass, www.alaskan.com/docs/ancsouth.

ATLANTA

The first time I flew into the Atlanta airport, I was taking advantage of a great deal offered only by Eastern: fly anywhere in the United States for twenty-one days for only $799. The only hitch was that, because of the way Eastern's routes were structured, if you wanted to fly between San Francisco and Los Angeles—you guessed it—you had to fly through Atlanta. As a result, although the price was right, my love-hate relationship with the airport and the now-defunct airline was born.

Back in 1978, the Atlanta airport was both huge and somewhat provincial. I'm not making this up: do you know what they sold at some of the airport stores? Sides of bacon! (How's that for a carry-on challenge?)

Thankfully, the airport—and the city—have improved. Atlanta continues to evolve, and, perhaps more than any other U.S. city, it is still trying to find its true identity while undergoing rapid and dynamic changes. But Atlanta is more than just a city; it's also a destination: more than seventeen million tourists and conventioneers visited there in 2001.

And yet certain things haven't changed. A scary (but true) statistic that one flight attendant told me is that there are more than two hundred waffle houses in Atlanta. You can get both foie gras *and* chitlins in Atlanta. It can get confusing.

Another curious fact about Atlanta is that no one ever eats at home. People dine out there more than in any other city I've ever visited. I've never been invited to anyone's home for dinner;

they always invite me out to eat, because that is how folks in Atlanta eat.

If you are a tourist, you can head for the Varsity for lunch (go for the cheese dog). But a pilot friend took me to what has become my real favorite: Fat Matt's Rib Shack, 1811 Piedmont Road NE. He also told me to wear a shirt I didn't mind ruining, and I soon found out why: this is a classic barbeque joint. And the ribs? They let me in the kitchen one night and I got to make my own. That's when I learned the secret recipe containing molasses and rum that they use to marinate the meat. Fat Matt's doesn't take credit cards, and beer is the strongest drink you can get. There are other reasons why this place is a flight crew favorite: it's a great place to hear jazz and blues, and it's not expensive. And while Atlanta boasts some of the more high-end restaurants in the South, I still prefer to hang out with the crew at Fat Matt's—another example of the flight crew showing me the way. (404) 607-1622.

AIRPORT TIPS

I fly to Fulton Airport in Atlanta, which is about thirty minutes away from the international airport. I tend to like historical places, and one day, close to the Marriott, I stumbled across an old hotel called Vinings Inn. (Vinings is a village about fifteen minutes from the airport.) The place looks like it was a tavern and meeting place in the early 1800s. The menu offers creative dishes, the presentation is good, the service is polished, and the prices are moderate. I had a seafood salad that cost about $8 for a large portion. It's a nice, fine-dining experience, polished but not stiff.
◆ Vinings Inn, 3011 Paces Mill Road, (770) 438-2282, www.viningsinn.com.

At the international airport in Atlanta, the store called Simply the Best Gifts has a sign that says, "Everything is $10. Really."

Some of the merchandise is junk, but there are good deals—lighters, pens, and costume jewelry are three things that come to mind.
◆ Simply the Best Gifts, Atlanta International Airport, Concourse A, (404) 669-0961.

Since the 1996 Summer Olympic Games were held in Atlanta, all of the wonderful sites and venues are there. The city also boasts efficient public transportation. You can take Atlanta's rail system, MARTA, to virtually all the Olympic sites, as well as to places like the Coca-Cola museum, Centennial Park, and Lenox Mall, all for $1.75.
◆ MARTA, (404) 848-4711, www.itsmarta.com.

CITY TIPS

Every third Saturday, wholesale antiques and furniture are sold to the public for great prices in McDonough, about twenty miles south of downtown Atlanta.
◆ Ragtime Antiques and Fine Furniture, I-75 South, exit 70, turn left, go three miles, left on Ice Street; 54 Covington Street, McDonough, (770) 898-0000.

Lakewood Antique Market is only open on the second weekend of every month. It is a huge warehouse filled with antiques such as brass beds, lamps, antique jewelry, lace, and old linens, at great prices.
◆ Lakewood Amphitheater, off Langford Parkway; 2000 Lakewood Avenue SE, (404) 622-4488.

Norman's Landing serves seafood and kebabs. It's a log cabin—nothing fancy—and you don't need a reservation. There's actually a Ping-Pong table in the room. Although they're always busy, the atmosphere is laid-back—but it's not a family restaurant. Prices start at $8 to $9 per person.

◆ Norman's Landing, take exit 13 on 400 North from Atlanta, make a right, and it's on the left, less than a block from the interstate; 365 Peachtree Parkway, Cumming, (770) 886-0100.

Piedmont Park is a beautiful place for a jog, a walk, or a Rollerblade ride. Inside you will find the Atlanta Botanical Garden, as well as beautiful rose and Japanese gardens. You can almost always catch a live band or an arts festival.

◆ Piedmont Park, www.midtownatlanta.org/ppark.htm. Hours 9 A.M. to 7 P.M., Tuesday through Sunday; admission $7.

◆ Atlanta Botanical Garden, www.atlantabotanicalgarden.org, 1345 Piedmont Avenue NE, (404) 876-5859. Public transportation is available.

If you are feeling a little tense at lunchtime in downtown Atlanta, check out the free yoga class at noon at the Fulton Library.

◆ Fulton Library, 1 Martha Mitchell Square, (404) 730-1700.

If we happen to be in Atlanta on a Sunday layover, we head to Burkhart's, where they have a gospel drag show on Sunday night. There is nothing else like it.

◆ Burkhart's, 1492 Piedmont Avenue NE, (404) 872-4403.

The Barking Hound Village is basically a pet mall, selling everything your companion animal might need: lodging, pet supplies, grooming services, pet wear, collars, and a bakery for pets. My dog likes the carob dog cookies, about $1 each. I also bought my dog a pearl collar for $28.

◆ Barking Hound Village, 1918 Cheshire Bridge Road NE, (404) 897-3422.

Eatzi's is a gourmet food market that's great for a sit-down lunch or a take-out picnic. The high-quality food will satisfy both carnivores and vegetarians, and Eatzi's also carries fresh-cut flowers.

◆ Eatzi's, 3221 Peachtree Road NW, (404) 237-2266.

Whenever I fly into Atlanta, I bring a very sturdy bag and go to a place called Highland Hardware. It has the best woodworking tools you could ever want and a great gardening section, too.

◆ Highland Hardware, 1045 N. Highland Avenue, (404) 872-4466.

Buckhead Bread Company and Corner Café is wonderful. I like the raisin-and-cinnamon baguette, which is perfect for the holidays. I also highly recommend the sourdough loaf. In early January through Mardi Gras, Buckhead sells their French king cake.

◆ Buckhead Bread Company and Corner Café, 3070 Piedmont Road, (404) 240-1978.

Outwrite Bookstore is a large independent that caters to Atlanta's gay community. Outwrite hosts a lot of informative events, and it is a great place to meet people, have a cup of coffee, and find out what is going on in the community.

◆ Outwrite Bookstore, 991 Piedmont Avenue, on the corner of 10th Street, (404) 607-0082.

Blakes is a pub a few doors from the Outwrite Bookstore. It is mainly a men's club, but women are welcome as well. It has two stories and an outdoor deck, and the drinks are reasonably priced.

◆ Blakes, 227 10th Street NE, (404) 892-5786.

One of my favorite places to browse (even though it's a bit pricey) is a little antique shop called Bennett Street, hidden behind a couple of restaurants, in Buckhead. Nottingham Antiques has a lot of stuff from Europe—armoires, tables and chests, desks and end tables—that are stripped down to the wood and then buffed with furniture polish. A five-drawer chest for the bedroom would cost maybe $500. They also offer reproductions that are quite reasonable. The Interior Market and Café has moderately priced salads, sandwiches, and cappuccinos. Various merchants and artists have stalls in the Interior Market. Ann Hathaway sells wonderful paintings done on canvas. The Stalls sells really beautiful, well-made European antiques.

◆ Bennett Street, 45 Bennett Street, (404) 352-1890.

◆ Interior Market and Café, 55 Bennett Street NW, (404) 352-0055.

◆ Ann Hathaway, 2101 C. Tula Bennett Street, (404) 352-4153. Hours 10 A.M. to 5 P.M.

◆ The Stalls at Antique Market and Café, 116 Bennett Street, (404) 352-4430. Hours 10 A.M. to 5 P.M., Monday through Saturday.

Spondivits is the only thatched-roof restaurant in Atlanta. Its specialty is delicious and reasonably priced seafood, and you can get a fantastic meal there for under $12. It's always busy after five in the afternoon, even though it's right by the airport, across the street from Delta's Flight Training Center.

◆ Spondivits, 1219 Virginia Avenue, (404) 767-1569; 599 Atlanta Highway, Cumming, (770) 844-9060.

The downtown Hilton Hotel has an agreement with the athletic club next door. If you stay at the hotel, you get a $15 pass to the gym for the day. The facilities include an indoor track, an indoor pool, and any kind of weights you can imagine, plus all the latest equipment.

◆ Hilton Hotel, (404) 659-2000; Hilton Atlanta, 255 Courtland Street NE; Peachtree Center Athletic Club, 227 Courtland Street, (404) 523-3833.

Sometimes we'll arrive on a red-eye that lands around 6 A.M. Instead of just going to bed, we go to the Silver Skillet. It was built in the 1940s, and its hallmark is genuine Southern cooking with red beans and rice and country ham. It's about as untouristy as you can get. A lot of the waitresses have been there for a long time, and they are really sharp. Last time I went I had the country ham, with gravy that was outstanding. It also came with eggs and a corn muffin—all for $6 to $7.

◆ Silver Skillet, 200 14th Street NW, (404) 874-1388.

One of my favorite places for an outing is the Silver Comet Trail, along an old railroad line, starting in Georgia and winding into Alabama. The beautiful thirty-five-mile round trip starts in town and then crosses the interstate, where you find yourself deep in the woods. The trail, a slow incline, is paved, so it is suitable for biking and Rollerblading as well as for people who just want to get out and walk or run. The starting point is a fifteen- or twenty-minute drive from the airport.

◆ Silver Comet Trail, enter at 4573 Mavell Road SE, Smyrna, (404) 875-7284.

If it's local flavor you want, have I got a pool hall for you. This place doesn't even have a name—everyone just calls it "the pool hall." The only way to identify it is by the Budweiser sign out front. It is dirty, cheap, and a good time. You'll see all kinds of people at this place, an intimate setting with about ten pool tables.

◆ E. Pace Street by Roswell and E. Andress Street.

I get my nails done at New Nails by Teresa, the owner. She is lovely, and all of the women who work for her are fantastic. Recently, Teresa put in a few massage chairs, where you can sit while you get your nails painted. They massage you from the back of your neck all they way down to your ankles. For $30, they give the best manicure and pedicure in the city by far. I hear the governor's wife gets her nails done there.

◆ New Nails, 3145 Peachtree Road NE, (404) 233-2202.

If you are in need of a dry cleaner, try Kay Cleaners. The owners, Michael and Sim, are quite accommodating and do a terrific job. I bring them my best clothes, and I've always been pleased with the results. I even trusted them with my $3,000 wedding dress, which was white silk and had grass stains all over it. For $80, they made it look as if it were brand-new again.

◆ Kay Cleaners, corner of Piedmont and Cheshire Bridge; 1740 Cheshire Bridge Road NE, (404) 733-5777.

BOSTON

The source of one of my favorite sayings about Boston is anonymous, but it's no less true for that: "Boston looks like a town that has been paid for."

There's a certain aura of aristocracy and security surrounding this city that is unmistakable. There is an overwhelming sense of permanence about Boston. Perhaps more than any other American city, Boston brings to mind a civilized place.

Although Boston is one of America's capitals of old money, it is now in conflict with newer generations and a fast-lane culture that is evolving more rapidly than the old-money people can, well, count their money. In fact, if you think about it, there are really two Bostons: the historic touristy attraction (which, old-timers will tell you, is older than the country it helped to create) and high-tech Boston.

Indeed, few cities so successfully contain such a juxtaposition. This capital city of Massachusetts likes to call itself the "Hub"—but of which universe? The battles of the revolution fought here are long over—except, of course, for the ongoing struggles of negotiating Logan Airport and navigating Boston's notoriously confusing streets and the continuing downtown construction.

For me, Boston means clam chowder so full of clams and rich with cream that I know, if I order even a single cup, a nap will soon follow. A cliché? Yes, but it's also true.

The beauty of tourist-oriented Boston is, at least for me, not that touristy at all. It's been preserved without being blatantly promoted, and has retained much that represents its heritage, not to mention its charm. For many flight crews, it remains a favorite layover destination.

AIRPORT TIPS

I'll often get a shoeshine on my way out of Logan Airport. It's cheap, and they do a good job. Including tip, it never costs more than $5. It's a good thing to do once you've checked in and are waiting at your gate.

◆ Dave's Shoe Shine & Repair, Terminal B.

The best way to get to and from the airport is to use the blue line on the "T" (subway system); otherwise, the traffic is just horrible. Tourists are lured into buying one- or three-day passes, but these are not worth it because Boston is so small that you really don't need to use the "T" once you get into town. You can pretty much walk everywhere. It costs only $1 to ride on the "T," and the one-day pass works out to be more than you would likely ever use.

◆ MBTA, www.mbta.com.

For trips to Boston, I recommend flying into Manchester or Providence. You can rent a car and drive to Boston in about forty-five minutes. It's an easy and well-marked drive.

CITY TIPS

In Boston, I go to Trinity Episcopal Church in the Back Bay, across from the Boston Public Library. The stained glass, stairs, and enormous lawn are so beautiful that they take your breath away. In addition, the church presents organ concerts on Fridays from 12:15 to 12:45 P.M.

◆ Trinity Episcopal Church, 206 Clarendon Street, (617) 536-0944.

In the summertime, we go jogging along the paved, five-mile path beside the Charles River, right next to downtown Boston. It's really tranquil and pretty, and is suitable for Rollerblading and running. There are also concerts from April to September at the Boston Hatch Shell, which looks like a miniature Hollywood Bowl.

◆ Metropolitan District Commission, Hatch Shell, (617) 727-9547, www.state.ma.us/mdc/hatchshellevents_2000.htm.

My favorite restaurant is Armida's, an Italian establishment operated by a family who has owned the building for thirty years. The mom, Mary, is the waitress; her daughter and husband do the cooking in the back. The food is excellent, and the people are warm and friendly. If I say to Mary, "I don't know what I'm in the mood for. Make me whatever you want," she'll serve me a great veal parmigiana or a terrific pasta dish. Entrées are $13 to $16.

◆ Armida's, 135 Richmond Street, (617) 523-9545. Hours 5 P.M. to 10 P.M., for dinner Wednesday through Saturday.

When I'm laying over in Boston, I actually look forward to reading. I'm serious—Boston has an impressive public library, with tiled floors and books everywhere, and that's where I go.

◆ Boston Public Library, average time from airport is thirty minutes on the "T," not including rush hour; 700 Boylston Street, (617) 536-5400. Hours 9 A.M. to 9 P.M., Monday through Thursday; 9 A.M. to 5 P.M., Friday and Saturday; 1 P.M. to 5 P.M., Sunday.

A great way to see the city is to take the water taxi from the airport to Rowes Wharf. It's $10 one way, and taxis run every fifteen minutes from 6 A.M. to 8 P.M., Monday through Friday. On Saturdays and Sundays, the taxis run every thirty minutes from 10 A.M. to 8 P.M. Rowes Wharf is near Faneuil Hall, the aquarium, and the Harbor Tower. The wharf is actually a tiny tugboat, and it's a really relaxing spot, especially if the weather's nice.

When you walk out of the arrival terminals at the airport, look to your right or left, for a bus stop with all of the Metro buses. The Water transport #66 bus goes to the Logan Dock, where the shuttle is located.

◆ Airport Water Shuttle on Logan Dock, (617) 951-0255.

I love Boston, and I'm always looking for a good deal on quality seafood. The Black Rose, a real Irish pub, usually offers a special such as twin lobsters for $19—and they're delicious! The pints cost about $4.50, and there's Irish entertainment nightly, although the music can be way too loud. The pub has an upstairs and downstairs, with tiny tables and plastic table covers. It's not the best first-date atmosphere; it's more of a place to go with a bunch of people—like we do with other flight crew members.

◆ Black Rose, 160 State Street, (617) 742-2286.

A lot of times when we land we're so tired we don't want to go out. In Boston, that's not a problem, because there is a fantastic place that will deliver the most incredible Italian food—and I know Italian because I lived in New York for six years! The place is Spinelli, and you can order just about any kind of Italian food, but their specialty is pasta. My favorite dish is an eggplant parmigiana and ravioli in marinara sauce, with a big loaf of bread—all for $5.50. In half an hour, Spinelli will deliver food right to the terminal. But be warned: the place closes at 8 P.M. Monday through Saturday, and Sunday at 6 P.M.

◆ Spinelli, 282 Bennington Street, (617) 567-1992.

The Omni Parker House in Boston's Financial District, one of our crew hotels, claims to be the oldest hotel in the United States. This is the place where the Parker House dinner roll was invented. The hotel is said to be haunted on the fourth and eleventh floors. People have reported feeling a presence and hearing doors shutting by themselves. Harvey Parker, original owner, used to personally shut and check all doors to make sure everyone was safe. The hotel has recently been remodeled, but there are some pie-shaped rooms—make sure you are not in one of those because they are small and very awkward.

◆ Omni Parker House, 60 School Street, (617) 227-8600.

If you stay at the Omni Parker House, you will be within walking distance of Filene's Basement, *the* place for bargain hunting. No secrets about that, but here's something people don't know about Filene's: it's a great place to buy wedding dresses. A $3,000 dress might go for $300, and Filene's sells both name-label and high-end designer clothes. None of this is advertised, but the place is always crowded. Be prepared to push and shove, and go as early in the morning as possible, when people are at work. There are rows and rows of everything, so you have to dig. It's a good idea to avoid carrying anything in with you, in order to keep your hands free for gathering bargains.

◆ Filene's Basement, 426 Washington Street, (617) 348-7934.

The minute we land in Boston and hit the crew hotel, we shower, change clothes, and head to a place called the Boston Sail Loft, in the North End. It's a rustic place—kind of a sports-bar environment, where a lot of the local people go. On game days, the place is really crowded and fun. The lobster is $16 and you get the tail and a couple of sides.

◆ Boston Sail Loft, 80 Atlantic Avenue, (617) 227-7280.

Across the street from the Sail Loft is Billy Tse's, where I ate the best lobster I have ever had, cooked in a delicious ginger sauce. Prepared for two, it costs $30.95. It's not fancy at all—it's just awesome food. Billy Tse's is usually crowded, so it's a good idea to call ahead for a table, or if you don't want to wait, you can eat at the bar. (Warning: people do smoke there.)

◆ Billy Tse's, 240 Commercial Street, (617) 227-9990.

Check out the New Balance Shoes corporate office. The bottom floor is a factory, where they sell seconds. Once or twice a year, they let you bring in your old shoes to recycle into bags, and they give you twenty percent credit when you buy a new pair.

◆ New Balance Shoes, 40 Life Street, (877) 623-7867.

In Touch is a gag gift store on Newbury Street that has reasonable prices and outrageous gifts. They have a great selection of funny/dirty greeting cards—let's just say you won't find this kind of card from Hallmark. One section of the store is devoted to gay-related gags and fun stuff to give as gifts.

◆ In Touch, 192 Newbury Street, (617) 262-7676.

Charlie's has terrific chili. It comes in a bread bowl, and it is really thick and spicy, with a lot of beans and meat. This is a very Boston restaurant, with a dark-wood-and-brass interior. There is outdoor seating with heat lamps during the winter, and the chili will warm you on a cold Boston day.

◆ Charlie's, 284 Newbury Street, (617) 266-3000.

We like going to the Vox Populi (Voice of the People) bar. It attracts a more sophisticated crowd—people in their twenties and thirties—which is hard to find in Boston because there are so many college kids. Located in a long, narrow, two-story building, it's a great place to go, and it's not too loud.

◆ Vox Populi, 755 Boylston Street, (617) 424-8300.

Vinny Testa's is a favorite with flight crews because the food is served family-style in the largest portions you will ever see. It rates about a seven, on a scale of one to ten. But really you go there to see Mike, the bartender, with the great Boston accent. He usually works weekends and has all the insider tips about where to go in the city. He makes a great martini, but ask him

for a cosmopolitan, too. Although it's a chain, the restaurant tends to be jam-packed, with lines going out the door.
◆ Vinny Testa's, 867 Boylston Street, (617) 262-6699.

I never go to Boston without going to Mike's Pastries in the North End, where the Italian community is located. I always buy their almond cookies, packed in a small box and wrapped in string. The cookies are $7.50 per pound, and they are just incredible—well worth the money. I buy enough to bring home, but sometimes they don't quite make it, so make sure you buy extra. Mike's is where the local people go for their wedding cakes. In the summer you cannot pass the place without treating yourself to an Italian ice. It's $2 per cup, and on a hot night it's almost better than a box of cookies, although it melts real fast.
◆ Mike's Pastries, 300 Hanover Street, (617) 742-3050.

One of my favorite things to do in Boston is to take the train to the State House, the city's oldest surviving public building. Inside, there is an incredible winding staircase, which appears to be almost entirely unsupported. This staircase is stunning; I have always wanted to photograph it—and nobody seems to know it's even there.
◆ State House, 24 Beacon Street, (617) 727-3676.

Marshall House in Faneuil Hall sits on the docks and serves the *best* Caesar salad in the world for $6.95. The plate is so huge that just the salad and a beer will fill you up. This place is a treasure—it was built during the Revolutionary War. It's very narrow and cozy inside, and it makes you feel warm the minute you walk in.
◆ Marshall House, (617) 523-9396.

One of my favorite stops on the Freedom Trail, which contains so much history, is the Old North Church, famous thanks to

Midnight Rider Paul Revere. This is where they hung lanterns from the steeple to warn the citizenry that the British were coming by land or by sea. The Old North Church has one of the oldest pipe organs, as well as one of the oldest clocks, in the country. Not many people know that George Washington worshipped there.

◆ Old North Church, 193 Salem Street, (617) 523-6676.

CHICAGO

For five years, Chicago was my escape. As a student at the University of Wisconsin in Madison, Chicago was only a three-hour drive down Interstate 90 to a brave new world. I conveniently forgot about the wind off the lake in the winter and a chill factor that often hit 10 or 20 below zero. That's how cool (in the hot sense) Chicago was and still is.

In the airline world of hubs and spokes, Chicago is one of those "fly over" cities. It's ironic to note that on a given day, about forty-seven percent of the people who fly to O'Hare have no intention of ever going to Chicago—they're only connecting through the airport. In my book, they're missing out.

Chicago is the great American city. Yes, the locals like to joke that there are only two seasons here: winter and construction. But for me, Chicago has always represented the perfect urban experience—high-rises and a wonderful lakefront, great neighborhoods and acres of parks.

The people of this city still embrace a strong work ethic and radiate Midwestern charm. Chicago has come a long way from the days of Upton Sinclair and Al Capone. And as modern as Chicago wants to be, you have to love a city with a major-league baseball team that plays in tiny Wrigley Field and has yet to beat a ninety-year World Series curse.

You also have to love a city that maintains Soldier Field for "da Bears" and Midway Airport for the smart travelers who know better. As far as flight crews are concerned, no one gets stuck in Chicago. They just get lucky, even when it's twenty below.

AIRPORT TIPS

I fly to Chicago O'Hare often, and it's one of my favorite airports. Burrito Beach is a brand-new place—friendly, fast, fresh food— and the servings are so huge you can't eat a whole one by yourself. I like the baja burrito with chicken and rice, priced between $4 and $5. Variations include the roasted veggie burrito for $4.49, black bean and goat cheese burritos for $4.69, and breakfast burritos and huevos rancheros for around $5. Their guacamole is pretty good, and fat-free black beans are available. This is a walk-up restaurant with a seating area right in front. They've also got one at the train station and at two downtown locations.

◆ Burrito Beach, Terminal 3 in the Food Court near K4, (773) 462-0190.

B Smooth, next to Burrito Beach, makes nondairy smoothies. The blueberry-banana smoothie is incredible. A medium-sized drink costs $4.95.

◆ B Smooth, Terminal 3 in the Food Court near K4, (773) 462-0190.

Ty Beanie Babies store in Terminal 3 has great gifts, and it's no more expensive than a regular store outside of the airport.

◆ Ty Beanie Babies, Terminal 3, (773) 686-0506.

If you want to go from Terminal 1 to Terminal 3 at O'Hare, the best way is to cross over to the Hilton Hotel and follow the signs for the Hilton. Once you see the entrance to the hotel, follow signs for Terminal 3. This will take you approximately ten minutes, whereas going from Terminal 1 to Terminal 2, then to Terminal 3, will take close to half an hour. Plus you can take a baggage trolley the whole way.

O'Hare tends to be very busy on Friday afternoons. If you have ordered a limousine, you will usually have to wait for your luggage before the limousine company will pick you up. Unfortunately, the limousine lot is five to ten minutes away from the pickup point. During rush hour, it takes the driver twenty to twenty-five minutes to get there. But there is a trick to successfully managing this: when you arrive at the baggage belt, identify the door that you're at, then call the limo service, and tell them you're ready to go. By the time you get out, your limo should just be arriving. I used to be a limo driver, so I know. Call AMMS Limousine at O'Hare and ask for Roy. Tell him Mickel sent you, and he'll provide you with a nice car from his fleet of stretch limos, Lincoln Town Cars, Cadillacs, and standard cars, including new models. It should cost $55 to $57 to take a private car to the city, with one stop. Going to the North Shore, the price will vary depending on whether you are charged a shared or a private rate; you should call AMMS to determine that.

◆ AMMS Limousine, 5509 N. Cumberland Avenue #509, (773) 792-1126, (800) 223-AMMS.

O'Hare Airport has a children's museum, to which I always direct parents.

◆ Chicago Children's Museum at Navy Pier, Terminal 2.

A great place to work out if you are stuck at the airport and have a few hours to kill is the Hilton Hotel O'Hare. It costs $10 for a one-time visit, and you can use the showers.

◆ Athletic Club, adjacent to Terminal 2, (773) 601-1723.

Chicago is one of the few cities with a public transportation system that takes travelers from the airport into the heart of the city. Locals call it the "El"—short for "elevated train." At $1.50 and $1.80 (for connections), it will take you from the heart of the city to both Midway and O'Hare. The Orange Line will take you from Midway, on Chicago's south side, into the city; the Blue Line will take you from O'Hare, on Chicago's northwest side. And since the trains dead-end on the northwest side, you can't get lost. While at Midway, stop at Pot Belly Sandwich Works for Chicago's best sub sandwiches. Since Southwest Airlines serves no meals, get your food to go and be the envy of your seatmates. Harry Carey was the voice of the Chicago Cubs for almost fifty years. If you have time, sit down for a taste of nostalgia at his restaurant.

◆ Harry Carey's, 303 W. Madison Street, (312) 346-1234.

The post office in the O'Hare Airport has a real live person at the counter. It's on the way to the F terminal.

◆ U.S. Postal Service, Terminal 2, (773) 686-0119.

At O'Hare, Heel Bar is a great shoe repair shop. It's a convenient service for flight attendants because we're always in such a hurry. One time the strap broke off my suitcase, and the skilled staff fixed it in no time.

◆ Heel Bar, B Concourse of the United terminal, Terminal 1, (773) 686-2741.

If you ever get stuck at O'Hare or have more than a three-hour layover (and believe me, we've all experienced this), then check out Maki Sushi. This great family-owned and -run sushi place is about fifteen minutes and a $12 taxi ride from the airport, in Park Ridge. The sushi portions are bigger than you get in the city, and the fish is really fresh. They have a martini menu with about thirty different variations. This place is child-friendly, and the kids' menu is kind of like sushi for beginners.

◆ Maki Sushi, 12 S. Northwest Highway, Park Ridge, (847) 318-1920.

CITY TIPS

Tails is a great little tailor shop run by Joseph and his wife, Irina. They've owned the place for about twenty years. Joseph can take stuff I've owned for ten years and make it look hip again—he's amazing!

◆ Tails, 1414 N. Wells, (312) 642-3711.

Need to buy a camera or get one fixed? Try the Triangle Camera Shop in the middle of Boystown. You can buy new and used equipment, including digital, and the best part is you can do your own developing, which saves you money. The darkroom is around the side entrance, down the stairs. There's an open area where you can mount your pictures and a drying area with lights to see your negatives. Buy paper and use the filter, chemicals, enlarger, and so on. There's also a private room where people can work on their own. There are eight to ten working stations in the communal area, and there's always someone around who can help you out. You can also take classes on subjects such as using the darkroom and lighting.

◆ Triangle Camera Shop, 3445 N. Broadway, (773) 472-1015.

Bin 36 wine bar and restaurant offers wine paraphernalia such as books, glasses, and corks, as well as wine tastings. It is spacious inside, with a minimalist decor. It also has a great dinner menu. The waiters are knowledgeable and they will tell you which wines to have with your meal, when they should be opened, and when they should be decanted. They match wines to the meal's courses as well to make sure that what you are drinking complements what you are eating. This is a place for wine connoisseurs or people who aspire to that position.

◆ Bin 36, 339 North Dearborn, (312) 755-WINE.

For the best deep-dish pizza in the city, I go to Gino's East Pizza, off Michigan Avenue. It's a little, old, dark pizzeria, where people carve their names on the walls and tables. A medium, deep-dish pizza is $15. (I recommend the deep-dish mushroom.) You can get a pizza with a pitcher of beer for about $10 per person.

◆ Gino's East Pizza, 633 North Wells, (312) 988-4200.

On one overnight layover, we discovered a great Thai restaurant, the Star of Siam, in downtown Chicago. It's a huge loft, and you sit on the floor with big cushions. The food is inexpensive—$4 to $7 per entrée. We liked the spring rolls and Pad Thai noodles, although everything we tried was good.

◆ Star of Siam, 11 E. Illinois Street, (312) 670-0100. Hours 10 A.M. to 10 P.M., Monday through Thursday; 10 A.M. to 11 P.M., Friday and Saturday; and 11 A.M. to 10 P.M. Sunday.

I don't have hair anymore, but I used to go to a barbershop called Gabby's. I still refer other crew members there. Gabby himself is no longer living, but the name has carried on, even though the current owner's name is Wayne. It's a family-run place—Wayne's niece, sister, and great-nephew cut hair. They have old-time barber chairs, and no flashy lights. It's a busy place because they only have four chairs. A haircut will run you about $12.

◆ Gabby's, 2860 N. Clark Street, (773) 549-8832.

You can get a good manicure at Old Town Nails. They get you in and out quickly and do a nice job. A manicure and pedicure will cost you $32 plus tip, which is good for the Chicago area.

◆ Old Town Nails, 1433 N. Wells Street, (312) 266-1614.

I'm a black guy, and I get my hair cut only in Chicago, L.A., or New York. In Chicago, I go to Terrell's Afro Barber Shop, in the Lakeview area, about forty-five minutes from the airport. In that neighborhood, there are three other hair places, but I like Terrell's the best because it has been there the longest and has more of a neighborhood feel. It's a small place—only seven chairs. I like to get a low fade, and they do a good job. They charge $15 for a regular cut.

◆ Terrell's Afro Barber Shop, 3943 N. Broadway, (773) 525-0022. Hours 9 A.M. to 7 P.M.; closed Sundays and Mondays.

American Girl is a doll shop with twenty-one different styles of dolls to choose from. You pick the hair color, eye color, skin color, and outfit. They also stock that same outfit in sizes to fit actual children so that the doll and the little girl can dress as twins. I wanted to buy a doll for my niece, so I brought in a picture of her and they helped to match the doll's appearance to that of my niece.

◆ American Girl, near the Water Tower, 111 E. Chicago Avenue, (312) 943-9400.

Arturo's is a Mexican restaurant that's got great food and is open twenty-four hours a day. It's really inexpensive, and the chips and salsa are outstanding.

◆ Arturo's, 7151 Western, (773) 776-0433.

The River Kwai Seafood II on Belmont is a great little hole-in-the-wall Chinese restaurant with a crooked floor and fantastic, cheap food. Everything on the menu is good, but I recommend the beef and broccoli. It is a good place to go after a late night, since the hours are 10 P.M. to 6 A.M. It has only two tables, but you can always just get the food to go. Only two guys work there—one who takes orders and one who cooks. Usually there is a long wait, so I suggest calling in your order.

◆ River Kwai Seafood II, 1650 W. Belmont, (773) 472-1013.

The Museum of Science and Industry is a bizarre old place, with some pretty unusual displays. For example, they have a frozen human body that has been sliced at eighth-inch intervals and spaced with glass to reveal all the layers of the human body—skin, muscle, organs, and bones. It's fascinating in a morbid sort of way. One of our crew favorites is the German U-boat—not a model, the real thing! We particularly like the cool film they show about how they got the sub to Chicago and then into the museum. (Think about it: a German sub on Lake Shore Drive—deeply weird!)

◆ Museum of Science and Industry, 5700 S. Lake Shore Drive, (800) GO TO MSI. Hours 9:30 A.M. to 4 P.M. weekdays, 9:30 A.M. to 5:30 P.M. weekends and most holidays; admission $9 for adults, $5 for children ages three to eleven, and $7.50 for seniors. Call ahead because there are certain days of the month that you can get in for free.

Chicago has a large community of runners, and a particular landmark for them is the ten-foot totem pole along the lake north of Belmont Harbor. Runners have been meeting there in the early evening for the past sixteen or so years. Anyone can join them to run between two and six miles along the lake. Times of the runs depend on the season.

Chicago is probably one of the finest sporting communities in the United States. People are competitive, but also friendly—they don't knock you from your bike. In the summer you can swim in Chicago. For training, triathlons, and swimming, it's a great city. Oak Street Beach at Oak Street and Lake Shore Drive; North Avenue Beach at North Avenue and Lake Shore Drive; and Ohio Street Beach on Ohio Street and Lake Shore Drive are three beaches in downtown Chicago.

When you're finished running and swimming, head from Lincoln Park over to a restaurant called O'Famé, in a residential area right off Oz Park. It's a wonderful fresh Italian place, small and inexpensive. It also has a great little bakery. I doubt many people know about it, because it's off the beaten path.

◆ O'Famé, 750 W. Webster Avenue, (773) 929-5111.

Chicago's lake waterfront is very beautiful. In the summertime, take the Chicago from the Lake tour, which offers ninety-minute architectural and historical cruises along Chicago's waterways. Head right for the upper deck—not surprisingly, it has the best views of the city. The Wendella Boat takes you on an hourlong tour of the city from the lakefront. It leaves just a few steps away from the Hyatt Regency on Wacker Drive.

◆ Chicago from the Lake Tour, 435 E. Illinois Street, (312) 527-1977, www.chicagoline.com. Boats depart regularly from the North Pier Docks at the River East Plaza, 9 A.M. to 4 P.M. Wendella Boat, 400 N. Michigan Avenue, (312) 337-1446. Boats depart regularly from the bridge on Michigan Avenue and Wacker Drive.

Tuman's Alcohol Abuse Center attracts a very eclectic mix of people and boasts the most interesting jukebox I have seen in quite a long time. It's got everything from punk to techno to rock, and a lot in between. The mix of people is likewise outrageous—gay, straight, purple hair, preppy, you name it. They have pool tables, pinball, and hardwood tables to sit around. The number one reason to go here is the name. They also have really cheap drinks—I know because I had a lot of them.

◆ Tuman's Alcohol Abuse Center, 2159 W. Chicago Avenue, (773) 227-6279.

Even in the middle of winter, people will line up on the street and around the corner for Garrett's popcorn stand. There are only three flavors: plain, caramel, and cheese—or you can mix the two flavors. It sounds absurd, but it's worth it. It's the aroma that attracts people—you can smell it from a block away. An eight-ounce bag costs $5. Four locations in Chicago.

◆ Garrett's, 670 N. Michigan Avenue, (888) 476-7267.

Crunch Fitness will make your heart pound with its dance and aerobic classes. The salsa class on Mondays and the funk classes on Tuesdays are the best, and Gloria is a popular instructor whose classes are always crowded.

◆ Crunch Fitness Studio, 350 N. State, (312) 409-4550.

In New York I would visit the Avon Center Day Spa at Trump Tower on Fifth Avenue to have my eyebrows arched and waxed by Eliza Petrescu, the eyebrow diva of the east coast, whose salon is dedicated exclusively to the art of the brow. It was the best I ever found (and at $50 per waxing it should be), until I found an even better one in Chicago: Anastasia's in Nordstrom's. Anastasia Soare and Eliza Petrescu have been dueling for the title of brow queen for years, as well as catering to an exclusive celebrity clientele. But with the recent opening of Anastasia's satellite makeup counters from her shop in Beverly Hills, she has made the task of obtaining the perfect brow easy and reasonable. For a mere $20 you can now have your brows perfectly waxed, arched, and groomed within an inch of their life. Ask for Alessandra, and call first for an appointment; waxing is performed only on Thursdays and Saturdays.

◆ Anastasia's, 55 E. Grand, (312) 464-1515, Ext. 1420, www. anastasia.net; Anastasia Skin & Body Care Salon, 438 Bedford Drive, Beverly Hills, CA, (310) 273-3155.

I don't land in Chicago without stopping by Sinequanon, a full-service salon offering facials, manicures, and massage. I go there to get my hair cut by a stylist named Holly. She charges about $45 for a cut. It is a two-story salon, and it has that young-and-hip feel. Frequently, the owner's dog is there sleeping.

◆ Sinequanon, 2766 N. Lincoln Avenue, (773) 871-2280.

Never use your hotel laundry or dry cleaning service. You'll need to get a second mortgage on your house when you get the bill. Instead, head to Gibson Couture Cleaners, one of the best dry cleaners in Chicago. It is a family-run business, and they have the cleaning facility on site. I would entrust my best evening gown to them.

◆ Gibson Couture Cleaners, 3432 N. Southport Avenue, (773) 248-0937.

Posh is a small shop with eclectic merchandise, run by two flight attendants, Karl and Steve. I once saw a gravy boat there that had come from an actual navy boat. They sell calendars, old flatware from hotels, soaps, lavender, champagne buckets that had been used at the Plaza, and many other such things.

◆ Posh, 3729 N. Southport Avenue, (773) 529-7674.

I get manicures at Spa Amelia from a super-duper manicurist named Suzanna. It's a high-end place, and they are well worth it. The atmosphere is quiet and very *feng shui*. A full French manicure and a pedicure are around $90. This spa is staffed by talented perfectionists. A manicure will take an hour and a pedicure sometimes longer. This is the place to go if you want to be pampered!

◆ Spa Amelia, 21 W. Elm, (312) 951-7415.

Sydney R. Marovitz Golf Course is an enjoyable nine-hole golf course right up Lake Shore Drive near Wrigley Field. It's public, so it's cheap! The locals call it "Waveland" because it's near Waveland Avenue. It's no little pitch and putt, though. The longest fairway is 515 yards, and it's a nice course to walk (although carts are available). The shortest hole is a 140-yard par 3.

◆ Sydney R. Marovitz Golf Course, 3600 N. Recreation Drive, (312) 742-7930.

Now for the really important stuff. I found the best place for bikini waxes! Jeannette used to work in the Marshall Fields Company, but she has her own salon now called Sisters, which she owns with her sister. She's fast and she's fabulous. I've had friends who were squeamish, but now they're hooked. I love her tell-it-like-it-is attitude, and I trust her. They also give great pedicures, but they are famous for the bikini waxes, which cost around $45.

◆ Sisters Salon, 845 N. Michigan Avenue, Suite 964W, (312) 943-8800.

The area on Lincoln Avenue from Irving Park to Belmont has a lot of little antique shops. In one shop, I found a chandelier for less than $100 that my husband loved. The candles are beautiful, too, and it's where I always get candles now.

◆ Old Sau's Resale and Antiques, 3845 N. Lincoln Avenue, (773) 665-7769.

I love to paint, so when I lay over in Chicago I buy supplies at the Art Institute at Utrecht. You can get a high-quality brush for $7 to $15 that might cost $10 to $50 in other stores.

◆ Utrecht, 332 S. Michigan Avenue, (312) 922-7565.

Franco's Hairstyling is a busy, local, traditional men's barbershop, where a cut costs about $20. Franco is a very friendly guy and a talented barber, who really takes care of you while you are in his shop—but he doesn't take appointments. Franco is there from Tuesday to Saturday, but the shop itself is open every day.

◆ Franco's Hairstyling, 2544 N. Clark Street, (773) 525-5499.

Sam's Wine and Liquors is one of the best places to buy wine. They have a huge selection and a very knowledgeable and helpful staff. Prices are reasonable, and the location is unbeatable. Plus they know where to get those firm Styrofoam wine holders, in which you can pack up to three bottles of wine in your luggage so they won't break.

◆ Sam's Wine and Liquors, 1720 N. Marcey, (312) 664-4394.

DALLAS

I first went to Dallas on a magazine assignment and had to admit I was afraid of the city. I flew on Southwest from Houston, and I'll never forget the flight attendants—dressed in hot pants—or their prelanding admonition: "OK, folks. We're about to set this piece of metal down on concrete, so sit up, strap in, and . . . chug-a-lug!"

Of course, having never been to Dallas, my only reference point to the city was a black-and-white image from November 22, 1963, and the assassination of JFK. I was going through Dallas on the way to northeastern Texas to do a story on latter-day cattle rustlers. First, I went on a tour of the old Texas School Book Depository building, and then I headed out with the last Texas Ranger who still uses a horse.

His name was Slim Hulen, and, yes, I got on a horse, too. As you can imagine, after three days on horseback chasing rustlers through the Red River and places like Paris, Texas, Hopalong Greenberg couldn't wait to get back to civilization—and in this case, civilization meant Dallas.

Dallas was—and still is—an enigma to me. But the saying "Everything is big in Texas" certainly applies. Big Money. Big Football. Big Hair. You get the picture. But then again, maybe you don't, and I certainly didn't until I spent some time in the Big D.

Just when you come to the conclusion that it's nothing but a hick town with skyscrapers, you meet Dean Faring, and he cooks dinner for you at the Mansion on Turtle Creek. Or you order the rib-eye steak at the Lone Star and swear it's the best you've ever had. And then, just about the time you start getting used to the sophistication of Dallas—whoops!—there's the Longhorn Ballroom or the frenzy of Friday night high school football, which is as close to organized religion as you can get without *being* organized religion. In fact, one of those Southwest flight attendants took me to my first Texas-style Friday night games. You didn't cheer, you worshipped.

Dallas and Fort Worth, Dallas's often-forgotten sibling, still struggle in the battle with Houston to see which city has the most money and can display it more garishly.

Dallas also has one of my least favorite airports—DFW, someone's version of a modern maze. Old-timers (and smart travelers would, if they could) chose Love Field over DFW any day of the week. But the hub-and-spoke machine of DFW just won't allow many defections. It's an airport you simply love to hate. Outside of DFW, if you can strap yourself in, there's a lot to, uh, chug-a-lug.

AIRPORT TIPS

There's a cool observation area by the south employee parking lot where you can watch planes take off and land. You can hear the radio transmission over the speaker, so you get to listen to the pilots and the air traffic controller talking.

At the Dallas airport, I never take the tram. It's more trouble than it's worth, and unless I have to go from C-36 to A-1, I won't bother with it; I can walk faster than it goes.

There's a shoeshine place by the C-7 area, with two of the nicest attendants. Once I said hi to them as I was passing and one of the guys told me to sit down. He proceeded to shine my shoes, and he didn't even charge me. I've been going back ever since.

Flight crew members normally are entitled to employee parking and then take a shuttle bus to the terminals, but if I pick up visitors at DFW, I always tell them to meet me outside the baggage claim area upstairs, right outside of the security office on the main level rather than on the busy lower level.

CITY TIPS

White Rock Lake is a great place to run or bike. It's about thirty minutes from the airport, and it's especially pleasant on weekends because people sail their boats on the lake. The homes around there are beautiful, too, if you like to look at things you could never afford.

◆ White Rock Lake Park and Recreation Center, 8300 Garland Road at Mockingbird Lane, (214) 670-8242.

It's $25 for an hour-long massage given by a student at the North Texas School of Swedish Massage.

◆ North Texas School of Swedish Massage, 2335 Green Oaks Boulevard W, Arlington, (817) 446-6629.

Here is a school closer to DFW (same price).

◆ Texas Massage Institute, 6301 Airport Freeway, (817) 654-9700.

Although it's not cheap, I get my hair done at Montana Salon. It's a twenty-minute drive from the airport, which isn't far for Dallas because the city is so spread out. Haircuts are $45 to $70.

◆ Montana Salon, 8313 Preston Center Plaza, (214) 368-8558.

Margaritas are the drink of choice during layovers in Dallas, and I like to get them at Blue Goose. They're $5, and you can order them with sangria swirled in. The chicken fajitas and quesadillas are good, too.

◆ Blue Goose, 2905 Greenville Avenue, (214) 823-8339.

Bikram Yoga on Mockingbird is a great place for a workout, at only $10 per ninety-minute class. It's in the Lakewood area near downtown Dallas. This session is not laid-back, so be warned! The classroom is heated (to facilitate stretching) and you do twenty-six different intense poses. By the end of class, your towel will be soaking wet with sweat.
◆ Bikram Yoga, 6333 E. Mockingbird Lane, Suite 253, 2nd Floor, (214) 824-YOGA, www.yogadallas.com.

Cacherel is a restaurant right across from Six Flags Over Texas theme park. They serve upscale French food, and a typical three-course dinner will cost about $40. I always have the salmon, and it's excellent.
◆ Cacherel, 2221 E. Lamar Boulevard at Highway 360, Arlington, (817) 640-9981.

Jack's Pub, my favorite hole in the wall in Dallas, makes strong drinks for a bargain. Monday night is mostly a college scene—all drinks are $2. Other nights, the mixed drinks are $3.50 to $4 and beers are $2.50. The place is outdoors, and it's huge. There are volleyball nets and a dance floor. Ask for Mike Turiaci, a really friendly bartender who makes a wicked-special drink: a blend of three alcohols plus amaretto and fresh fruit in a pint glass.
◆ Jack's Pub, 5550 Yale Boulevard, (214) 360-0999.

Near Southern Methodist University, check out the Burger House. The Greek owner started it as a little joint serving burgers, French fries, and really good chocolate shakes back when his kids were still going to the school. The place is known for the excellent seasoned salt they put on their fries and burgers. You can eat inside or sit outside at picnic tables.
◆ Burger House, 6913 Hillcrest Avenue, (214) 361-0370. Hours 11 A.M. to 9 P.M.

Roses is an interesting dive started by three men in 1940. It's located in an alley behind a restaurant/bar—look for a little door with roses on it, in a red building. Roses only serves burgers ($4.50 for a cheeseburger). There are only a handful of tables, and you get the impression that they decorated with things brought from home. Before it became a hamburger joint, it was the last stop for buying beer before heading off to Greenville. Nowadays, it's in the heart of Dallas and the SMU campus. One of the waitresses writes all the orders out by hand and doesn't use a calculator—she works everything out by long addition. Roses is that kind of place. Once we saw Ross Perot there.

◆ Roses, 4515 Greenville Avenue, (214) 891-0631.

I go to Dyer Street Yoga because the instructor, Ally David, has an infectious kind of energy. She keeps the classes small to weed out the people who are not serious. Ally teaches Iyengar yoga, the type that uses props, and she keeps up-to-date by constantly going to workshops. Classes last ninety minutes, and a one-time class costs $15. The studio is in Lower Greenville, so a lot of young professionals go there.

◆ Dyer Street Yoga, 5539 Dyer Street, (214) 365-9642, www. dyerstyoga.com.

Ahab Bowen is a fun secondhand consignment store, reminiscent of something you might find in New York. I bought a Jackie O–type three-piece suit from the 1960s, originally from Neiman Marcus, for $36. I also found a black Bill Blass blazer made of wool for $25. The store carries a lot of upscale, name-brand things (I don't know how he finds this stuff!), but they also have no-name things, such as a sleeveless dress I bought for $12. The merchandise is separated by era—from beaded, empire-waist dresses from the 1940s to go-go dresses from the 1960s.

◆ Ahab Bowen, 2614 Boll Street, (214) 720-1874.

Gloria's is a Mexican and Salvadoran restaurant best known for its wide variety of margaritas—my favorite is topped with amaretto. A recommended dish is the seviche, a marinated whitefish served atop greens, with tomatoes, avocados, and lemon juice, which costs $8 to $10. I always have leftovers to bring home because the portions are so big. I also love the chips and black bean dip that they serve when you are seated. Gloria's has a patio outside, and the interior is decorated with authentic-looking pueblo painting. The servers tend to speak limited English. There are several locations throughout the Dallas area.

◆ Gloria's, 3715 Greenville Avenue, (214) 874-0088, www.gloriasrestaurants.com.

Café Izmir is a wonderful family-run Mediterranean restaurant. They serve one meat entrée and one vegetarian entrée per evening, as part of a five-course meal including cucumber and pita bread, the entrée, and dessert. I recommend the Turkish coffee, which is really thick and similar to Cuban coffee, but with more of a sweet, mochalike taste. The restaurant is tiny, dark, quaint, and intimate, and it displays an ever-changing selection of local art for sale.

◆ Café Izmir, 3711 Greenville Avenue, (214) 826-7788, www.cafeizmir.com.

Razzoo's Cajun Café has four locations in the Dallas area, but the one we like to visit is in Irving. Its Cajun cooking is simply the best. The restaurant is large, not overly noisy, and caters to families. It has a large, raised bar that makes you think you are on the bayou, with the tin roof and the old tin signs surrounded on both sides by tables. This place is nothing fancy—no tablecloths, just wooden tables. You definitely should try the gator tails—fried pieces of alligator tail available as either an appetizer or a main course. They also have the freshest seafood, such as crawfish and oysters on the half shell. It makes my mouth water just thinking about them. The prices for main courses range from $7.95 to $18.95. Reservations are not needed, and there are smoking and nonsmoking areas.

◆ Razzoo's Cajun Café, 1414 Market Place Boulevard, Irving, (972)-373-9400.

Dallas has a Neiman Marcus resale shop for bedding and home accessories, called Horchow Finale. I found a sterling silver cheeseboard in the shape of an artist's palette with the cheese cutter as the paintbrush—the perfect gift for my artist friend, and I paid only $25 for it. I later found the same thing at Nordstrom's and Neiman's for between $75 and $80. You can also buy comforters for $85 rather than the list price of $300. It's near the university.

◆ Horchow Finale, 3046 Mockingbird Lane, (214) 750-0308.

DENVER

Every time I land in Denver, I know I'm in for a physical challenge. No, it's not that it's the mile-high city and the air is thinner there. In addition to the altitude, it's the *attitude*. Every one of my friends there wants to take me higher—to hike, to run, to ski. In Denver, you experience the city outdoors. It's as simple as that.

During the day, you dress like an escapee from a Timberland catalogue and, with few exceptions, that's also considered formal wear in the evening. And then there's Denver as the embodiment of the history of a nation that continually moved west: Native Americans, the transcontinental railroad, and more than a few cowboys and explorers, all of whom seem to drink Coors.

Folks in Denver like their statistics—because of the mile-high altitude, water boils at 202 degrees Fahrenheit instead of 212. (Yes, that means it takes four minutes to soft-boil a three-minute egg.)

I've been told that golf balls travel ten percent farther in Denver, and the old Mile High Stadium still holds the record as the site of the longest field goal ever kicked—sixty-three yards!

But Denver is also a city of surprises, starting with the fact that it boasts more high school and college graduates per capita than any other metropolitan area.

Perhaps one of the most attractive stats about Denver, as one flight attendant told me, is its three hundred days of sunshine per year. She also told me (and, yes, she's a hiker) that Denver has America's largest city park system, with two hundred parks and another twenty thousand acres in nearby mountains.

Then there's Denver International Airport, the once-troubled, sprawling complex sitting on fifty-three square miles—the largest airport in the United States. When it first opened—actually, when it was first planned to open—the joke about DIA was that it meant "Doesn't Include Airplanes." The much-delayed, much-maligned facility (who can forget those awful videos of the state-of-the-art baggage sorting and handling system literally eating bags?) has now come into its own. While a few diehards still insist they miss Stapleton (only because it's closer to the city, and not for any other reason), it's become one of my favorite airports.

AIRPORT TIPS

At the Denver Airport it's a good idea to park at one of the independent parking lots across the street; there are only two on Tower Road. It is door-to-door service if you do that, and they take you right to your car. Friends have told me that they park there even when they have to pick someone up. US Airport Parking is the best. The airport's parking structure is huge and it is a hassle, with passing checkpoints, getting the ticket, finding a parking place, and walking forever to get to your terminal. You have to allow an hour just for parking.

◆ US Airport Parking, 8100 Tower Road, (303) 371-7575, (866)-PARKING. For directions, discounts, and calculating payment, visit www.usairportparking.com. Rates $2 per hour, $7 per day, or $45 per week (seven days); prepaid is $125 per month or $1,250 per year.

Denver is my favorite airport. It has roomy taxiways and doesn't shut down too often because it has three Category III runways, meaning that the plane (if it has the proper guidance equipment on board) can land without much runway visibility.

Colorado Collections carries a variety of jewelry such as sterling silver, semiprecious stones, and turquoise. All of it is hand-crafted, and some has a Native American influence. I bought a couple bracelets made out of glass beads with a sterling silver clasp. Each handmade bracelet was about $55, including my crew discount. It is a bit pricey, but worth it, because every piece is so unique.
◆ Colorado Collections, United Terminal, B Concourse, (303) 342-7878.

Executive Shoe Shine in the United Terminal is a great place for a shoeshine. The people who work there seem genuinely interested in their customers and do a fine job. A great shine costs between $4 and $5.
◆ Executive Shoe Shine, B and C Concourse.

I got a $1-per-minute walk-in massage a while back at A Massage. It's a great way to pamper yourself after being cooped up and dragging around luggage. There are two locations inside the airport.
◆ A Massage, Main Terminal and B Concourse, (303) 342-7485.

Que Bueno has the best burritos in the Denver airport. A local newspaper proclaimed it the best airport food for several years running. If you are hungry when you get off the plane, this is the place to go. They make their famous burritos right before your eyes.
◆ Que Bueno, Concourse B, (303) 342-0940.

You know how airports are known for bad food? Well, there are two places I eat at in the Denver airport. The first one is Que

Bueno (see above); the second place is Lefty's Grill. Although they charge airport prices—$8 to $9 for a burger—it's worth it because the food is so good! It's got a backyard-barbeque flavor to it. The portions are huge, and you can see what you are getting because it's grilled before your eyes.

◆ Lefty's Grill, B Concourse, (303) 342-7178.

My favorite place for junk food is the Rocky Mountain Chocolate Factory in the Denver airport, and my favorite things to order are the chocolate pecan turtles. I've tried turtles everywhere, but the ones there are the best because they have the thickest caramel. You pay by the pound—and you might not be able to resist eating the whole pound by yourself!

◆ Rocky Mountain Chocolate Factory, B Concourse, (303) 342-7178.

In the Denver airport, there's no reason to take the train if you don't have to because the security lines downstairs are horrendous. But if you're lucky enough to be on Frontier, America West, or Continental, then you can walk across the bridge and save yourself a lot of time. In addition, United has that steel plate that your luggage has to fit into, but they don't use the steel plate if you cross the bridge on Concourse A. So you can stuff your bag in. If you take the train to go to Concourse B or C, you can't walk, because the train is the only way to get there.

CITY TIPS

One of my favorite places for lunch is the Corner Bakery, in the 16th Street Mall in what is called the Pavilion, at the Barnes & Noble bookstore. Food is served cafeteria style, so there's no tipping. It's a hidden treasure that flight crews love. A meal will run about $8.

◆ Corner Bakery, 500 16th Street #150, (303) 572-0166.

Delectable Egg has a unique menu of egg dishes for breakfast and lunch. My favorite is the Santa Fe, a slightly spicy egg dish. Three locations.

◆ Delectable Egg, 1625 Court Place, (303) 892-5720. Hours 6 A.M. to 2 P.M.

Wazee Supper Club in downtown Denver is called a club, but no memberships are necessary. The menu includes pizza and spaghetti dishes, all of which are great. Prices run about $18 for a big tray of pizza. It's in an old building appointed with lots of mahogany and a nice ambience. There is also an old-fashioned soda fountain bar, which is pretty cute.

◆ Wazee Supper Club, 1600 15th Street, (303) 623-9518.

The Cherry Cricket is a Mexican place off the beaten path in the interesting Cherry Creek area of downtown Denver. Lunch and dinner are always busy.

◆ Cherry Cricket, 2641 E. 2nd Avenue, (303) 322-7666.

Senor Pepe's has been around for probably thirty years, and their prices haven't changed much in that time. They serve large portions, and there is no way you'll be able to finish your whole plate. Everything I've ordered there is good. The place is family-run, and the menu tells the history of the place.

◆ Senor Pepe's, 1422 Poplar, (303) 321-1911.

My hobby is weight lifting. I've been to gyms all around the world, and I'm picky with facilities. There's a really nice gym in Denver called the Colorado Athletic Club, which is open to the public. This place is loaded with equipment, including several floors of machines, free weights, cardio equipment, racquetball and basketball courts, a steam room, a pool, and a massage area. We get a crew discount, but it's free to everyone two days out of every month. There's no set date for this, so you can call ahead to ask.

◆ Colorado Athletic Club, 600 S. Holly Street #2, (303) 377-0800. Rate $10 for one-day pass.

I actually take artwork to Denver with me on my flights to have it framed. The Carolyn-Edward Gallery is a wonderful gallery with a framing store in the back called Creative Hangups. They specialize in framing and shipping from the store, and they offer sound advice about what type of frame will look good. (Both Carolyn and Eddie have great taste.) They sell original works of art as well as prints and lithographs.

◆ Carolyn-Edward Gallery, 5702 E. Colfax Avenue, (303) 394-9700.

Sally Starr Antiques is a great little shop that sells all kinds of things: knickknacks, furniture, mirrors—you just never know what you will find. I went there and my friend and I found two unique brass candleholders and loved them so much that we decided to split the pair and each take one. Sally, the owner, is knowledgeable and informative, and a very gracious woman.

◆ Sally Starr Antiques, 2940 E. 6th Avenue, (303) 399-4537.

When I have a bit of time in Denver, my friends and I rent a car and take I-70 west for about fifty miles to the little mountain town of Georgetown, where there's a seasonal train called the Georgetown Loop that passes antique shops and pubs.

◆ The Georgetown Loop Railroad, Inc., take Exit 228 (Georgetown exit) off I-70; at the four-way stop sign, turn right onto Argentine Street and follow it to 11th Street; turn left over the creek to Rose Street. The Old Georgetown Station is right next to the Georgetown Motor Inn, 1106 Rose Street, Georgetown, (303) 569-2403, (800) 691-4FUN, www.georgetownloop.com/map.htm. Rates $14.50 for adults; $9.50 for children ages three to fifteen; no charge for children under three if they sit on a parent's lap.

The little town before Georgetown is called Idaho Springs, home of Beau Jo's, the best pizza restaurant I have ever been to in my life. The pizza is fresh and you can have your crust any way you like it. You can build your own pie, selecting from different sauces, or you can have their house specialty. An average large pizza costs about $16. They also have pastas, sandwiches, and more. Beau Jo's is located in a historic building decorated with Colorado paraphernalia pertaining to mining, skiing, and the like. The salad bar is made from an antique bathtub! The place is always packed, but you can usually get a seat within ten minutes. And there is an ice cream shop next door that has really good homemade sugar cones!

◆ Beau Jo's, 1517 Minor Street, Idaho Springs, (303) 567-4376.

I ask about hikes at the downtown REI store, where official park rangers give information about outdoor activities, including hiking, biking, skiing, and ice and rock climbing.

◆ REI, 1416 Platt Street, (303) 756-3100.

I definitely recommend the Denver REI to shop for ski equipment. Rented boots never fit well. REI's Boot Doctors make a mold of your feet, from which they can outfit you with insoles for your boots in forty-five minutes, all done by computer. To create the mold, the Boot Doctors put you in the ski stance position and determine where the pressure points are in your foot. It's expensive—about $100—but if you're serious about skiing, it's worth it.

If you go to the city before hitting the slopes, any gas station or grocery store from Denver to the mountains will give you coupons you can use for $5 or $7 off your ski pass. If you're not familiar with Denver, stop at REI, tell them what kind of skier you are, and they will direct you to an appropriate mountain.

Copper Mountain is a fun and inexpensive place for the beginner or intermediate to ski, although it has gotten somewhat crowded as a result of their $65 five-day pass that you can use on nonconsecutive days. Copper Mountain is about an hour and forty-five minutes from the airport. Denver airport makes it really easy for skiers—it has baggage belts made strictly for skis, and all the rental cars are equipped with ski racks. This might cost you an extra $5 a day, but it saves on ski rentals.

◆ Copper Mountain Resort, 0509 Copper Road, Copper Mountain, (970) 968-2882, www.coppercolorado.com.

Want to meet some fit, really great-looking flight attendants? Head to Vail, about one hour and forty-five minutes from the airport. As flight crews we get good airline discounts, which save us about fifteen percent every time we travel. Vail is a huge, wonderful resort, but you can save money by staying outside of the city. We usually stay in a tiny town called Avon, which is about half the price of staying in Vail and is right off I-70. Remember, you can ski Vail but you don't have to stay there.

FORT LAUDERDALE

I can vividly remember my first Fort Lauderdale experience: being thrown out of a local hotel during spring break. And I wasn't even drunk! Luckily, the statute of limitations has expired, and I am back there frequently—and with good reason.

Today, of course, Fort Lauderdale has turned around 180 degrees. It has gone from being a mecca of deranged college kids to a more sophisticated city of islands, canals, rivers, and bays, not to mention the hottest new library (that's right, *library*) in America—at Nova Southeastern University. Until you see it, you might think I'm still recovering from spring break when I tell you that I now make it a point to visit this library every time I'm in Fort Lauderdale.

My other must-do, thanks to one of my American Airlines pilot friends, is to hop a ride on his forty-footer and cruise the backwaters of the city, and then out into the open ocean. (Hint: make friends in Fort Lauderdale with folks who have a boat. It's one of the few boating capitals in America where people actually use their boats!)

The quality of the food and nightlife has soared, whether on Las Olas Boulevard or along the river behind it. One of my favorite spots, which a flight attendant showed me, is Indigo, right in the landmark Riverside Hotel, a great sidewalk café on Las Olas inside the city's oldest continuously occupied hotel. Imagine a menu that says it is "colonial southeast Asian" cuisine with some South Florida thrown in. I won't try to explain it—I'll just say the food is really good.

Perhaps the best news is that when it's time for spring break these days, no one gets thrown out—the city now embraces all visitors.

CITY TIPS

Café Moderano is a little Italian restaurant right by the beach. It doesn't look like much from the outside, but the atmosphere inside is appealing. People are dressed up. (You wouldn't want to go in shorts.) It seems like a South Beach crowd, but it looks like it should be in New York City—and it was packed the last time I was there. The homemade meatballs are fabulous—as though Grandma were in the back, cooking. It can be expensive, though, and last time I went, no prices were listed on the menu. The place has about fifteen tables, the waiters are all Italian, and they have a good wine list. Café Moderano is about ten minutes from downtown and twenty minutes from the airport. Lake Hermitage, luxurious condos, is right next door.
◆ Café Moderano, 3343 E. Oakland Park Boulevard, (954) 561-2554. Hours 5 A.M. to 12 P.M. No reservations.

Wings and Things, in Wilton Manors, is a major find. It's not in a great part of town, located west of Federal Highway about ten minutes from downtown, but it has the best wings that I have ever tasted, with a mild and buttery sauce, and curly fries. The staff is really friendly, and a lot of local people go there. A basket of wings for lunch will cost about $5, there's a lunch special for $6.20, or dinner for $6.
◆ Wings and Things, 2199 Wilton Drive, (954) 566-2199. No reservations.

Cafe Tipico is a Spanish-Mexican restaurant right by the Gateway Theatre. It's relatively new and is an excellent deal. They serve huge portions of refried beans, rice, and whatever kind of meat you want. I love the pounded meat with lime, garlic, and caramelized onions. They serve delicious salsa and chips, along with sangria, wine, and beer. The place is very casual, a shorts-and-a-shirt kind of place. The folks who run it are very nice. Prices range from $5.95 to $12.95.

◆ Cafe Tipico, 1910 E. Sunrise Boulevard, (954) 463-9945.

The beaches in Fort Lauderdale are packed, but if you go to Hollywood, between Fort Lauderdale and Miami, Sheridan Street is a good beach. You can bring a picnic there, and the water is very pretty. It is a quieter beach, with the feel of being in the Bahamas.

◆ Take U.S. 1 to Sheridan and go a little east.

Red Reef Beach in Boca Raton is north of Fort Lauderdale and is great for snorkeling right off the beach, so you don't have to go out on a boat. It's about a twenty-five-minute drive from Fort Lauderdale.

◆ Red Reef Beach, 1400 N. Ocean Boulevard, Boca Raton, (561) 393-7820.

Another place close to Sheridan Street is the Taverna Opa, on the intracoastal. I took an entire crew there for dancing, drinking shots of ouzo, and eating traditional Greek dishes. (I'm Greek, and this place is authentic.) You can mash up chickpeas with a mallet and add garlic and oil on bread.

◆ Taverna Opa, 410 N. Ocean Drive, Hollywood, (954) 929-4010.

Casbah Spa and Salon is very exclusive. If you have money, this is the place to go. They have a water pressure machine for the massages and everything you could think of for massages, nails, and hair. The place is beautifully decorated, with flowing curtains, vanilla-scented candles, and lovely couches. You might think you were in Morocco.

◆ Casbah Spa and Salon, 1010 Seminole Drive, (954) 630-0633.

One of my favorite places is family-owned and -operated Ireland's Inn, where the people are very down-to-earth. The hotel is right on the beach and it serves irresistable breakfasts—home cooking, made to order, at very reasonable prices. You can get a bowl of fresh oatmeal for about $3; omelets are $5 to $8. They have a smoked salmon platter and fresh fruit platters. Tables are set with linen tablecloths and napkins, they use real china, and the waiters wear starched shirts with bow ties and cummerbunds—all of this for prices equivalent to those at Denny's or less. The place is casual, but they do require shirts and shoes. Go on a Sunday if you can. It is kind of off the beaten path, on A1A between Sunrise Boulevard and Oakland Park Boulevard.

◆ Ireland's Inn, 2220 N. Atlantic Boulevard, (954) 565-6661.

There is a pier at the end of Commercial Boulevard past A1A, toward the ocean. I like to walk along the ocean to a little place called the Pier Restaurant. You can sit outside or inside and order one of their great specials or breakfasts. The deluxe breakfast runs about $3.95, including eggs, bacon, sausage, grits or homefries, juice, and coffee.

◆ Pier Restaurant, 2 Commercial Boulevard, Lauderdale-by-the-Sea, (954) 776-1690.

Danny's Sly Fox is a favorite, serving excellent seafood. There is an outdoor grill, and they make their own barbeque marinade. It is a very popular place to hang out for a beer, both reasonably priced and casual. You'll also enjoy the glider swing.

◆ Danny's Sly Fox, 3537 Galt Ocean Drive, (954) 561-8444.

You must check out the services of Pierre at the Sullo Salon and Day Spa. He will give you a cut and color for $180 that is worth every penny. If you have time for a massage, ask for Pam. For $40, she will give you the best thirty-minute neck-and-shoulder massage you've ever had. One time I was so tense that she worked on me for an hour because she felt sorry for me.

◆ Sullo Salon and Day Spa, 3045 N. Federal Highway, (954) 563-9217, www.sullosalonspa.com.

Aunt I's is a lively, reasonably priced Jamaican/Caribbean restaurant, where the servings are huge. I love the tasty chicken with brown rice and beans, as well as the jerk chicken. I also enjoy the fried plantains and the fried dumplings. Believe me, you will be full when you walk out of this place. Yummy!

◆ Aunt I's, in Lauderhill on Highway 441, north of Sunrise Boulevard; 1178 N. State Road 7, Lauderhill, (954) 321-0190.

Blue Moon Fish Co. is a great place for lunch (it's a little pricey for dinner). Located right on the intracoastal at Commercial Boulevard, the ambience is wonderful. You can sit there and watch all the boats that you know you will never be able to afford. Recommended dishes include salad with baby shrimp and goat cheese rolled in pecans. They have a wonderful entrée of steamed mussels. The menu changes all the time, but there's always fresh fish. They serve a delicious swordfish sandwich with a pesto mayonnaise and meat loaf with garlic mashed potatoes. Lunch for two will run you about $15.

◆ Blue Moon Fish Co., 4403 W. Tradewinds Avenue, (954) 267-9888.

HAWAII

It exists on the threshold of a dream. Within a six-hour radius of San Diego, Los Angeles, San Francisco, Portland, Seattle, and Vancouver, the Hawaiian Islands are a breathtaking archipelago. One hundred and thirty-two islands make up this chain of submarine volcanoes, each with great beaches, large verdant valleys, and staggeringly beautiful sea cliffs. The state of Hawaii comprises eight major islands, seven of which are inhabited. The islands exist—and, in fact, thrive—on tourism. But, thankfully, most of Hawaii has not been ruined by it.

I've been going to Hawaii for more than thirty years. It's actually a part of my family. My uncle, one of the original California surfers and a former Santa Monica lifeguard, sailed from Los Angeles to Honolulu on a forty-foot catamaran in 1954, married a Hawaiian, and never left. My cousins, Nohea and Pua, took me to the right beaches, laughed as I tried to surf— and together we celebrated the magic that was, and still is, their home.

But even my family isn't always hip to the real local secrets. Once again, it's the folks who fly for a living who get out, see, and experience the best the islands have to offer. They know how to do Hawaii up close and personal, immersing themselves in the culture without being smothered by it.

AIRPORT TIPS

Honolulu Airport

Honolulu Airport basically surrounds a park. In the center of the airport is a five-acre triangle garden, which is subdivided into three sections: the first is a garden with Hawaiian plants and Hawaiian architecture, another is Chinese, and the third is Japanese. It's a very peaceful place to get away. Often, people (especially Americans) are so busy getting somewhere that they pass it—although somehow the Europeans always manage to find it.

The unique, hidden Japanese garden in Honolulu Airport is open to the public, but no one seems to know about it. It's on a subterranean level right next to Gate 14. We go down there sometimes to sit and eat. There is an employee cafeteria, likewise open to the public, or you can bring your own food. You reach it via a glass elevator. The garden is very relaxing and beautiful, but the airport doesn't have any loudspeakers, so you must keep track of your departure time.

Leis are probably more expensive in the airport than they are on the island, but there are some stands outside of the airport terminal, behind the post office, where they sell leis for all departures to the mainland. They have everything, including the solid fanned orchid leis, the little pikaki ones, and the masculine green-leaf ones, as well as the run-of-the-mill—meaning carnation and plumeria. The cheap orchid leis start at $5.

Honolulu's airport seems stuck in the 1960s. It's spread out and inconvenient. There's one central check-in area, and if you're going to United, for example, you've got a long walk. Also, it's completely open, so there's no air-conditioning except near the gates. If you're coming from Minneapolis in the winter, you're stoked! But if you're in your uniform and rushing to a gate, you get drenched in sweat.

Don't take the Wiki Wiki trams; it's much faster to walk.

Kona Airport

The Allison Onizuka Museum at the Kona Airport is named after one of the astronauts who died in the *Challenger* tragedy. There's a scaled replica of the space shuttle. This museum is especially good for kids.

◆ Allison Onizuka Museum, (808) 329-3441.

CITY TIPS

Oahu

The Silent Dance Center in Moili'ili, a town near Honolulu, teaches Iyengar yoga. This type of yoga uses props such as blocks, chairs, and ropes as aids because not everyone has equal abilities in terms of flexibility and strength. This workout makes you feel fantastic. My favorite instructor, Ae Ja, has been there forever and she's like a comedian and instructor rolled into one. She teases you a little bit, but she does it in such a way that you love her by the end of class. Classes are $10 for ninety minutes.

◆ Silent Dance Center, behind the Down To Earth health food store; 2535 S. King Street, Moili'ili, (808) 526-YOGA.

Fujioka's Wine and Spirits in Honolulu is a find. Knowledgeable proprietors Lyle Fujioka and his wife can recommend a good wine for under $20. They also have champagne, specialty vodkas, port wines, and a counter for wine tasting.

◆ Fujioka's Wine and Spirits, 2919 Kapiolani Boulevard, Honolulu, (808) 739-9463.

The Royal Kitchen in Chinatown is known for its baked manapua. Traditionally, manapuas are steamed, but the baked ones taste more like bread. Manapuas can be made with chicken, curry, Portuguese sausage, Chinese sausage, black bean, or other vegetarian fillings. Each is about three inches across, and if I'm real hungry, then I'll eat four of them, at about 75¢ apiece.

◆ Royal Kitchen, Chinatown Cultural Plaza #175, Honolulu, (808) 524-4461.

The Curry House originated in Japan, but they now have locations all over Oahu. You can choose how mild or spicy you want your food and how much rice and sauce you want with it. You also select the meats or vegetables you prefer. I recommend chicken with spinach, but they also have a good chicken katsu. It's the perfect curry. There are about twenty individual items to choose from, based on eggplant, spinach, pork, beef, and so on. The prices start at about $5 and depend on how many ingredients you add.

◆ Curry House, 2310 Kuhio Avenue, Honolulu, (808) 922-9441.

If you're going to get an aloha shirt, get a Reyns Spooner. It's the Armani of aloha shirts. They run about $65, but are well worth it. Whereas on the mainland an attorney would wear a suit and tie, in Hawaii an attorney would wear a Spooner. The shirts are top quality and they even have a signature print: the neni goose and Hawaiian crest with the lehua blossom (that's the tree with red flowers that looks like a gathering of red hairs). Reyns stores have four locations throughout Oahu.

◆ Reyns, 1450 Ala Moana Boulevard #2067, Honolulu, (808) 949-5929.

I don't know whether I should tell you about my hairdresser in Honolulu because I might not be able to get an appointment anymore! Renee is a crew favorite, and she's a one-woman show. She runs her own salon called Felipe's Beauty Salon, and a haircut there will cost you only $12. She's not into the trendy scene; she does very basic haircuts, and that's what I like about her. If you want a good, cheap haircut, see Renee.

◆ Felipe's Beauty Salon, 1641 Kalakaua Avenue, Honolulu, (808) 949-8780. Closed Sundays and Wednesdays.

Most tourists don't know that Waikiki Beach is home to a living legend. Across from the Hyatt, right next to the statue of Duke Kohana Moku, an instructor named Rabbit Kekai still gives beginning surfing lessons. In surfing terms, he's an institution. A contemporary of the Duke's, Rabbit even beat him in the big canoe race once. He's in his eighties now, but everybody there still knows who Rabbit Kekai is. Lessons cost $35 including the board, or you can just rent a board for $8.

◆ Ask for Rabbit at the beach boy stands on Kuhio Beach, Waikiki. For events and contests visit www.toesonthenose.com.

Kahala Nails is a good place for a manicure, with a great staff. They charge $19 for a manicure, and it will take about an hour. Owners are Mike and Michelle. Appointments are recommended.

◆ Kahala Nails, 4210 Waialae Avenue #B107, Honolulu, (808) 739-1668.

There are a lot of mom-and-pop shops in Hawaii that make sushi, but cone sushi is not the kind everyone's used to. Instead of raw fish, cone sushi is rice and vegetables in rice and wine vinegar wrapped in a seaweed cone. You can get it at Young's Fish Market, a small general store above Liliha Bakery, for 75¢ to $1. At Young's you can also find boiled peanuts, which kama'ainas like to eat (so do Southerners). These peanuts are boiled in salt, which makes them taste sweet.

◆ Young's Fish Market, 1210 Dillingham Boulevard #19, Honolulu,
(808) 841-4885.

Japanese Buddhist churches often compile Hawaiian cookbooks
for door-to-door fund-raising; you can often get them at bookstores in the Hawaiiana section for about $10. I have one called
Favorite Island Cookery, written by Honga Hongwanji and put
out by a Buddhist temple. It contains over two hundred recipes
from different cultures on the island, including recipes from Ko-
reans, Filipinos, Chinese, Japanese, and Hawaiians, for such
dishes as steamed fish, chicken longrice, pineapple cucumber
salad, and chicken curry.

Whenever I drive to the North Shore of Oahu, I stop at Matsumoto's Shaved Ice in Haleiwa. In Hawaii, this treat is called
"shaved ice," which is smoother and finer than a snow cone, with
thick syrup. It's a must to have it with ice cream, which blends
with the flavors of the ice. You can also add azula beans, and there
is a coconut cream to top any syrup. The smaller size is $2.50, but
it's big enough to be a large! My favorite flavor is the blue vanilla.
◆ Matsumoto's Shaved Ice, 66-087 Kamehameha Highway,
Haleiwa, (808) 637-4827.

A favorite place for Hawaiian food among locals is the Side
Street Inn. With a sports bar and karaoke, it's usually a packed
scene—popular even with the police. The food is delicious, and
an average meal will cost about $15, not including drinks.
◆ Side Street Inn, 1225 Hopaka Street, Honolulu, (808) 591-0253.
Open weekly for lunch and dinner; open for dinner only on weekends.

Here's a little flight crew secret from Hawaii: down the street
from the Ala Moana Hotel near Iolani Palace is a YMCA that
offers $5 day passes. It's not exactly modern, but it's a nice set-

ting and very popular with local people. It has a courtyard, a pool, machine and free weights, and aerobics classes. Sometimes there are yoga classes, too. There's a bus stop right outside.
◆ YMCA, 1040 Richards Street, Honolulu, (808) 538-7061.

Central YMCA offers yoga and aerobics, and has a $10 day pass.
◆ Central YMCA, 401 Atkinson, Honolulu, (808) 941-3344.

A pair of pantyhose can last a few days or a few hours, depending on the brand and the stresses to which they are subjected at work. I've found that the ones at St. John's Knits in Ala Moana Shopping Center last the longest. They're rather opaque, although thinner than tights, but they last for months. However, at $17, they're a bit expensive. You can find St. John's in other cities, but the pantyhose are the only things I can afford!
◆ St. John's Knits, 1450 Ala Moana Boulevard 3220, Honolulu, (808) 973-1166.

Waikiki Beach is crowded, noisy, and has too much suntan oil in the sand and water. My choice? Head for Lanikai Beach. It has white, white sand and blue, clear water; it's never too hot because it is on the windward side; and it is very secluded.
◆ Lanikai Beach, from the airport, take H3 Highway toward Kailua, just past Kailua Beach Park; park along the road near the public access signs and walk down the path to the beach.

The Ross in Honolulu is a wonderful place to shop, and there's one located near the Ala Moana Hotel. One advantage is that they stock a wider selection of men's XXL T-shirts because Polynesians tend to be larger than average.
◆ Ross Dress for Less, 711 Ke'eaumoku Street, Honolulu, (808) 945-0848.

Keo's is my very favorite restaurant in Honolulu. It's a beautiful Thai restaurant, with orchids around the dining room. A lot of people know about it, so the key is knowing when to go: exactly at noon for lunch, or for an early dinner at 6. (That's when the local people go.) They have delicious spring rolls wrapped in lettuce leaves and a dish called Evil Jungle Prince, which is chicken, beef, or pork with a nice, spicy flavor. They also sell a recipe book.

◆ Keo's, 2028 Kuhio Avenue, Waikiki, (808) 951-9355.

Christy's & Harry's Café is a true hole in the wall, but is considered a best-of-Honolulu attraction. It serves 99¢ breakfast specials consisting of eggs, bacon, and two scoops of rice. On Friday you get larger portions, just because it's Friday. The place is near everything, but it's a little tricky to find.

◆ Christy's & Harry's Café, 1101 Waimanu Street, Honolulu, (808) 593-7798.

The Ala Moana Park is where local triathletes and swimmers swim in Honolulu. The Waikiki Swim Club meets there regularly. Just show up, get to know them, and you're in. It's a great place for beginners to swim: it's safe to go alone, there are lifeguards, and it's not very deep.

◆ Waikiki Swim Club, 1109 12th Avenue #202, Honolulu, www.hawaiiswim.com.

Every Wednesday at 5:30 P.M., starting at the Nike Running Store in Waikiki, there's a three-to-six-mile run along the beach. Just show up, go running, and meet new people.

◆ Nike Running Store, 2080 Kalakaua Avenue, Honolulu (808) 943-6453.

I get waxed religiously everywhere I go. In Honolulu, Premier Salon in Macy's is a stand-out. I see a very fast and thorough woman named Shereen Boyajian, who has a great talent for eyebrows.

◆ Premier Salon inside Macy's, Ala Moana Shopping Center, Honolulu (808) 945-5377.

I usually bring my wife flowers or leis from Hawaii, but I also like to take her a terry-cloth robe from the Royal Hawaiian, the legendary pink hotel where flight crews used to stay before it got too expensive. (They still have a great mai tai beach bar, but don't order a mai tai, because the pina coladas are better. Go figure.) You can get the robes, which only come in pink, from the gift shop for about $100. They have a full-length one to the ankle, and a shorter one to the knee.

◆ Royal Hawaiian Hotel, 2259 Kalakaua Ave, Honolulu (808) 923-7311.

I ran into a friend who was on a layover and she looked as though she was walking on a little pink cloud. She told me she had just come from having a massage done by Lloyd Fujimori. He doesn't have an office, but he will come right to your hotel. Although Lloyd is young, he is quite accomplished and professional, and will put you at ease. He'll do the massage as hard as you want. A one-hour massage runs about $45, plus tip.

◆ Lloyd Fujimori, (808) 271-5474.

I have always wanted a Tahitian black pearl, but they cost a fortune if you buy them in finer jewelry stores. The Gardenia, in the International Marketplace in Waikiki, run by a woman named Gean Lamtang, has 14-karat fine jewelry and Hawaiian heirlooms. I shopped around for a long time for a black pearl that I liked and could afford. The pearl I found there was large and cost less than $300. The same ring from a fine jeweler would likely cost $800 or more. Gean also sized it for me. All the jewelry is made at the store. Don't be afraid to haggle about price, either.

◆ The Gardenia, 2330 Kalakaua Avenue, Booths 49 and 91, Waikiki, (808) 923-2223.

Island of Hawaii

Since virtually every flight to Hawaii is a long haul, you're definitely ready to chill when you land. There are thermal springs in

Pohiki, outside of Hilo, that even some of the local people don't know about because they usually go to a bigger spring at Isaac Hele Beach Park. If you're coming from Hilo, there's no public transportation so you will need to rent a car. Drive south six miles in the direction of the volcano to the next major town, Keaa. It's another twenty-five miles to Pohiki, and there's a boat lodge parking lot. There's only one road, so you can't get lost. From the parking lot, you'll see a house. Walk in the direction of the house until you see a trail. Down the trail, about fifty yards from the beach, is a natural heated pool that fits about ten people comfortably. The water temperature gets to the high eighties and a lot of the surfers will jump in the springs after a ride.

◆ For general information about this area, call (808) 961-8311.

The best time to visit Hilo is on Wednesdays and Saturdays, when the whole town comes alive for the Farmer's Market. You can find fresh produce—everything from organic, vine-ripened tomatoes to kalamungai, a bitter melon from the Philippines. Dazzling anthuriums and orchids of all shapes, sizes, and colors are also sold for dirt-cheap prices.

◆ Farmer's Market, Kamehameha Avenue and Mamo Street, Hilo, www.hiohwy.com/h/hifamahi.htm.

Nori's is a very simple restaurant, where seating consists of wooden benches. Try the Big Plate for $15, which feeds two hungry locals or four average eaters and includes two huge musubis, barbeque meat, barbeque chicken sticks, noodles, and fried fish. Nori's also has really good saimin and plate lunches, ranging from $3.95 to $8.95. A nice woman named Beth Ann Nishijina owns the place.

◆ Nori's, 688 Kino Ole Street #124, Hilo, (808) 935-9133. Open until 12 A.M. weekdays, until 2 A.M. weekends.

In Hilo, you should go to Two Ladies' Kitchen, run by a woman and her niece, and known for its mochi. Mochi is made from sweetened black beans and the texture is like that of a marsh-mallow. Two Ladies' Kitchen makes about twenty different kinds of mochi, including Asian-style, strawberry, and Lilikoi (made from fresh passion fruit). They make the mochi into different shapes of fruit, which is fun. Although they will box it for you to take out, the best thing to do is eat it fresh. They open early in the morning, but they'll always answer the phone or come to the door, even if they're closed.

◆ Two Ladies' Kitchen, 274 Kilauea Avenue, Hilo, (808) 961-4766.

There is a ten-acre flower farm in Kona specializing in tropical exotics such as anthuriums, proteas, and ginger. They will ship cut flowers, and their prices are below average for a generous quantity of blooms.

◆ C and K Ohana, Lehualani Farm, on Mamaloha Highway between land markers 104 and 105, and one-half mile mauka (toward the mountain) from the telephone exchange building; Honaunau (South Kona District), (808) 328-8028.

Guess where I did my Christmas shopping in Kona? Wal-Mart. Everything that you could possibly want in a tourist store you can find at Wal-Mart, cheap. They have two huge sections of Hawaii-ana, including aloha shirts, food, candy, notepads, and stationery. I bought two pounds of chocolate-covered macadamia nuts for $7.49, and I also bought Maui Caramacs for $1.50 per box.

◆ Wal-Mart, 75-1015 Henry Street, Kailua-Kona, (808) 334-0466.

In Kona you can try some of the famous Iron Man events. The bike ride is 112 miles from the King Kamehameha Hotel in the center of Kailua-Kona to Hawaii and back. Or you can swim the two-and-a-half-mile Iron Man course. It's ideal for people seeking adventure vacations who want to go at their own pace. No wetsuit or goggles needed. Hawaiiswim.com will put you in touch with the events around town.

◆ Hotel King Kamehameha, 75-5660 Palani Road, Kona, (808) 329-2911.

Maui

If you want to experience the Hawaii of a hundred years ago, go to the Hana Hotel, about a three-hour drive down a very winding road in a sleepy little town called Hana. Jacqueline Kennedy stayed there on her honeymoon, but we don't have that kind of budget. Eating, however, is a different story. The restaurant is very casual and, because it doesn't get very crowded, you don't need a reservation. The General Store has everything from groceries to hardware! Local sights include a bamboo forest in the Seven Pools Park, and you can go horseback riding through Hana.

◆ Hana Hotel, 5031 Hana Highway, Hana, (808) 248-8211.

The all-time best restaurant in all of Hawaii is hard to find and harder to get to, but once you go there, you won't go anywhere else. The first time one of the crew members told me about the Haliimaile General Store, I thought it was just some tourist place. Not even close. It's a forty-five-minute ride from either Kapalua or Wailea, and about thirty minutes from Lahaina. It's run by Beverly Gannon and her husband, Joe, and the cooking is unbelievable. Beverly has a way with lamb, tuna, and chicken, but her signature dishes are meat loaf and chocolate peanut butter banana cake. However, my favorite dish is the simplest: Beverly cooks up some sugar snap peas in a wok with soy sauce and ginger to accompany the lamb.

◆ Haliimaile General Store, 900 Haliimaile, Makawo, (808) 572-2666.

Kauai

Kauai Fruit and Flower Company makes beautiful, extremely high quality arrangements that are well worth the price. Their unique and exotic arrangements may include anthuriums, birds of paradise, wood roses, ginger plants, and orchids.

◆ Kauai Fruit and Flower Company, 3-4684 Kuhio Highway, Lihue, Kauai, (800) 943-3108, www.kauaifruit.com, mail to pineapple@kauaifruit.com.

The most beautiful beach I have ever been to is Donkey Beach, a nude beach. It is an eleven-mile-long stretch that is never crowded. You can't see Donkey Beach from the main highway, but traveling north from the airport at Lihue, look for the second dirt road on your right, after passing the eleven-mile marker.

HOUSTON

My first trip into Houston was, let's say, memorable. It was 1972, and I was flying on a Texas International prop plane. Plane hijackings were front-page news, and the flight attendant made quite a dramatic scene in explaining that this plane had a locking door to the cockpit, equipped with a combination lock.

That was somewhat reassuring, but the comforting feeling didn't last. We roared down the runway, and just as we lifted off from New Orleans, the cockpit door suddenly swung open, then fell off its hinges!

We laughed all the way to Houston.

I survived similar flights on TI and, later, on Braniff, flying often in their ugly green and maroon 727s throughout Texas, and in the early days on Southwest, hopping between Houston and Dallas.

I lived in Houston for a while, roasted by the hottest summers I'd ever experienced. I spent the entire month of August one year curled up next to my window-mounted air conditioner.

Once, when I tried to find a beach, a young Southwest flight attendant cautioned me against it. "A lot of folks drive to Galveston, but I wouldn't. It's not exactly my favorite beach."

I didn't heed her advice, and I got into my car and headed south on I-45. I should have listened to her. I stayed in Galveston about twenty-five minutes—long enough to put more gas in the car—and jumped right back on I-45 North, back to

Houston. A week later, that same flight attendant pointed me in the direction of Corpus Christi and Padre Island.

It was hard then, as it is now, to believe that Houston is America's fourth-largest city. The summers are still unbearable, but at least these days downtown Houston has tunnels and overhead air-conditioned walkways to ease the pain.

Braniff is long gone from Texas. So is TI. Continental now reigns supreme in Houston, and the city is hotter than ever. My Continental flight crew friends still recommend Padre Island, and for laughs—especially when the thermometer rises over 100—they head over to Barren Springs Drive and check out the National Museum of Funereal History, which features a fascinating display of fantasy coffins, including one in the shape of a KLM jet.

OK, so they may have to rename Enron Field. Not a problem. They still have Otto's barbeque on Memorial Drive.

CITY TIPS

Baubles and Beads is a great secondhand store for quality clothes, purses, and shoes. For $60, I bought a Moschino jacket that I had seen elsewhere for $800, and this one was almost brand new.
◆ Baubles and Beads, 9715 Katy Freeway, (713) 468-3544.

I've been to all the fancy restaurants in New York, but I think Mark's right here in Houston has the best food of all. You can get a great risotto, a lamb chop, a pork chop—he'll cook anything you want, with emphasis on continental food. It's considered one of the better restaurants in Houston, and the service is good, too. Mark's is considered "inside the loop" in Houston, and they just redid the decor. Entrées run about $16 to $25; appetizers, $9; salads, $7.
◆ Mark's, 1658 Westheimer, (713) 523-3800.

La Griglia, an Italian restaurant, is another of my favorites. It features a very pretty circuslike atmosphere, with large murals on the walls. An average dinner is about $17, and the salads are $8. I really like the penne amatriciana, and they also have a very good autumn salad.

◆ La Griglia, 2002 W. Gray Street, (713) 526-4700.

Stracks Farm is the best barbeque restaurant in the world. I went there on my first date with my husband, over twenty years ago. The place used to be a roadside stand, but because it got so popular they ended up turning it into a nice restaurant. There's nothing like their potato salad—it has baby back rib meat in it and chunks of cheese, and—oh my gosh!—it is so incredible. Their sausage and brisket is also amazing. And so is the cornbread—it melts in your mouth. You can have a rack of ribs, or any meal, for around $15, plus drinks, and that will give you tons of food. You're likely to walk out with a doggie bag.

◆ Strack Farm Restaurant, 5707 Louetta Road, Spring, (281) 376-0901.

Battenberg ATA Black Belt Academy is a martial arts facility that also teaches kickboxing. Renee Battenberg, the owner, is personable, dedicated, and professional. She's also a master in Tae Kwon Do and a sixth-degree black belt. She teaches a rape assault class every two months, and it is open to the public. I have taken this class, and I now feel confident I would be able to defend myself if put in a vulnerable situation. The class costs $50, and refresher classes are free. This is a family-oriented facility, staffed by friendly people.

◆ ATA Black Belt Academy, 4333 Kingwood Drive, Humble, (281) 360-5460.

The Kingwood Yoga Plus Studio has state-of-the-art machines to help you stretch and flex.

◆ Kingwood Yoga Plus Studio, 1202 Kingwood Drive, Kingwood, (281) 359-4663. Hours 9 A.M. to 7 P.M., Monday through Thursday; 10 A.M. to 5 P.M., Friday.

Kingwood Cove Golf Club offers special deals and coupons on its website so that you can print them out and bring them in when you play golf. It's a challenging course. There is a dress code and, although it is not strict, my advice is to dress in a respectful manner.
◆ Kingwood Cove Golf Club, 805 Hamblen Road, Kingwood, (281) 358-1155.

Latifee's Alterations is the place to go for alterations and embroidering. Latifee, the owner, is usually at the store and she's very friendly, cooperative, and fast.
◆ Latifee's Alterations, 22844 Loop 494, Humble, (281) 359-5500.

The Camera Care Center does repairs for both professionals and amateurs. If you have a minor problem they can fix it for you right away, and if it is a major repair then they will send it out. They will fix any type of camera, and they are trustworthy. Prices are reasonable.
◆ Camera Care Center, 2113 Richmond Avenue, (713) 521-1441.

The Camera Co-op sells used and consignment cameras, as well as brand-new ones. If you are looking for a certain type of a camera that you have not been able to find elsewhere, you might just find it here. They stock cameras, lenses, tripods, equipment, and film.
◆ Camera Co-op, 3514 S. Shepherd Drive, (713) 522-7837.

Salon in the Park was recommended to me by other flight attendants. Christy McDonald styles my hair, and she has a great personality. She knows all of the latest styles and is very good about keeping mature ladies like myself up-to-date without trying to get me to look like a teenager. She knows what looks good on people of different ages. A cut, color, and highlights will cost about $120.

◆ Salon in the Park, 17776 Tomball Parkway #22, Houston, (281) 517-6100.

Essential Skin Care is upscale, professional, and very clean. The ladies who work here are quite nice and will take you to your own area to listen to soothing music that relaxes you while they work. The facials usually last about an hour and cost anywhere from $45 to $70. I get the glycolic peel facial for mature skin. Melissa Coleman is the owner of the salon, but the entire staff is very knowledgeable. They do a relaxing Swedish massage for $60 to $65, too.

◆ Essential Skin Care, 1259 Kingwood Drive, Kingwood, (281) 359-4122.

Vanna Nails is a great place for a quick manicure and pedicure for about $30. Vanna is the owner and she is very good, but if you want her to do your nails, then you have to call and make an appointment. Otherwise, you can usually just walk in and not have to wait. They offer a wide selection of OPI nail polish colors.

◆ Vanna Nails, 9640 Fm 1960 Bypass Road W, Humble, (281) 446-4909.

Jan Liebsch has mastered Rolfing, which is similar to chiropractic techniques but goes even deeper. Jan looks at the overall structure of your back, determines the problem areas, and then works on those. It is not painful—it feels as if she is pushing your bones back into place as well as giving you a deep-tissue massage. The shop itself is darkly lit, with candles glowing and soft music usually playing. Jan has a soothing voice, which puts you at ease. She explains exactly what she will be doing so that you are not surprised by anything. It's worth trying if you have pain and are open-minded about new experiences. A session costs about $100 for an hour—and sometimes lasts a little longer.

◆ Jan Liebsch, 3701 Kirby Drive, Houston, (281) 360-0473.

The Scott Chiropractic Clinic uses the Activator Method to detect spinal joint dysfunction, body mechanics, and neurological reflexes. The activator is a long instrument that is put next to the area that needs adjusting to slip the vertebrae back into place. This process is very quick, easy, and painless. It's also very effective. The business is family-owned, and I see Elaine Scott, a very soft-spoken, positive, and uplifting woman. The initial exam may run up to $200, but subsequent sessions cost about $40. They take the time to explain what is wrong in terms that you can understand. They prefer to use homeopathic medicines and techniques.

◆ Scott Chiropractic Clinic, 1380 Stonehollow Drive #1, Kingwood, (281) 358-7101.

I've been sending plants from Flowers by Glenda as gifts for twenty-three years, and I've never been displeased and neither has anyone who's received them. They have a huge selection of flowers, and they are really dependable. A basic bouquet or plant starts at about $40.

◆ Flowers by Glenda, 3040 Fm 1960 East #141, (281) 443-3811.

I trust Unik Cleaners to clean my uniform and all of my best clothes. I take my wife's clothes there, too, and we've been consistently happy with the quality of service. They know how to fold clothes just right, which seems to be a vanishing art. The service is prepay.

◆ Unik Cleaners, 7802 Louetta Road, Spring, (281) 251-2712.

Mina's Cuts & Styles, only seven minutes from the airport, does a great job on my unique head of hair. Tracy gets it right. Now I take my whole family when I can, so she can cut my wife's hair and my two daughters', too. My cut costs $14; it's $70 to $80 for a cut and highlights for my wife. Tracy is there Tuesdays through Saturdays.
◆ Mina's Cuts & Styles, 233 Fm 1960 Bypass Road E, Humble, (281) 548-7767.

I attend Sunday Mass at St. Ignatius Loyola. The sermons are interesting, but what keeps me going back is the choir, the best I've ever heard. It is well balanced between men and women, and they have a mixed repertoire of traditional and contemporary music.
◆ St. Ignatius Loyola Catholic Church, 7810 Cypresswood Drive, Spring, (281) 370-3401.

The San Jacinto Inn is way cool, an antebellum house up on stilts that is now a restaurant. It occupies the site on which Santa Anna's army was defeated by Sam Houston and where Santa Anna was captured while sneaking out dressed as a private. A lot of history, as well as a monument in a beautiful park, comes with the San Jacinto Inn. The park features bike and running trails and gazebos. At the inn, you pay a flat fee ($59 per person) for all you can eat and drink (excluding alcohol). My favorite dishes are softshell crab and steak, which are simply delicious.
◆ San Jacinto Inn Motel, Highway 150 W, Coldspring, (936) 653-3008.

In the old warehouse district in Galveston you can visit the burnt-down house and last known residence of the notorious pirate Jean Lafitte. He was given a stay of execution and that is when he moved to Galveston. If you are a history buff, then this little-known attraction is for you.
◆ La Maison Rouge, 418 22nd Street, Galveston, (409) 763-0717.

Galveston holds a haunted-house tour at night, which is pretty spooky. Everyone in the town knows that these beautiful houses are haunted—people have been hearing noises coming from them since the 1800s. The tour will make you believe all these stories! Contact Galveston Historical Society for more information about the haunted-house tour.

◆ Moody Mansion Museum, 2618 Broadway Street, Galveston, (409) 762-7668.

Ghost Tours of Galveston, (409) 949-2027; admission $10 per adult and $5 per child for the hour-and-a-half tour.

LAS VEGAS

I remember my first trip to Las Vegas because of my departure from the city. I was on a Western Airlines 737 headed for Los Angeles—more or less a forty-minute flight. We taxied toward the runway, and after takeoff the pilot's voice came over the speaker: "Welcome aboard. We'll be making a left-hand turn over the Las Vegas strip, which will allow those in window seats to look down and wave good-bye to your money."

Element of truth? Of course. But also, an element of style.

Las Vegas, with the most hotel rooms of any U.S. city, the most neon, the most glitz, and not necessarily the most glamour, still ranks high with me—and with many flight crews. In fact, a growing number of them have moved to Las Vegas and commute to their official bases.

It is still a young city, growing exponentially, and has often been called the largest consumer-marketing laboratory in the world. The folks who run Las Vegas have figured out what America wants, and they give it to them. An escape, a thrill, and for the past decade, a really great meal. Would you believe that a majority of the master sommeliers in America now work in Las Vegas restaurants?

And the beauty of Las Vegas is that you don't have to gamble to go there. You can horseback ride, water-ski on Lake Mead, rock climb, go deep beneath the Hoover Dam—and some of the best spas in the United States can be found in the middle of the desert.

If any city is a challenge to flight crews, Las Vegas is it. It's a potential affront to anyone's wallet, but also a challenge to get beyond the obvious temptations and discover some really great, affordable secrets.

You want tasteless? It's right in front of you. You want something approaching greatness or that, at the very least, won't require you to mortgage your house? Ask the flight crew. I did.

AIRPORT TIPS

There's a multilevel twenty-four-hour fitness center at the Las Vegas Airport. That's pretty unusual. It's a full gym, and you don't have to be a member to use it. Take the elevator between the T-shirts Ltd. store and the post office to "0" level.
◆ 24 Hour Fitness (702) 261-3971. $15 for nonmember one-time use; call for weekend hours; otherwise, open 24 hours, Monday through Thursday.

The Las Vegas Airport also has a full-service Wells Fargo Bank, with tellers.
◆ Wells Fargo Bank, just south of the A-B security checkpoint, (702) 765-1551.

The airport also boasts an aviation museum located one floor above the baggage claim area. It is a great place to kill an hour, plus it's free. The museum focuses on the golden age of aviation, but also covers the history of aviation. It is in an open area and there are some public displays.
◆ Howard W. Cannon Aviation Museum, Level 1, Terminal 2, (702) 455-7968.

CITY TIPS

In back of the forgettable Peppermill is the old-school Vegas-style Fireside, a '70s- and '80s-era glamour-chic lounge that should not be missed. There is indirect blue and red lighting and mirrored walls. All the seats are very low to the ground, so when you sit down you have no choice but to relax. There are plum blossom trees over all the tables, so every table is its own private nook. The waitresses are glamorous and wear wonderfully sexy dresses. Drinks are tasty and reasonably priced. The scorpion is the signature drink and it's a monster, with something like seven shots in it. The place is called the Fireside because in the middle of the bar there is a pool of water with a gas flame bursting out of it. As for the ambience, let's put it this way: if I were going to have an affair, I would go to the Fireside because it is extremely intimate, sexy, and very private. It is the kind of place that makes you feel just a bit secretive and naughty.

◆ Peppermill's Fireside Lounge, 2985 Las Vegas Boulevard, (702) 735-7635. Open 24 hours.

If you want a good workout, climb the seventy-foot rock wall (the commercial world's highest) at Steven Spielberg's Gameworks, for $10. Gameworks is right on the Strip, across from New York, New York, and is open late. It costs $27 for three hours of unlimited games.

◆ Gameworks, 3785 Las Vegas Boulevard S, Suite 010, (702) 432-4263.

Another fun thing to do is indoor skydiving at Flyaway Indoor Skydiving, near the Frontier Hotel. They've got a BC3 propeller, from a plane like the ones in *Casablanca,* on the floor, facing straight up and with wire mesh over it. It creates a 120-mile-per-hour blast of air. They outfit you with a padded suit and a helmet, skydiving goggles—the whole works. Then you jump right over it as if you're free-falling. It's difficult to get hurt, but you still need to be in good shape to do this. The "dive" lasts about fifteen minutes and is a real aerobic workout. (Afterward, our heart rates were around 170 beats per minute.) It costs $45 for the first flight, and $65 for a double flight.

◆ Flyaway Indoor Skydiving, 200 Convention Center Drive 1, (877) 545-8093.

Princess Liquidators is a great place for shopping and unusual finds. Row after row of items are stacked and boxed in a huge warehouse. On one side of the building is lots of furniture, new and used, and some of it from various hotels in Las Vegas. I saw a large gold bed with Egyptian flair that came with a matching dresser and nightstands. They also had some cute Christmas lamps, lots of hand-painted flowerpots, pottery umbrella stands, picture frames, and seasonal accessories for Halloween and Thanksgiving. The inventory is subject to change, depending on what businesses are being liquidated. The prices vary, depending on the condition of the item and how unusual the piece is, but for the most part the prices are fantastic.

◆ Princess Liquidators, 3455 Boulder Highway at Sahara, (702) 737-2078.

Wild Sage Cafe is a wonderful restaurant off the Strip. The food is superb—innovative and imaginative. The owners/chefs are usually there and are very accommodating. They only serve wine, but they have an impressive selection. They take reservations, and I recommend that you make them.

◆ Wild Sage Cafe, 600 E. Warm Springs Road, (702) 944-7243.

Cappozzoli's Italian Restaurant is on a very busy corner in an older strip mall and looks like a dive from the outside—with a sign that says "Open twenty-four hours," and advertisements for video poker and the like. You don't go for the food—although it isn't bad; you go because you never know who might show up after hours to perform. Tom Jones and Robert Goulet have been there. They show up very late—after the shows on the Strip are over, around 1 A.M. or so. I have known some performers to sing until the wee hours of the morning, just for fun. You have to go and take your chances, since everything there is impromptu, but if you get lucky and someone special comes, it is an evening you won't forget.

◆ Cappozzoli's Italian Restaurant, 3333 Maryland Parkway, (702) 731-5311.

Pianist Jimmy Hopper performs a free show at Bellagio's Fontana Lounge Tuesdays through Saturdays. He and his band play everything from Andrea Bocelli to rock and roll. Usually there are four or five other people playing with him, including a female vocalist. It's all about the music—no costumes or anything—and, amazingly, he performs for free! (I think there's a two-drink minimum, though.) A bonus with the Fontana is that it overlooks the lake and fountains.

◆ Fontana Lounge at the Bellagio, 3600 Las Vegas Boulevard S, (702) 693-7111.

Avoid most hotel dry cleaners in Las Vegas at all costs. They're usually overpriced and, more often than not, don't get your stuff back to you on time. But Village East Dry Cleaners is an exception. They put tissue in the sweaters and in the sleeves of the blouses. They automatically spot-clean, which some other cleaners won't do, and they put the folds where the folds are supposed to be. Diana, the alterations lady, is skilled with everything from beaded gowns to jeans. For $14 she's taken in pants at the waist, and she's done hemming for $10. This is quality; you know that they're going to take care of your clothes. My good stuff always goes there. There are four locations throughout Las Vegas.

◆ Village East Dry Cleaners, 5025 S. Eastern Avenue #1, (702) 736-1366.

I fly to Las Vegas specifically to get my hair cut and highlighted at Static Salon by Jodi Jensen, the rock star of hair stylists. I will not go anywhere else, and I will not let anyone else touch my hair. Everyone that works here has energy you can feel when you step inside. The place has metallic walls and ceilings, and the floor is polished concrete. There is a pool table inside and sometimes even a DJ spinning. A cut and color costs about $60.

◆ Static Salon, W. Russell Road #13, (702) 253-7055.

The best-kept secret in town is the Paul Addi Salon. I get my hair cut by a guy named Al Seaquist. He charges $30 for a cut and outperforms anyone I've ever gotten a cut from. His chair overlooks the MGM pool, and while he works, he tells you what he's doing, why he's doing it, and how to take care of your hair. He never pressures you into buying anything.

◆ Paul Addi Salon, 3799 Las Vegas Boulevard S, (702) 597-0104.

LOS ANGELES

My first flight as an adult to Los Angeles was on an American Airlines 747. The aircraft had an electric piano/organ in the back of the coach section. It was a publicity stunt by the airline to introduce its transcon service on the 747, and on the first flight, Frank Sinatra Jr. and his band performed.

"This will never last," a flight attendant told me, rolling her eyes as child after child jockeyed for a seat on the piano bench. "After all, there is a limit to how many times and how long you want to hear chopsticks played at thirty-five thousand feet." (She was right. American removed the piano bars shortly thereafter.)

I asked her where she lived. "The beach," she replied.

That didn't exactly narrow things down. In Los Angeles, that could be just about anywhere. And as I soon learned, moving to Los Angeles as the west coast–based correspondent for *Newsweek,* anywhere is about as close as anyone gets to Los Angeles.

For me, Los Angeles isn't a city. It's a state of mind. To try to describe it as a city is to do injustice to all other cities. In fact, you can't even define Los Angeles as a community, although people try all the time. Instead, Los Angeles is eighty-seven separate incorporated cities in desperate search of a community!

The "beach" can be any one of a dozen or more places. The "hills"? Same thing. The "desert"? You get the picture. Imagine trying to negotiate a population of more than fifteen million people, five counties, and 34,149 (more or less) square miles.

People who visit for the first time are often given terrible geographical advice. On more than a few occasions, I've asked people coming to L.A. for the first time where they planned to stay. "Oh," they say excitedly, "we're staying downtown."

Downtown in New York means one thing. In L.A., it means you've never been there before!

When I worked for *Newsweek*, the east coast bias of the magazine (and its editors) dictated that, as a matter of routine, they had to criticize Los Angeles. There was no culture west of the Hudson River. No one read a newspaper, except to find the movie listings. Everyone was (or wanted to be) in a hot tub with Goldie Hawn. We had style, but no substance.

And all the ephemeral cultural fads started in Los Angeles, right?

Nothing could be further from the truth. In fact, Los Angeles has more museums per capita than any other American city, more than 150 art galleries, and shockingly, more theaters than New York City.

As for the cultural fads, they get perfected and *publicized* first in Los Angeles. Period.

Is Los Angeles a manageable city? Hardly. We live in our cars, and we get lost frequently. I've never taken a bus in Los Angeles because, I have to admit, I have no idea where the buses go.

As a result, we seek out our own sense and definition of community, usually within a twenty-minute driving radius of where we live, or in the case of flight crews, where their airline puts them. As a result, I'm always learning new things about a city that refuses to be defined by community.

Flight crews who lay over in Los Angeles feel the same way. Some airlines put them in Hollywood. Some in Manhattan Beach. Some even farther south in one of L.A.'s great secrets, Long Beach. So there's no single set of great Los Angeles tips, but a series of wonderful suggestions based on what the flight crews have discovered within their own twenty-minute areas.

Then there's LAX. Most of us who live in Los Angeles will do anything we can to avoid it. The alternatives are often better deals: Ontario, John Wayne, Burbank, and lately, Long Beach, one of the cutest airports I've ever experienced. (If you're walking out on the tarmac to your plane and you suddenly feel you've been transformed into Humphrey Bogart about to kiss Ingrid Bergman in *Casablanca*, you're not alone. That's where they filmed it! And nothing much has changed since, except that the propellers have been replaced by jets.)

But if you have to fly out of LAX, always do what I do: embrace the contrarian view of airport design and operation. Flying out early in the morning? Avoid the upper-level departure areas at all costs; head to the lower-level arrivals area. No traffic. No lines. Having someone meet you on an arriving flight in the evening? Reverse the process. Get your bags, then take the elevator upstairs to departures, and meet them there. You'll save between fifteen and twenty minutes of exasperation and frustration every time.

AIRPORT TIPS

In the Southwest Terminal 1 of LAX, you'll find good, fast, and relatively healthy Mexican food. It's the only place I eat in LAX. I order the chicken tacos, which cost about $5 for a couple of them.

◆ El Paseo, Terminal 1, (310) 645-9984.

I don't like driving to LAX, but once you're there it's a good airport. You can often walk from one terminal to another without having to take any connecting transportation, if you're not in a rush. There's a shortcut if you need to go from Terminal 4 to Terminal 5 or 6. There's a tunnel underneath Gate 46 that goes beneath the runway, and you can walk right on over to Terminal

5 or 6, which are the Delta and United terminals. Someone might want to do that if they have a connecting flight. Go down to baggage claim, look for signs for Terminal 5 and Terminal 6 or Delta Airlines or United Airlines.

Sometimes there are more flights arriving than departing. So it's often easier to go downstairs when you're trying to catch a departing flight because it won't be as crowded.

Enter the United Terminal through Terminal 6 and walk over to Terminal 7. There is rarely a wait at the security line in Terminal 6, whereas Terminal 7 always seems to have a line. Terminal 7 has a good Mexican food stand, which serves a decent burrito (although they don't offer knives to cut the burrito).
◆ La Salsa, (310) 646-6470.

Usually, we all go to Starbucks because it's directly across from our gate. But one day we had a delay, so we went to Terminal 5—and we found Euro Coffee Shop, which has twenty different flavors of ice cream and frozen yogurt. You can order frozen shakes, which blend a frozen mocha with any flavor of ice cream or yogurt. A small shake is about eight to ten ounces, and it costs less than $5. I had a frozen mocha with butter pecan ice cream. It was so good that I want to go back to the airport.
◆ Euro Coffee Shop, (310) 645-3606.

CITY TIPS

Genghis Cohen is a real find, on Fairfax, just north of Melrose. You'll find great Szechuan food and the hottest new music groups in town. A former record company A&R man opened it two decades ago, and twenty years later it still rocks. No tourists here, just locals. Order the crackerjack shrimp or the ma-bu beef, served in its own potato basket. The garlic string beans are to die for. And if you hear a familiar guitar riff coming from the adjoining performance room, don't be surprised to see Taj Mahal working out his new stuff or Joni Mitchell trying out some new songs. Want to see the great acoustic groups before they break? This is the place.

◆ Genghis Cohen, 740 N. Fairfax Avenue, (323) 653-0640.

Welcome to Jerry's Famous Deli. The menu is huge (about six pages), and they have everything. There are also Jerry's locations in Marina del Rey and on Beverly, near the Beverly Center. What flight crews really like about it is, one, they're open all day every day, and, two, the portions are large enough for us to share. If I'm on my own, I order half a sandwich.

◆ Jerry's Famous Deli, 12655 Ventura Boulevard, Studio City, (818) 980-4245.

Thai Talay is a real find, with some of the best Thai food in Los Angeles. If you drive too fast, you'll miss it. It's right across the street from a Lucky grocery store on Lincoln, between Jefferson and the airport. Don't be surprised if you're the only non-Asian in the joint. They do a great job with the Pad Thai and both beef and chicken satay. Definitely affordable.

◆ Thai Talay, 11314 Santa Monica Boulevard, (310) 477-3189.

I collect wines, so I go to the Wine House. It's off I-405 by the 10 Freeway. If they don't have a bottle you want, they'll try and get it. They offer a lot of consignment wines from private sellers, and they have stuff from the 1960s for a good deal. They stock wines from every imaginable place on earth.

◆ Wine House, 2311 Cotner Avenue, (310) 479-3731.

The Beach Hut, run by Hawaiians, is a tiny, surf-hut-food kind of thing. Very local, very famous. People will wait outside for thirty minutes to be seated. You'll find both surfers and guys in suits. It's a little bizarre, but definitely worth the wait.

◆ Beach Hut, 3920 Highland Avenue, Manhattan Beach, (310) 545-8911.

The Hacienda is the classic airport hotel because it's the cheapest. You've probably figured out that airline people are frugal—probably because we're used to being ripped off. When you pay for a hotel out of your own pocket, it's hard to swallow, particularly if you stay for only four or five hours. So everyone stays here because it costs only $69 for one person, $6 for each additional person.

◆ Hacienda Hotel, 525 N. Sepulveda Boulevard, El Segundo, (310) 615-0015.

My nomination for the best restaurant in California—maybe in the country—is the Mariposa Restaurant in the Hacienda Hotel. Think coffee shop with vinyl booths that haven't changed since 1970. Many of the people who work there have been there almost that long, too. You can actually hop on the Hacienda van to go eat there. Many places in California try to imitate retro, but this place *is* retro. There's nothing on the menu that costs more than $10.

◆ Mariposa Restaurant, 525 N. Sepulveda, El Segundo, (310) 615-0015, Ext. 4111.

I love riding horses. The Broken Horn (near Los Angeles) is a good place for supplies, and it's cheaper than the equestrian shops. It's a Western type of place, where real cowboys go. They've got saddles, shoes, and clothes. Pants cost about half of what you'd pay elsewhere.

◆ Broken Horn, 1022 Leorita Street, Baldwin Park, (626) 337-4088.

In Torrance, O-Nami offers an awesome all-you-can-eat sushi and seafood buffet for $21.95 during the week and $22.95 on Friday and Saturday. It's casual—shorts and T-shirts are fine. There's one in Carlsbad, too.

◆ O-Nami, 1925 West Carson Street, Torrance, (310) 787-1632.

The Venice Whaler on the Venice Pier offers one of the best views of the ocean. It's not a terribly classy place, but a lot of airline crews go there. Happy hour is from 5 P.M. to 7 P.M.

◆ Venice Whaler, 10 Washington Boulevard, Venice, (310) 821-8737.

We like to browse in used bookstores, such as Read It Again Sam, which has a big selection. Buying used books can save you as much as forty and fifty percent. You can turn in the books you are finished with and then get credit toward more.

◆ Read It Again Sam, 6208 W. Manchester Avenue, Westchester, (310) 641-2665.

A lot of my running shoes and almost all of my uniform shoes come from Marshalls. It has bargains all the time, for example, leather shoes for half price. I never spend more than $25 on a pair of shoes.

◆ Marshalls, 11270 W. Olympic Boulevard, (310) 312-1266.

At Masters Swimming Clubs, adults can swim and get coached workouts. It's really good for people who want to improve at swimming as a sport, but who don't want to enter a race. The hourlong workouts are offered at 6 A.M. and 6 P.M. The largest Masters club in the country is based here in California: SCAQ (Southern California Aquatic Masters). You can buy ten visits for $70, or you can buy monthly passes for about five pools. The Loyola pool is the most beautiful outdoor pool I've ever seen.

◆ Masters Swimming Clubs, (310) 390-5700, www.swim.net/scaq.

Before I started flying, I worked at the Venice Beach House. A lot of people think there are no places to stay in Venice, but this is right on the Speedway and is one of the family homes once owned by Abbott Kinney. There are four large suites and three smaller rooms. My favorite is the Abbott Kinney Suite because it has a fireplace. Rooms without a bath are $65. The Abbott Kinney Suite and the ones with a Jacuzzi cost $135. Keep in mind that this is a house, not a big hotel.

◆ Venice Beach House, 30th Avenue #15, Venice, (310) 823-1966.

In Los Angeles, you can rent a car for a buck an hour from the Crowne Plaza if you are a hotel guest.

◆ Crowne Plaza, 1150 S. Beverly Drive, (310) 553-6561 (Thrifty Car Rental).

I love playing golf, and Rancho Park is a public golf course in Beverly Hills where you can play for $25.

◆ Rancho Park, 10460 W. Pico Boulevard, (310) 838-7373.

Thanks to dehydration, if you're a flight attendant, there's a good chance you need a dermatologist. I recommend Dr. Ralph Kamell in Thousand Oaks. I had a girlfriend with a scalp condition who went all over the country for help until I suggested him. She was diagnosed and on her way in thirty minutes.

◆ Dr. Ralph Kamell, 227 W. Janss Road #230, (805) 497-7529.

There is a beautiful church in L.A. called the Self-Realization Fellowship Lake Shrine. The most peaceful place I have ever been, it leans toward Buddhism but is oriented more toward self-discovery than toward a specific denomination. It has a pond full of swans, ducks, and koi fish, but it's the energy of the people that makes it so serene. The grounds include the Court of Religions, honoring the five principal religions of the world; the Mahatma Gandhi World Peace Memorial, where a portion of Gandhi's ashes are enshrined; a small museum with exhibits on Paramahansa Yogananda's work; and a gift shop featuring arts and crafts from India. The hilltop temple overlooking the lake was opened in 1996.

◆ Self-Realization Fellowship Lake Shrine, 17190 Sunset Boulevard, Pacific Palisades, (310) 454-4114.

One of my daughters is into retro style and bought her beautiful wedding dress at Aardvark's Odd Ark, a vintage clothing store. It was from the 1920s and cost only $20. (She paid more to have it dry cleaned!) Aardvark's has formal and informal clothing for both men and women. The original owner chose that name because he wanted his store to be first in the phone book, and since its opening in 1972 it has always been first in the vintage clothing section of the Yellow Pages. There are four locations in Los Angeles.

◆ Aardvark's Odd Ark, 7579 Melrose Avenue, (323) 655-6769.

For haircuts, I go to Tammy at Bob Roy's in Manhattan Beach. I've probably sent twenty colleagues and passengers to see her. The clientele consists of young, trendy types, but she never pressures you into doing something you don't want. Tammy's real down-to-earth, and she'll cut both men's and women's hair. Call ahead to make sure she's there.

◆ Bob Roy's, 327 Manhattan Beach Boulevard, Manhattan Beach, (310) 545-2500.

For facials, I go to Manhattan Health and Beauty Center. It's just a little room in the back of a beauty supply store. There's not a sign that says "facial," so you have to ask for it. I go to Rima for facials and waxing. Facials are $85 for a vitamin C or mini dermabrasion treatment, or $65 for a regular facial. I've been going four years, and I have noticed a big improvement in my skin.

◆ Manhattan Health and Beauty Center, 1006 Manhattan Avenue, Manhattan Beach, (310) 374-9890.

There's a really cool, affordable wine shop in Manhattan Beach called Bacchus—the least intimidating wine shop I've ever been to because every wine has the rating listed below it, along with suggestions for food that complements it. It's real easy to maneuver yourself around the store and find what you want. You can get an Italian A+ wine for $12. The wines are stored on the walls in "beehives," like wine cases that you'd have at home.

◆ Bacchus, 1000 Manhattan Avenue, Manhattan Beach, (310) 372-2021.

I found a good chiropractor in Manhattan Beach, Dr. Steven Saber. I sometimes get lower back pain, and after I see him the pain is gone. I referred a few people to him, and they've been happy with him as well. He's an athlete himself, so he can show you some appropriate stretches.

◆ Dr. Steven Saber, 1104 Highland Avenue, Manhattan Beach, (310) 376-0781.

My favorite manicurist is a hardworking Vietnamese woman named Vicky at EXP Nails. She has many regular customers, because she really cares about the people who come to her shop. It's $16 for a straightforward manicure and pedicure, $3 extra for a French manicure. The shop is a ten-minute drive from the airport.

◆ EXP Nails, 1015 Aviation Boulevard, (310) 374-5272.

Just off I-405 is Havana Mania. I was shocked at how killer the food is there. I am not one to recommend food to flight crew, but this place is not to be missed. The first time I went, I felt immediately relaxed by the comfortable atmosphere. Three dishes that I have had there are absolutely to die for: pollo asado, the garlic chicken, costs $8.95; pargo frito, deep fried snapper, is $12.95; and lechon asado, which is fresh-daily roasted pork, goes for $8.95—and is the favorite dish of my husband and me. Every Tuesday is really special: they roast a whole pig for eight hours. All of the local people know about it, and they usually sell out before 8 P.M., so get there early. They also serve a Cuban beer called Hatuey that complements the food beautifully. They even have live music on the weekends.

◆ Havana Mania, 3615 Inglewood Avenue, Redondo Beach, (310) 725-9075, www.HavanaMania.com.

MIAMI

South Beach may have the buzz, but all of Miami is hot. "That's a nice outfit you've got on . . . How'd you like to wear it to work tomorrow morning?" is not just a bold pickup line, it's a reflection of a way of life in Miami. People do wear their nighttime outfits to work, because no one seems to sleep at night in this city.

There's an excellent reason why flight crews like arriving in Miami around 8 P.M. Things don't get going until two or three hours later, and with normal turnaround and layover times, many of them get a chance to leave the next afternoon—plenty of time not just to party, but to visit some of their secret haunts for shopping and services. Every once in a while they even get a chance to sleep.

But Miami is more than a singular destination—it's a Caribbean hub. Flights to everywhere from the Cayman Islands to the Turks and Caicos are less than two hours away. Nassau is just a short commute—even by speedboat. So are the Keys.

Lenny Bruce once said that Miami Beach is where neon goes to die. Not anymore. The transformation of Miami from God's Waiting Room to a population worshipping the nonstop pursuit of nighttime ephemeral pleasures is complete.

Miami is also a culinary treat—not just great Cuban food in Little Havana, but great restaurants like Azul at the Mandarin in Biscayne Bay.

Yet for such a happening city, the airport—seven miles from downtown—is, sadly, a galaxy away in terms of creature comforts, efficiency, and design. MIA is a disgrace—poorly lit, long walks, bad shopping. And the commuter flights resemble the last flight out of Saigon. It is not an exaggeration when I tell you I have yet to board an American Eagle flight leaving Miami that ever left on time.

Even the airport hotel isn't much to write home about, though they do have a decent health club.

If you can, make that seven-mile trip into town.

AIRPORT TIPS

La Carreta, a Cuban restaurant, is the kind of place that has flight crew sprinting from the other end of the concourse on a thirty-minute stop. The gate agents are screaming at us to get the airplane out and one guy says, "I'll get the airplane ready, and you go for the beans and rice!" The black beans and rice with fried plantains and the tamales are really good. There's also a dish called Pollo Imperial that's fantastic. They serve a tuna sandwich on flat Cuban bread that costs about $3.50, and you can get a pretty decent meal for under $10.

◆ La Carreta, Concourse D, (305) 871-3003.

I love going to the Miami airport because we get long layovers there. I go up to the top floor to the gym and use the steam room, pool, and Jacuzzi, which not many people seem to know about. It costs $8 for the public, and they have lockers and a snack bar. It's an open area, so you can see all the planes landing and taking off. There's also a carpeted running path on the roof.

◆ MIA Hotel, Concourse E, 2nd Level, Departure, (305) 871-4100.

If you are trying to get to Miami Beach, avoid the bus because it will take at least two hours. Trust me, the taxi ride is worth it.

CITY TIPS

Books & Books is an inviting, old-fashioned independent bookstore with locations in Miami Beach and Coral Gables. There's hardly a layover when I'm not there. The decor consists of mahogany bookshelves, and you can find just about any book you might be looking for. There are conference rooms, a café, and even a happy hour on Friday evenings. Mitchell Kaplan, the owner, has stayed in business for a long time, even though a large chain bookstore moved in right around the corner. You can even buy gifts there, such as funky reading glasses.

◆ Books & Books of Miami Beach, 265 Aragon Avenue, (305) 442-4408.

Stone crab is a delicacy associated with the Miami area, and Joe's Stone Crab, out on Miami Beach, has its own vessels that go out and collect crabs and bring them back. Everyone knows about this place, although not everyone knows that you can get take-out there. During the Super Bowl, the place is booked solid, so take-out is definitely the way to go.

◆ Joe's Stone Crab, 27 Biscayne Street, (305) 673-0365.

At El Globo Beauty Salon you can get a manicure for just $5. They do French manicures, but they don't do acrylics. The place is decorated in wild, Cuban style, and the staff doesn't speak any English—but you can get by with Spanglish. It's a full-service salon, but they don't take reservations. There are about ten manicurists and they're all very good, but I ask for Amanda.

◆ El Globo Beauty Salon, S.W. 17th Avenue, (305) 541-5887.

Albert will give you a great haircut right in his own home. Next to his old Florida-style house in Coconut Grove, he has a studio with one chair in it. A haircut costs about $35 and he does color as well.

◆ (305) 442-9544.

Las Vegas Restaurant has excellent Cuban fare. They prepare a grilled chicken with onions and lime that is outstanding, and the pork is delicious, too. Located about six miles north of South Beach, it's not touristy at all. I found it when a local person recommended it to me. It gets a little crowded later in the day, but at lunch it's not busy.

◆ Las Vegas Restaurant, 6970 Collins Avenue, (305) 864-1509.

I go to Porky's Gym, which is open twenty-four hours a day and is only twenty minutes from the airport. You can get a one-day pass for $5. They don't offer any classes, but there are machine and free weights. It does get crowded between 5 and 8 P.M., but the mornings are pretty empty.

◆ Porky's Gym, 10000 S.W. 56th Street, (305) 279-0610.

Parrillada Las Vacas Gordas is a family-owned Argentinian restaurant, decorated with pictures of cows out front and with wine bottles and garlic hanging from the ceiling inside. They serve rolled-up steaks with a variety of garlic sauces. A recommended dessert is crepes with ice cream. You should be able to get a table if you go at 6 or 7 P.M. Prices range from $8 to $15.

◆ Parrillada Las Vacas Gordas, 933 Normandy Drive, (305) 867-1717.

Jimbo's Shrimp is a little dive known for its marlin and salmon, as well as its unique clientele. It's been around for fifty years and used to be a bait house. Rather than selling side orders to go with your fish, they just give you some hot sauce. Then you sit out back on picnic tables and eat your fish and drink beer. On one side of you there might be a biker, and on the other side maybe a doctor or a lawyer. They don't have silverware, and you can bring your own side dishes and drinks if you want to have a picnic. The place is usually packed, but the food is so good and the people so great that it's worth it. They do not have a sign or even a street address. To get there, take I-95 and exit at Key Biscayne. Get on the Rickenbacker Causeway. Cross the bridge and drive for approximately two miles. Turn left after the first light; you'll see Mast Academy on your left. Go down that street for about one and a half miles, and look for the Water Treatment Plant sign. You will run right into Jimbo's.

◆ Jimbo's Shrimp, Rickenbacker Causeway, Key Biscayne, (305) 361-7026. Hours 6 A.M. to 6:30 P.M., Monday through Friday; 6 A.M. to 7:30 P.M., Saturday.

Every winter for the last eight or nine years, Alex Fox, a famous Spanish guitarist, has played at the Breakwater Hotel in South Beach. He sets himself up on the porch in front of the bar, facing Ocean Drive. He is so wonderful that he literally stops traffic on the beach. The bar gets so crowded that people set up chairs and blankets across the street at the beach.

◆ Alex Fox at Café Med in the Breakwater Hotel, 940 Ocean Drive, (305) 674-6776.

Doral Floral makes a beautiful arrangement for about $35 to $40. My favorite combination is sunflowers with another type of summery flower to complement them.

◆ Doral Floral, 8031 S.W. 138th Plaza, (305) 592-3373.

Biscayne National Park is right on the beach, ten minutes south of Miami. There are palm trees, sand dunes, pavilions, and bike and Rollerblading trails. This is a quiet park, where the beach is about ten miles long. The farther south you go, the more isolated you will be. The park is nine miles east of Homestead. From the turnpike, go south to exit 6; turn left on Speedway

Boulevard. Go straight on Speedway until S.W. 328 Street, and turn left. The entrance to the park will be on your left.
◆ Biscayne National Park Headquarters/Information: (305) 230-PARK, (305) 230-7275.

The last thing I want to do after a flight is open the door to a minibar in my hotel room. Who can afford that? Instead, I make a trip to Latin American, a great grocery store that sells Spanish and Cuban food. It always has fresh baked bread and in the back is a deli where you can get a fantastic Spanish meal. Breakfast costs no more than $4, lunch no more than $6, and dinner no more than $8. Breakfast is typically American eggs, pancakes, and waffles, but lunch and dinner are Spanish food only. Everybody loves the carne rey, which is a shredded beef stew that comes with rice and beans and a side of plantains. I recommend tres leches for dessert—it's like flan but is made with three types of milk. They sell it for $2, and you get a huge portion.
◆ Latin American, 7365 W. Flagler Street, (305) 261-4401.

At Dry Clean USA, you use a computer to enter your information, including what you brought in and what you want done, as well as when you would like it back. If you drop off your stuff before noon, you can get it back the same day. You deposit your clothes in the bag next to the computer. There is always an attendant there in case you have questions. They also do alterations; I got a pair of pants hemmed and cuffed for only $8. A man's shirt costs 75¢, 25¢ for extra starch.
◆ Dry Clean USA, 1515 Alton Road, (305) 538-0722, www.drycleanusa.com.

It sounds silly, but when I fly to Miami, I always bring extra shoes to Joe's Shoe Repair Store. Joe will resole a pair of shoes for $15, and he does it fast. If necessary, he will fix whatever you need while you wait. One time I took him a belt that needed extra holes and he only charged 25¢ per hole.

◆ Joe's Shoe Repair Store, 5386 Palm Avenue, Hialeah, (305) 823-4111.

Club Space is a great club that only local people seem to know about. It does not even look like a club from the outside, but inside there are two rooms for dancing. One is the rock-and-roll room, painted with clouds, and the other is the techno room, which is painted in stripes. It's very bizarre but so much fun—and it's only a $10 cab ride from Miami Beach. It keeps strange hours, and at 5 A.M. they set out huge containers of all different kinds of fruit so that people can cool off and get refreshed.

◆ Club Space, 142 N.E. 11th Street, (305) 372-9378, www.clubspace.com.

NEW ORLEANS

"New Orleans is American Voodoo," the Continental flight attendant cautioned me on my first flight into the Crescent City. "But it's nothing to worry about," she reassured me. "It's just this weird subterranean energy in New Orleans. It's as if they already know you're coming and where you're going before you even get here. One more thing," she cautioned, "New Orleans is the town last call forgot . . ."

About forty-five minutes later, as I got into my cab to drive downtown, her prophecy came true. A big, happy man drove an old, big, happy Oldsmobile 98. We were riding a whale into town. "Welcome, Mr. Greenberg," he said. "Continental treat you right from Houston?" he asked. "Well, you're in for a treat at the Windsor Court." Wait a minute. How did he know my name, the airline I flew in on, and the hotel where I was staying?

"Just a lucky guess," he chuckled, and drove me in.

It was just the beginning. My flight had landed around 8 P.M., and I was tired. But at 9 P.M., the phone rang in my hotel room. It was one of my friends who lived in New Orleans. "Welcome," she said. "So . . . what are you doing later?"

Later? "What do you mean by later?"

"Honey, we're just getting started. We'll pick you up a little later."

It is safe to say that when in New Orleans, you must redefine the word "later." It really means *much later.* Four hours later, in fact, and a little before one the next morning, my hotel phone rang again. "Okay," she said, "we're downstairs. Get down here."

"Now?" I asked. "No," she joked. "Later. No . . . I mean right now."

I pulled myself out of bed, threw some water on my face, and hastily dressed. And in retrospect, I'm glad I did—my friends grabbed me, drove only a few blocks, and by 1:30 that morning I was floating down the Mississippi on a riverboat with a few hundred of their closest friends, jamming with the Neville Brothers.

My flight crew friends will take their friends to Bourbon Street or Café du Monde only once—those places are for amateurs. They know the secrets of the French Quarter, the out-of-the-way jazz clubs, the aboveground cemeteries, and the haunted places that populate the city. They also know the hidden palaces of indulgence and decadence outside of town.

In the subsequent years when I've been to New Orleans, I've never forgotten my first piece of advice from that flight attendant, and the two lessons I've learned. The first: as Mark Twain once said, "There is no architecture in New Orleans, except in the cemeteries." The second lesson? Only in New Orleans is "later" a really good thing.

AIRPORT TIPS

The best way to get into town from the airport is the $10 airport shuttle. Unless you can get two or three people to share a cab with you, it's a better deal because it's a flat rate of $25 from the airport to the city.

CITY TIPS

Every Friday, the local newspaper has something called a Lagniappe, an extra pullout section dealing solely with entertainment for the upcoming weekend.

If you have a few hours to kill between flights, head to the Harbor Seafood and Oyster Bar, which dates back to my old Navy days, before I started flying commercially. It is a five-minute cab ride from the airport, and it's my favorite place. Half of the building is a fish market and the other side is the restaurant. So you can either order in the restaurant or go over to the left side, pick out anything you want, and have it sent over and cooked to your liking. They will pack the fish for plane travel or ship it for you. The owner once told me the secret of why his fish is so good. He uses only peanut oil and changes it twice a day. Other restaurants change it every few days. I discovered it one day while talking to the mechanics. The clientele is all locals, no tourists, and very low-key and casual.

◆ Harbor Seafood and Oyster Bar, 3203 Williams Boulevard, Kenner, (504) 443-6454.

R Bar Royal Street Inn, just a half block from the French Quarter, is a darling little place with only five rooms. You really feel like you are in New Orleans there. A second-floor balcony runs all the way around the building, and each room has a different name and a different New Orleans theme. One of the rooms is called Storyville, after the legal red-light district that was around at the turn of the century. Another is Ghost in the Attic, decorated to feel haunted. It's an alternative B&B, which in New Orleans means "bed and beverage." My friends Tom and Heidi Epps (both retired Delta employees) are the owners, and Kimmy is the manager. If you stay at the inn, they give you a token for a free drink at the bar. The R Bar clientele is mostly local, and with all the music elsewhere in the area, it's a nice place to have a quiet conversation. The ceiling is decorated with a full band of instruments hanging upside down, a surfboard, and a flight attendant mannequin wearing an oxygen mask. There's also a full-size motorcycle sitting on top of the cooler.

◆ R Bar Royal Street Inn, 1431 Royal Street, (504) 948-7499, (800) 449-5535. Bar hours 3 P.M. to 5 A.M., Sunday through Thursday, and till 6 A.M., Friday and Saturday.

The muffalata is a local sandwich originated at an Italian deli in the French Quarter called Central Grocery. It is a round loaf of Italian bread hollowed out and filled with Italian meats, olive salad, and different kinds of cheese. They cut it into pie shapes, and it's usually enough for several people. You can get them all over town, but Central Grocery is the most famous place because they're the best. There is a little counter in the back where you can sit, but I like to take my sandwich to Jackson Park, a big, well-known park in the French Quarter. Whatever you do, don't bring it back with you on the plane. It's a very messy sandwich and you'll ruin whatever you're wearing if you're not careful.

◆ Central Grocery, 923 Decatur Street, (504) 523-1620.

At Bella Donna Day Spa you can get just about everything done to pamper yourself. Not only do they do a great job, but because the place caters mostly to locals, you can pick up information about things to do in town that week.

◆ Bella Donna Day Spa, 2900 Magazine Street, (504) 891-4393.

Yvonne La Fleur is an inviting boutique named after the owner, a quintessential Southern belle. The place is upscale but not so pricey that the average person couldn't afford something. Yvonne will send a taxi to pick you up or she might send clothes to you if she knows you. She goes all over the world to get her merchandise. She has her own fragrance line and is also well known for her hats, which she learned to design and style from an aunt who had a millinery shop. Check out Sugar Daddy Night, when female models parade in lingerie, for men only.

◆ Yvonne La Fleur, 8131 Hampson Street, (504) 866-9666.

Pilots are notorious for being a little tight with money. Characteristically, one thing they love to do is figure out ways to get a free morning paper. In New Orleans, I do that—and get coffee—at Morning Call Coffee Stand. It's a small coffee shop that serves great New Orleans–style coffee, half chicory espresso and half steamed milk. Make sure you get some of the beignets, powdered-sugar-covered pastries. Next door is a well-stocked newspaper stand with papers from around the world. Definitely a local hangout.

◆ Morning Call Coffee Stand, 3325 Severn Avenue, Metairie, (504) 885-4068.

I've been in the business for twenty-one years, and I'm devoted to two things: flying and my dog. So when I'm in New Orleans, I stop at a very special place, the Three Dog Bakery. This place only makes dog treats, and they're not too expensive. They have bones, cookies, cakes, and all sorts of things. My dog, Bear, goes crazy for the treats I bring him.

◆ Three Dog Bakery, 827 Royal Street, (504) 525-2253.

I get my hair cut by Tom at Golden Shears, a tiny barbershop with only four chairs. The place is probably fifty years old and definitely has that old-time feel to it. There is always a stream of customers waiting because there are no appointments. Tom has been in the business for a long time. He gives me the classic buzz cut, which costs $12, but he will do whatever you want.

◆ Golden Shears, 6008 Magazine Street, (504) 895-9269.

When I have shoes that need fixing, I head to Edward's Shoe Service. The place is amazing. At least two hundred pairs of shoes—those that people have left and never claimed and those still waiting to be repaired—sit up on shelves all around this small store. Mr. Edward is the only person who works there, and this man can fix anything! It usually takes just a couple days, but if you are desperate and speak kindly to him, he may fix them while you wait.

◆ Edward's Shoe Service, 3704 Magazine Street, (504) 895-4993.

On one of my layovers, I was so sick that I couldn't even go out to get medicine. Then one of the crew members told me about Uptown Delivery Pharmacy. These guys are just the ticket in such situations. You call and say what you need or tell them what is ailing you, and they will recommend something (over-the-counter) and deliver it directly to you for free (you tip, of course). You pay by credit card over the phone and they accept a variety of insurance providers.

◆ Uptown Delivery Pharmacy, 741 Nashville Avenue, (504) 897-0141.

This comes under the "difficult to pack" heading, but Clement's Hardware Variety sells great antique gas space heaters from the 1920s and 1930s. They also have a huge selection of cast-iron cookware. The employees are knowledgeable and helpful, and prices very reasonable. I bought a cast-iron skillet for around $15.

◆ Clement's Hardware Variety, 6000 Magazine Street, (504) 899-0711.

Le Salon is the in place for many of us. Trudie, the owner, and her daughter, Valesca, are the only two employees. I love this place for the pedicures because you sit in a chair that vibrates. Le Salon does manicures, pedicures, waxings, facials, and more. A pedicure will cost about $30 with tip, and includes a fabulous leg massage. You definitely have to make an appointment with her before you go.

◆ Le Salon, 222 N. Rampart Street, (504) 529-9968.

Want to get a little crazy in New Orleans? (But then again, doesn't that come with the territory?) Fifi Mahoney's is the perfect place to release that alternate persona by buying a wild wig.

I never thought I was a wig person until I went there. Now I own at least five. The wig selection here is wide, with a variety of good-quality items to pick from. In addition to wigs, they sell makeup, wallets, purses, earrings, and funky T-shirts.

◆ Fifi Mahoney's, 934 Royal Street, (504) 525-4343.

Sally Ann Glassman is a voodoo priestess, and she is the real deal. Her shop, Island of Salvation Botanica, is not one of those New Orleans tourist places. She does readings, blessings, and cleansings. She did a cleansing at the bar we own, and the following Monday was the biggest Monday we'd ever had. I had never had a reading done before, and my first one with Sally was a truly wild experience. She has written a few books, including *Vodou Visions*, one of the best.

◆ Island of Salvation Botanica, 835 Piety Street, (504) 948-9961.

A few years ago I was going out with a man who sent me a bouquet of flowers from Tommy's Florist every week for a year. The man is gone, but Tommy's is still there. Tommy's is well known around town for doing unusually creative things, as well as for being really dependable. It's a small shop that does great business because of its wide variety of flowers and very reasonable prices. Tommy's will supply you with simple arrangements or really extravagant ones.

◆ Tommy's Florist, 1029 Chartres Street, (504) 522-6563.

William "Billy" Rau runs an antique shop called M S Rau Antiques, which has been in the family since his grandfather opened it many years ago. The antiques come from all over the world. He has furniture, perfume bottles, hairbrush sets, and much more. It is one of the foremost antique shops in New Orleans. Billy is almost always there, and he will help you find whatever you need. His knowledgeable staff has worked for him forever.

◆ M S Rau Antiques, 630 Royal Street, (504) 523-5660.

Croissant d'Or Patisserie is a pastry shop that is well known to local people. I usually go there on the weekends to read the paper, have a croissant and coffee, and relax. I always try to get a window seat so that I can do some people watching. I like their almond croissants, but you can get any kind of filling you want. A large croissant is about $1.25, and coffee is about $1.

◆ Croissant d'Or Patisserie, 617 Ursulines Avenue, (504) 524-4663.

La Marquise Pastry Shop is a tiny shop that is not the least bit touristy. You follow a little alleyway to a courtyard where you can sit and have your pastry and coffee. It is just the cutest place. They have little round tables, most with umbrellas.

◆ La Marquise Pastry Shop, 625 Chartres Street, (504) 524-0420.

The Grace Note is the only place I go to buy something to wear for a special occasion. I bought a beautiful sheer silk tie-dyed dress to wear for my twin brother's wedding. I also bought a $45 porkpie hat with a feather for my husband. The hats, for both men and women, vary in style and price, but they are works of art in themselves. However, you really go there for the ambience, which is truly bohemian. The buyer patronizes artisans from New Orleans, and nothing in this store would be found at a mall.

◆ Grace Note, 900 Royal Street, (504) 522-1513.

NEW YORK

In the interest of full disclosure, I am partial to New York. I was born there, went to school there, summered there, and survived there. In public school, I played baseball on cement playgrounds and dreamed of weekends on grassy fields in Central Park. At seventeen, I became a volunteer fireman in my summer community on Fire Island, and I am still a volunteer fireman today.

I'm very lucky because my job allows me to be in New York about once every six or seven days. And I give the city full credit for allowing me to succeed elsewhere. I am a firm believer that if you have the chance, and you weren't lucky enough to be born in New York, you should spend at least a year of your life in the city. Why? Because living in New York teaches you to be streetwise; you may not always know where to go, but you soon—and surely—learn where *not* to go, in New York, and for that matter, everywhere else.

Flight crews who live in the city are the quintessential New Yorkers—they process information quickly, do not suffer fools well, and are not shy in the least about telling you exactly what you need to know.

Flight crews who fly to New York are streetwise by association. If they can master this city, they can master any city.

New York is, by definition, crowded, expensive, and frenetic. There is a certain synergy to the bedlam that is New York, a certain organizational level that can only be experienced, never described. This is a city where you hit the ground running—or you get hit back. And that is both the attraction and the danger of this city. It is energy, nonstop.

About the only time I have ever seen the city slow down was during the week following the tragic events of September 11, 2001. On that morning, I was at NBC at the *Today Show* studios at Rockefeller Center, about six minutes away from doing one of my segments, when the first plane hit the building, and our lives changed forever.

In the first days following the terrible tragedy, I witnessed a city in dazed disbelief, and for the first time in my life, I watched New Yorkers walk, speak, think, and act in slow motion. But then I saw the very same people bounce back with a newfound resilience that other cities would be hard-pressed to match.

On that terrible Tuesday morning, my first thoughts went out to my many flight crew friends—and I knew a number of them who died that day. Three of those four planes were headed to Los Angeles, and for a short period of time, many of my friends thought there was a high likelihood that I had perished.

Since September 11, I've been with numerous flight crew friends as we made the necessary pilgrimage to Ground Zero, to pay honor to those who died in the buildings and on those planes. It is a tribute to the spirit of thousands of flight crews who, confronted with this terrible disaster, still manage to fly, to smile, to serve. For a number of months, it was difficult for many of them to talk to me for this book. Slowly, surely, they have recovered, but they will never forget.

New York has always been *the* international gateway city in the United States. Between JFK, LaGuardia, and Newark, more than 115 airlines fly into the region, ranging from Royal Jordanian to Cathay Pacific, from Air France to Japan Airlines, and some airlines (and countries) from newly emerging, independent, and previously unknown states.

For such a popular area, it also has some of the worst-designed, most user-unfriendly airports. It's not exactly the welcome you want or need when you come to New York. But if you can get past the chaos and frenzy of the airports, there's more than just hope.

As any flight attendant or pilot can—and will—tell you, New York is one of their most popular layovers.

And they will also tell you that they hate New York's airports. Kennedy is poorly designed, LaGuardia boasts the most delays, and Newark is . . . well, Newark—although a new train service from Penn Station now makes getting there a breeze.

Someone once described New York as a city where everyone mutinies but no one ever deserts. That is certainly true of its airports.

AIRPORT TIPS

JFK

Kennedy is the worst airport I've ever been to. It's a mess. It's so difficult to make a change from terminal to terminal, which I must do every week. I go from Terminal 3, which is Delta, to Terminal 6, and sometimes it can take as long as forty minutes. That's how it was pre–September 11, and it will probably be the same way in 2025. Changing terminals in Kennedy is a nightmare. People are treated like sardines; their luggage is all over the place. God forbid there is ever an accident—nobody will be able to get to the exits.

In the American Airlines terminal, cigarettes are the best duty-free bargain. You can get them for a lot less than what they cost now in a regular store. However, there's a limit on how much you can purchase.

◆ International Shoppes

Pickles, Deli and Soups makes good New York–style sand-wiches. In the morning you can get a pretty decent omelet made to order, for $4.86, which includes home-style potatoes, bacon or sausage, and peppers or onions if you ask.

◆ Pickles, Deli and Soups, Terminal 8, (718) 553-6717.

The New York Express Bus (nicknamed "The Carey") is the best way I have found to get into the city from JFK or La-Guardia. It stops every twenty to thirty minutes at every termi-nal in the airport. The bus is red, white, and blue—ask for it and anyone at the airport will be able to tell you where to find it. From Kennedy it costs $13, and from LaGuardia it costs $10. It takes you to Grand Central and the Port Authority, from which points you can take the subway or a cab anywhere. A cab from LaGuardia will cost about $20, and from JFK it's $35.

◆ New York Express Bus, (718) 875-8200.

If you're in a hurry between connections, take a cab from termi-nal to terminal. Just tell the cab driver to get a short call and then tip him $10. At the most, it will take ten to fifteen minutes. I got out of the Delta terminal at 4:30 and I made it onto my 5:20 departure with a little room to spare. So bite the bullet and spend the money.

For $5 it's an easy five-minute ride to the "Ronkonkoma" train station. For $7 you can take the train to New York's Penn Sta-tion. It takes about an hour and twenty minutes and avoids all the traffic going into New York. It will probably save you hun-dreds of dollars on last-minute flights.

LaGuardia

The M60 bus is an inexpensive way to get into the city from the airport. It takes about forty-five minutes and costs only $1.50. It makes five or six stops in the city, all with easy access to any subway. The last stop is at 106th and Broadway. You have to have exact change, but there is no problem taking your luggage on the bus. Usually the bus drivers are helpful with directions as well.

◆ M60 Bus, located downstairs, between the taxi stands.

Asian Chow is fantastic Chinese food. It's downstairs in the airport, next to the deli, so not a lot of people know about it. I tried a free sample one day, and I was hooked! The place is famous for Bourbon chicken, which you can get with rice for $5.

◆ Asian Chow, Baggage Claim Level, (718) 898-6665.

Newark

Here is a warning: the bar/restaurant in the American terminal at Newark Airport takes at least forty minutes for each order. It's actually famous for making you wait. So these days, when no one wants to go through security twice and a lot of flights aren't serving food on board, make sure you get food outside and bring it along with you.

After a long flight, get a neck rub at d-Parture Spa. You can also get manicures and pedicures for $25, chair massages, and waxes. It's a great place to kill time and pamper yourself a little bit. They also do mini makeovers in which they analyze your skin type and colors.

◆ d-Parture Spa, Terminal C, Gate 92, (973) 242-3444.

CITY TIPS

One of the ways I avoid jet lag is by not eating on the planes. But once I land in New York, I want organic food. Josie's is the best. The prices are moderate and you can get a wonderful tuna burger for $8. There are multiple locations.

◆ Josie's, 300 Amsterdam Avenue, (212) 769-1212.

Mike's Coffee Express "roach coach" has all the food you would expect in New York, such as sausage, pepper, and onion sandwiches, but my favorite is the black-and-white cookie. Although there was a line when we went, there were cops in that line, too, so that tells you right there that it's good.

◆ Mike's Coffee Express, Ditmars Boulevard and 100 Street, Queens, (917) 559-2917.

Viand is an amazing Greek coffee shop on Madison. It seats about forty people, and the kitchen is tiny. Viand specializes in turkey, meat loaf, cheeseburgers, and rice pudding. When we get to the city after a flight, if Viand is open, we're there. I can definitely vouch for the cheeseburgers. Regardless of whether you order the cheeseburger medium or well done, be sure to lean forward when eating it—it's that juicy! On certain days they make great hot bread pudding, but you have to ask. Viand is also just three blocks away from the Metropolitan Museum of Art.

◆ Viand, 1011 Madison Avenue, (212) 249-8250.

At the Redeye Grill, the thing to order is Chinese chicken salad. It costs about $14.50, and you can only eat about half. Also, don't miss their shrimp quesadilla appetizers—really good!—for $9.75.

◆ Redeye Grill, 890 7th Avenue, (212) 541-9000.

There are very few flight crews that don't know about Carmine's, near Times Square, by the Milford Plaza (dubbed the "Mildew Plaza" when it was our crew hotel; it's not the best hotel, but a good location). Carmine's was the savior. The bartenders know the flight crews and are very generous with drinks. But what we really like are holidays. Many of us fly on Thanksgiving and Christmas, but we still want a Thanksgiving or Christmas dinner when we land. At Carmine's we're served family-style, so we feel really comfortable, like at home. Last year, they gave us a rate of $120 for a table seating eight people. They served us turkey and stuffing and a couple of side dishes. The pièce de résistance is their bread pudding, which satisfies about twenty people. Ask for John—he's our favorite bartender.

◆ Carmine's, 200 W. 44th Street, (212) 221-3800.

I always go with one of the other flight attendants to Montebello Ristorante Italiano. The people are extremely pleasant there—and as someone who works in the service industry, I notice how we are treated. The quiet music makes it easier to talk, and because of its setting—it's a little more formal—it draws an over-thirty crowd. Main courses can range from $18 to $30. The portions are ample, but not excessive. But mostly it's the service that keeps me coming back.

◆ Montebello Ristorante Italiano, 120 E. 56th Street, Fl. 11, (212) 753-1447.

The Amish Market on East 45th Street has nothing to do with the Amish, but it's a high-quality delicatessen and gourmet food service. It's a regular grocery store, too. We buy what we want, and take it back to the hotel—it sure beats the minibar!

◆ Amish Market, E. 45th Street, (212) 571-4232.

I like to go to the flea market on Columbus Avenue. Here you can find antiques, architectural paraphernalia, old doorknobs, and even jewelry. I bought some handmade glass bead earrings for about $20. If you look hard, you'll find great fabrics, even Persian rugs. There's the usual assortment of clothing, and it's not all junk. I've found some bargains on designer stuff.

◆ Flea Market, Columbus Avenue, between 75th and 76th Streets. Sundays only.

If you like sushi, then go to Tony Sushi King. It's a take-out place with free delivery. I'm a vegetarian, so I order inari and edi-mame—the basic stuff. Prices are very reasonable. Vegetarian rolls are $3.25. They've got a family jumbo platter for $60. A small sushi platter is $13.95. There's a friendly Japanese girl who will make special orders. It's take-out all the way, but the food is healthy and fresh.

◆ Tony Sushi King, 200 W. 57th Street, (212) 957-5151.

On one New York layover, a Korean flight attendant took us to Woo Lae Oak in SoHo. They have grills right in the center of the tables, on which people cook their own fish. All the wait staff is friendly and helpful. I tried grilled vegetables and a seaweed salad there, and of course, they have great kimchi. It's a little pricey, but not over the top. Order à la carte and share if you want to save some money.

◆ Woo Lae Oak, 148 Mercer Street, (212) 925-8200.

Strider Records in Greenwich Village is the place to browse if you collect vintage records from the 1950s and 1960s. Records cost anywhere from $15 to $2,000.

◆ Strider Records, 22 Jones Street, Fl. 1, (212) 675-3040.

The Firehouse Restaurant is a Mexican-American restaurant that is decorated with badges from police and fire precincts throughout the city.

◆ Firehouse Restaurant, 522 Columbus Avenue, (212) 595-3139.

I buy cheese at Di Palo Fine Foods, where the little old Italian ladies shop. They make all the mozzarella balls for the restaurants in the neighborhood, and the Parmesan cheese is the best you'll ever get. They educate you and help you find your favorite treats. They will even ask what season of Parmesan you want because cows eat different things depending on the time of year, which flavors the cheese. In addition to cheeses, they have prosciutto and other Italian deli items. My pilot friend brings bread from San Francisco and trades it with the owner for deli items.

◆ Di Palo Fine Foods, 206 Grand Street, (212) 226-1033.

Tout Va Bien, a little French restaurant a few blocks from Times Square, was opened in the 1920s and is still owned by the same family. It's a small place, frequented mostly by locals and theater people, and it feels more like an intimate café in Paris. They've had the same grandmotherly French waitresses there for twenty years, and they always make me feel welcome when I walk in the door. You can call for a reservation, but you shouldn't need one. Everything I've had there is good, especially the steak with *pommes frites.* Appetizers range from $6 to $10, and entrées are $15 to $22. They have an extensive wine list and great food, but what makes this place special are the people who work here and the ambience.

◆ Tout Va Bien, 311 W. 51st Street, Fl. 1, (212) 974-9051, (212) 265-0190.

As a black guy, I find Astor Place Hair Designers in Greenwich Village to be a great place for a haircut. Actually, I think this is the best place to go in the whole country. It costs $15, and there must be at least fifty barbers.

◆ Astor Place Hair Designers, from Times Square, take the N train and get off on Astor; 2 Astor Place, (212) 475-9854.

There are great Italian restaurants in virtually every neighborhood in New York, not just in Little Italy. Sistina is a small, intimate, uptown place that stays open late. The portions are huge, so just about every dish can be split. When the waiter tells you the specials, you better pay attention—there are more specials than menu items. Order the frico salad (mushrooms and potatoes) or the risotto with black truffles. It's not expensive, but it's still fun to share. One night Giuseppe, the owner, gave us a corner table in the back, and ten minutes later the entire cast of *The Sopranos* came in! Reservations are a must, unless you go after 10 P.M. Going in late is cool because that's when the old regulars come in. Giuseppe will often sit down at your table and tell great stories.

◆ Sistina, 1555 2nd Avenue #816, (212) 861-7660.

St. Clement's Episcopal Church is in an old theater in midtown. Services are held in the early morning and afternoon on Sundays. It's not the most beautiful church, but it has a wonderful spirit and an eclectic mix of people of all ages and socioeconomic groups. This is New York at its best and most colorful.

◆ St. Clement's Episcopal Church, 423 W. 46th Street, (212) 246-7277.

The Renaissance is a traditional American-Mediterranean restaurant open twenty-four hours a day. They serve Greek salads with olives that are as big as your fist. The Renaissance is like Denny's—the only difference being that at Denny's there's some guy with an apron and a tattoo of his mother doing the cooking, while at the Renaissance, there's a guy with the apron and the tattoo of his mother, but while he's cooking he's thinking of the recipe passed along for generations by his mother's family. The place was recently remodeled, so check it out.

◆ Renaissance, 776 9th Avenue, (212) 246-9873.

If you want to see a great show without paying the price of a Broadway ticket, go to Don't Tell Mama, an L-shaped bar with a backroom cabaret revue. The performers are phenomenal—all of them incredibly talented, struggling actors, just waiting for someone to figure that out. The place is standing room only, with a line out the door, spilling onto the street. Audience members sing and bartenders perform. I saw a girl who looked like she just got off the farm get up and belt out "Son of a Preacher

Man" like her voice was coming up from her feet! If you get there after 10 P.M., you'll be listening from the outside, so get there early.

◆ Don't Tell Mama, 343 W. 46th Street, (212) 757-0788.

Whenever we're in New York, I drag the other crew members over to ABC Antiques, where you find floor after floor of unique home furnishings. One floor is devoted to china and crystal, one has lovely linens, and another displays antiques. The building is huge, and it could take the better part of a day to go through this store. If you get hungry or tired of walking, they also have a café. Across the street is an adjunct store, with area rugs of every style and size imaginable. If you are looking for something special and unique for your home or if you just enjoy browsing, this is the place to do it.

◆ ABC Antiques, 888 Broadway, (212) 473-3000.

Across the street from ABC Antiques is Fish's Eddy, where you will find discontinued china and pottery from hotels that have either gone out of business or changed their patterns. It is fun to look over all the dishes, recognizing the logos of some very famous hotels. Furthermore, the prices are great. They also carry glassware and other small kitchen items.

◆ Fish's Eddy, 889 Broadway, (212) 420-9020; 2176 Broadway, (212) 873-8819.

Nu Look Sauna and Spa (it also goes by Nu Hong Yong Beauty Salon) is a Korean place offering massages for women—and it's *very* Korean. The Korean masseuses, most of whom must be about sixty years old, dress in black bras and panties, which they change after every customer. First you take a hot shower, then a twenty-minute sauna, and then they put you on a table and exfoliate you from head to toe with a pumice stone. When they are done, they start all over again, exfoliating for an hour. After scrubbing you down, they give you a massage over every inch of your body, and when they are done, they do it again! Finally, they give you a facial, wash your hair, rub you all over, rinse you off, get you back into the room, dry you off, and get your clothes. The whole process takes about two and a half hours and costs about $200. For many of us, it's the greatest thing in the world. Except for the receptionist, no one there speaks English, and you can't be shy about being naked in front of your friends. As in Korea, no one is that modest—no one really cares.

◆ Nu Look Sauna and Spa, 11 E. 36th Street, (212) 447-6666.

New York's running club meets every weeknight. It's a treat for out-of-towners who don't know the city and want to be safe when they run. Group runs are at 6:30 A.M. and 6:30 P.M.; the morning run meets at the Safety Kiosk inside Central Park at 90th Street and East Drive. In the evening, go to 9 East 89th Street approximately ten minutes before the start of the run.

◆ NYRRC Safety Office, (212) 423-2205, www.nyrrc.org/nyrrc/org.

Javon is where I go to get waxed in New York. Sara Savage is from Buenos Aires, and she's fast, thorough, and knows what she's doing. She also does excellent electrolysis, facials, and laser hair removal. I would never recommend anyone that wasn't exceptional, and I've been waxing for twenty-five years. She will fit you in if you are from out of town, but definitely book in advance if possible. I'm usually in and out in an hour. She lives nearby and if you have some kind of emergency, she might come in especially for you.

◆ Javon, 66 W. 84th Street, (212) 874-1327.

At Bon Sofi, near the Empire State Building, Ilona Taithy gives exceptional facials. I've been going to her for four years. She's got a gentle touch and a European graciousness (she's Hungarian). She goes out of her way to accommodate her regular customers. She uses a rose-scented cream and tea tree oil. When she finishes, my skin is absolutely glowing. Facials cost $60, and she also does waxing.

◆ Bon Sofi, 333 5th Avenue, Fl. 2, (917) 256-1234.

Diane Young is an aesthetician who appears on the QVC channel on television fairly regularly. If you want advice on hiding your flaws with makeup and making the most of what you've got, then schedule an appointment with her. It's not cheap, but she's right on target with her advice.

◆ Diane Young, 38 E. 57th Street, (212) 753-1200.

Idlewild—the bar—is designed like a 747 airplane. When you open the door, you walk down a hallway that looks exactly like a jetway. The lounge area feels like the upper deck of a jet. The bathrooms are small and designed just like the lavatories on planes. There are airplane seats with seat belts, airplane windows, and curved walls. The bartenders dress like pilots, the waiters and waitresses dress like flight attendants, and the busboys wear grounds-crew ramp uniforms. The menu looks like a safety card from an airline. Try the drink called the Tokyo Red Eye, which is one of my favorites. Even the air-conditioning system in this place sounds like that hum you hear when you are on an airplane.

◆ Idlewild, 145 E. Houston Street, (212) 477-5005.

Angelica Kitchen is a great macrobiotic vegetarian restaurant. I recommend the dragon bowl—rice, beans, seaweed, and carrots with homemade tahini dressing, for about $9.95. All the desserts are made with honey or unrefined sugar. Contrary to what you might expect, the food is very filling and tasty. There are tables for two or four people, but if you are alone you can eat at a communal table.

◆ Angelica Kitchen, 300 E. 12th Street, (212) 228-2909.

Temple in the Village, near NYU, is a vegetarian buffet, serving anything a vegetarian might want, including four different kinds of rice, cabbage with red pepper, kale, radishes, beans, and potatoes. They weigh your food and charge by the pound.
◆ Temple in the Village, 74 W. 3rd Street, (212) 475-5670.

Anna and Jeanne Marie are two of the wonderful instructors at the Iyengar Yoga Institute of New York. They are open from 8 A.M. to 8 P.M. Classes cost about $15 for an hour and a half.
◆ Iyengar Yoga Institute of New York, 27 W. 24th Street, Suite 800, www.yoga-ny.org.

Body Logic is where I go for body alignment, a kind of therapeutic touch or holistic physical therapy. What a chiropractor does with bones, owner Yamuna Zake does with the muscles. First, she works from your feet to your hips, and then she works on your back and shoulders. She tries to teach your muscles to be properly aligned. The first hour costs $200, and you definitely need to make an appointment.
◆ Body Logic, 295 W. 11th Street 1F, (212) 633-2145, (888) 226-9616.

Wilner Chemists carries a natural sleep aid from France called Sibilium that's great for jet lag. I take three, which puts me right to sleep so that I wake up refreshed in the morning. Ask for Ronald, who sells natural homeopathic products. They will ship all over the United States.
◆ Wilner Chemists, 100 Park Avenue, (212) 682-2817, (800) 633-1106.

The Cajun is a great place to hear live music every night and on Sunday for brunch. They play New Orleans music, jazz, and big band, but I go on Mondays and Thursdays to see Vince Giordano. He plays bass, but he's also the bandleader, and his band plays music from the 1920s through the 1940s. Meals are priced from $13 to $18, and reservations are required.

◆ The Cajun, 129 8th Avenue, (212) 691-6174.

If you like to get dressed up and go ballroom dancing, go to the Red Blazer. They have a fantastic continental cuisine, with entrées starting at $16 to $17. There is also a bar where you can just sit with a drink and listen to the music. The weekends are usually busy, but during the week it is pretty quiet. It's a place for all ages to go and have a good time. Spiro, the maître d', will set you up.

◆ Red Blazer, 32 W. 37th Street, (212) 947-8940.

International ballroom dance champion Pierre Dulaine has a studio in New York, where you can sign up for a particular kind of dance class (mambo, swing, ballroom, etc.), or you can take private lessons.

◆ Pierre Dulaine studio, 25 W. 31st Street, (212) 244-8400.

ORANGE COUNTY

When I first moved to Los Angeles, Orange County was thought of as the uncle no one wanted at the family reunion. With the possible exception of Disneyland, no one went there.

People who lived in Orange County were thought of as way behind the curve, ultra-right-wing John Birch Society members and poster children for the polyester telethon.

No one admitted to being from Orange County, either. But somehow, a few million people happened to live there.

Of course, while everyone in Los Angeles and San Francisco treated Orange County folks either with condescension or derision, a funny thing happened: it became the population base of California and it became a money capital. California went the way Orange County voted.

But slowly and surely, Orange County has become a hot destination. Even the airport works, although it is pretty much stretched to flight capacity. Smart travelers head out to Gate 9 to Catarina's Candies, where chocolate fudge or other candy can be bought by the pound. You can also get delicious smoothies near Gate 6. Perhaps my favorite aspect of John Wayne Airport is that the entire wall facing the airfield is glass—so if you're a plane junkie like I am, grab your smoothie, head for the intersection of the two airport concourses, and enjoy.

Orange County essentially merges with San Diego County. Laguna Beach and La Jolla are just two of the must-sees for anyone driving down I-405. Between December and March, head to the Dana Point harbor for some fascinating whale watching.

I have had an ongoing love affair with San Diego since I wrote a story about Lindbergh Field for *Newsweek*. It had—and still has—the steepest approach of any major city airport in the world. The direction of the approach takes you over Balboa Park and through the city's downtown before you finally flare over the runway.

I remember that when I first wrote about the airport, that approach was demonstrated to me by a pilot, who—along with many others—thought Lindbergh Field was unsafe. To say it was a steep approach was an understatement. In fact, then, as today, if you're in one of the city's hotels with someone you're not supposed to be with, better draw the curtains when a plane approaches, because the entire left side of every incoming flight can see you!

Despite the terrifying airport approach, San Diego is as close to a perfect city as I can imagine. The weather is ideal, there is access to both the desert and the Pacific Ocean, and it has one of the great zoos of the world.

I've got two favorite things to do in San Diego. If I'm not flying, I'll take my boat down from Los Angeles to the San Diego harbor. Thanks to the abundant presence of the U.S. Navy, it's one of the most interesting harbors on the west coast. I go under the bridge and over to Coronado, where I park and leave my boat at Loews Coronado. Sometimes my friends will accompany me and drive me back into San Diego, where I rent a motorcycle and cruise back over the bridge to Coronado.

When I'm not on the motorcycle, I cruise the harbor in the boat. If I'm feeling particularly bold, I'll head to Harbor Island, where I watch the jets land at Lindbergh. If you don't have a boat, check out San Diego Yacht and Breakfast, which consists of nine vessels that offer overnight accommodations on yachts and sailboats.

Some flight crews like to head south to Baja's Gold Coast and take day trips at Rosarito Beach and Ensenada. It's only a ninety-minute drive from San Diego. You have to go through Tijuana, but that's part of the fun. Just remember: if you're renting a car, be sure to get Mexican accident insurance. If an accident happens south of the border, they arrest everyone first and ask questions later—sometimes much later. If you've got a flight to catch . . . well, you get the picture.

AIRPORT TIPS

John Wayne Airport is the most convenient airport in the country. If you walk out of Aloha's Gate 9, you are literally ten yards from the escalator, and it drops you right in front of the baggage claim. Directly across the street are the rental cars. It is a long and very thin airport with a lot of glass and air. In spite of all this, I don't think the food is all that good. The food court is located on the second level near Gate 8.
◆ General information: (949) 252-5200.

California Kids baby store is not a big brand-name store, but it has really cute baby clothes. The merchandise might be a little pricey, but that's nothing unusual for an airport. They stock sizes ranging from three to six months to 6X.
◆ California Kids, second level near Gate 8, (949) 242-6148.

CITY TIPS

Orange County

In Costa Mesa, we all go to a bar called the Corner Office, where they serve a mean cosmopolitan.
◆ Corner Office, 580 Anton Street, Costa Mesa, (714) 979-9922.

We can get around in Costa Mesa without a car because our crew hotel is adjacent to the South Coast Plaza. Statistically, this is the safest neighborhood in the country. Costa Mesa's corporate parks, where there are excellent restaurants and hotels, are conveniently connected via sky bridges to the South Coast Plaza, so you don't even have to cross the street.

◆ South Coast Plaza, 3333 Bristol Street, Costa Mesa, (714) 435-2000.

Jerry's Famous Deli and the Clubhouse (owned by actor Kevin Costner) serves some of the best American food in Southern California. Try the meat loaf sundae, which looks like a brownie sundae but is made with meat loaf, mashed potatoes, and gravy. The desserts are oversized and sure to please any dessert freak.

◆ Jerry's Famous Deli and the Clubhouse, 3333 Bristol, Suite 2802, Costa Mesa, (714) 708-2582.

Last Long Nail, a Vietnamese place, lives up to its name. Their manicures are long-lasting and inexpensive—and they charge only $14.99. (I live near Charlotte, where they charge $45 for a manicure.) Some of the staff speak English, but most don't. However, they might sing to relax you—a low-pitched and soothing melody in Vietnamese.

◆ Last Long Nail, 688 Baker Street, 6b, Costa Mesa, (714) 751-3417.

For a girls' night out, we like to go to Sing Sing in the Irvine Spectrum. The cover is under $10, but it's hard to get in on weekends—try to get there before eight or nine. The entertainment features dueling pianos, and the pianists rib members of the audience. It's the kind of place that a lot of bachelorette parties wind up. They offer a full bar menu.

◆ Sing Sing, 71 Fortune Drive, Irvine, (949) 453-8999.

Walt's Wharf, in Seal Beach, is famous for its fish and steaks cooked on an oak grill. The service is good and the price is right, too.

◆ Walt's Wharf, 201 Main Street, Seal Beach, (562) 598-4433.

You generally need a car in Orange County, and we recommend Budget Rent-A-Car in Long Beach. They are open Sundays, are very friendly, and provide excellent service.

◆ Budget Rent-A-Car, 249 E. Ocean Boulevard #104, Long Beach, (562) 495-4316.

San Diego

Great News is a cooking supply store and cooking school in Pacific Plaza, which offers short, one-day classes for $39 to $49; sushi classes are $59.

◆ Great News, 1788 Garnet Avenue, (858) 270-1582.

At French-style Cafe Champagne you can get delicious coffee and pastries, as well as breakfast and lunch. The almond croissants and the omelets are particularly tasty.

◆ Cafe Champagne, 32575 Rancho California Road, Temecula, (909) 699-0088.

Jim Johnson at the Golden Touch Hair Salon is another professional dedicated to the best in his craft. He is quiet, competent, and cares about his customers.

◆ Golden Touch Hair Salon, 6110 Friars Road, Suite 106, (619) 296-7800.

Jim Jessop's family has owned George Carter Jessop Jewelers for generations, and although the store is off the beaten path, the quality of their inventory is unmatched. They work with a wide variety of precious stones and metals, and they have a large selection of estate jewelry. The quality of the selections is exceeded only by the quality of the customer service. Jim and his staff can make you happy—just tell him how much you want that happiness to cost.

◆ George Carter Jessop Jewelers, 401 W. C Street, (619) 234-4137, www.JessopJeweler.com.

A friend went to Williams-Sonoma intending to stay five minutes and buy a gift for an upcoming wedding, but she met resident chef Jean-Marie Carrett, who charmed her into staying for two hours for one of his cooking classes—ironic because she hates to cook! On her recommendation, my husband and I went on one of his cooking tours of Provence, where it was clear that Jean-Marie is adored by people in every village we visited. If you can't make the tour, the next best thing is to register for one of his cooking classes. They cost $50 per person, but you get to eat the results!

◆ Call Marga Fountain for schedules and reservations, (619) 225-9014 or (800) 456-7389; e-mail Margafountain@aol.com.

Although Ramada Inn has taken it over, the St. James Hotel, in the Gas Lamp District, has remained essentially an early-nineteenth-century hotel. The gorgeous and unique lobby contains a marble staircase to the first floor, graced by stained-glass windows with a dolphin motif above. The two elevators—one of which, built in 1907, was the world's fastest—still open and close with gates. These elevators will hold only five crew members and their baggage, so if you're claustrophobic, you may want to wait for the next elevator. The rooms are tiny, but they all have charming features like ceiling fans and vintage bathroom tiles. Often we'll take drinks and sandwiches to the roof of this ten-story building, where there is seating, and on Thursday nights in the summer, wine tastings are held. You can see all of San Diego from there.

◆ St. James Hotel, 830 6th Avenue, (619) 531-8877. Room rates $119 to $269.

Ralph's grocery store, four blocks from the St. James, has the best deli in town. This is where we get those sandwiches (for $4.95) that we take to the rooftop of the hotel.
◆ Ralph's, (619) 579-7929.

My favorite restaurant is the Blue Point, a family-run place in the Gas Lamp District. The dark-wood interior is quaint and there is a wonderful bar, where they serve the best martinis in San Diego. The seafood is equally good.
◆ Blue Point, 565 5th Avenue, (619) 233-6623.

If you ever have a toothache in San Diego, call Dr. Steven G. Ward. His services include teeth cleaning, fillings, and bleaching.
◆ Steven G. Ward, 3500 5th Avenue, Suite 201, (619) 298-2893.

The Cottage House in La Jolla is a casual restaurant in a private home setting, where all the tables are in a garden. The food is as inviting as the atmosphere. Try the turkey Benedict. Breakfast and lunch are served year-round (from 7:30 A.M. till 3:00 P.M.), and during the summer months they serve dinner till 9 P.M., Tuesdays through Saturdays. They take reservations for dinner only.
◆ Cottage House, 7702 Fay Avenue, La Jolla, (858) 454-8409.

El Pescadore Fish Market in La Jolla is both a market and a sidewalk café. Not only is it a good place to buy fresh fish, but they also make fresh grilled seafood sandwiches, which you can order to pick up or eat there. You can even order lobster, which they will steam so that you can take it out and eat it on the beach. It's open seven days a week.
◆ El Pescadore Fish Market, 627 Pearl Street, La Jolla, (858) 456-CLAM.

The man to see for haircuts and color in the San Diego area is Kerry Welch at Model Call Hair Salon. He keeps up on the latest styles, and he loves to talk about movies—he knows them all!

◆ Model Call Hair Salon, 7553 Girard Avenue, La Jolla, (858) 454-3812.

Word of mouth or pure luck is the only way you would find out about Pietro's, since they don't advertise. Owned and operated by Pietro DiMeglio, the place hasn't changed in the twenty-six years he's been there, seven days a week. Sit in the comfy red booths, listen to Frank Sinatra, and order a pizza for less than $15 or a meatball sandwich for under $5. And one more thing: be sure to wear elastic-waist pants.

◆ Pietro's, 8378 Parkway Drive, La Mesa, (619) 462-1162.

Singer/pianist Steven Orr and bartender Bud Falls make an entertaining combination at the Monterey Bay Canners restaurant at the Oceanside Harbor in north San Diego County. Orr performs original compositions as well as requests from his large repertoire of tunes by the likes of Eric Clapton and Steely Dan. Falls wears a headset and, while making drinks, joins in and sings along, which makes for a hilarious performance that has actually acquired a local cult following. The restaurant serves surf-and-turf style cuisine, but it's just as much fun to have a drink and enjoy the show.

◆ Monterey Bay Canners, 1328 Harbor Drive North, Oceanside, (760) 722-3474.

In Coronado, everybody knows about the famous hotel where they filmed *Some Like It Hot* with Marilyn Monroe, but on the beach side, at the last mile of North Island, is an immaculate dog beach. Most dog beaches are unpleasant because you have to dodge what other dogs have left behind, but this place will surprise you. The people who regularly bring their dogs here want to keep it a secret. But even if you don't have a dog and you just want to see the interesting variety of breeds on this mile-and-a-half strip of beach, it's a fun place—and a dog lover's heaven.

◆ Coronado Dog Beach, Coronado.

If you have the whole day, spend a buck to catch the ferry from the Waterfront area to Coronado Island. Ferries run every half hour, starting early in the morning. You can spend as much time as you want on the island. Take a walk to the Hotel Del Coronado, which has a rocky beachfront where you can sit and watch the waves crashing or the sun set. Be sure to wear jeans and something to keep you warm, because once that sun goes down it gets kind of nippy. Ferries stop running around 9 P.M.

ORLANDO AND TAMPA

Is Orlando a city or a huge chunk of Central Florida that just happens to be the theme park capital of the entire planet? Don't worry. It was a rhetorical question. I always laugh when I'm in Orlando and someone wants to show me "old town." Old town dates back to . . . 1955?

Orlando seems more invention than real city. And if it's not theme parks, it's convention-goers. Next to Las Vegas, Orlando is tops in the number of hotel rooms—more than 100,000.

Many if not most of the thirty-six million visitors to Orlando each year do precisely the same thing at least once: fly to the airport, hit the Beeline expressway and then Interstate 4, head directly to the fifty square miles that make up Walt Disney World, stay about three days, and then drive back to the airport.

But my flight crew friends can only take so many rides on "It's a Small World After All." These repeat travelers to Orlando know that if you head north, about thirty minutes from downtown Orlando, you hit the Wekiwa Springs State Park, a nearly eight-thousand-acre wilderness with thirteen miles of hiking trails. But the real gem here, as one flight attendant once showed me, is the headwaters of the Wekiwa River. You can rent a canoe and play with turtles, dodge cypress branches and, of course, the occasional alligator.

There are also beautiful lakes around Orlando—Osceola, Virginia, and Maitland—and you're not far from the Kennedy Space Center.

But don't get me wrong. I'm not that hung up on reality. Thanks to a counter agent at the airport, I was introduced to the Spider Man ride at Universal Studios. And now, every time I go to Orlando, I bookend my trip between that ride and the Tower of Terror at Disney/MGM. A little dose of fantasy goes a long way.

The reality, of course, is the airport, which, to its credit, actually works. Good access, good shopping, not too many long walks. And a hotel within the airport (the Hyatt) that has figured out a way to streamline the process. You land, call the hotel, and a bellhop comes to the baggage carousel. Very cool.

AIRPORT TIPS

Orlando

At the Orlando airport, a lot of the flight crews and ground personnel eat at "roach coaches," a term used disparagingly to describe those trucks with the sides that flip up that sell sandwiches. But the appellation is not always justified. Sometimes the food is absolutely delicious. If you exit the airport terminal on side B and walk through the parking garage, you will see two or three trucks in the same area as the taxis. They make Asian dishes such as kung pao chicken, curry chicken, beef, and sesame chicken, as well as Puerto Rican dishes like pork chops with rice. It's mostly Chinese food, but it's good and cheap. You can get a meal for as little as $2.50; for $4 you get a plate that's big enough for two.

Nathan's hot dog stand sells the best ice cream. I'm partial to a flavor called strawberry cheesecake. A waffle cone will cost you $3.50.
◆ Nathan's, Main Terminal, third level.

Tampa

One day while stuck at the airport I discovered the Museum Company in a nice shopping area at the main terminal. Here you can find gifts appropriate for children, including educational toys from the National Geographic Society and from other museums. For example, I bought my brother a Galileo thermometer for $49.

◆ Museum Company, Main Terminal, third level, (813) 876-4403.

CITY TIPS

Orlando

Room 1500 at the Radisson actually has a refrigerator and a microwave. And there is a real grocery store (as opposed to a convenience store) a couple of blocks away, so you can actually make a decent meal in your room.

◆ The Radisson, 8444 International Drive, (407) 345-0505.
Goodings Supermarket, 8255 International Drive, (407) 352-4215.

A lot of professional women get their hair cut at Strand's. The quality of the cuts and the personable service are the attractions at this clean, friendly shop. Cuts cost about $15; appointments are suggested.

◆ Strand's, 9318 E. Colonial Drive, (407) 381-8111.

Bikram's Yoga College of India is a good place for beginners or those like me who want to get back into yoga or need to do some stretching for health reasons. Classes are conducted at all skill levels and usually consist of fifteen to twenty people. The rate depends on the number of classes you take.

◆ Bikram's Yoga College of India, 2415 E. South Street, (321) 663-7526.

I've been all over the world for eyebrow waxing, but Tina, at Galaxy Nails, is the *best*. She's talented and personable, and she also does nails. Waxings cost around $7; pink-and-white nails, resembling a natural French manicure, will run about $30 for a full set. Tina is popular, so appointments are suggested, especially on the weekends.

◆ Galaxy Nails, 2514 S. Semoran Avenue, (407) 736-0021.

At Wallaby Ranch, an old, two-hundred-acre cattle ranch that's a thirty-minute drive from Orlando, you can get towed in a hang glider behind an ultralight plane for $75. It's a tandem ride with an instructor. They take you up to two thousand feet, where you glide over forty-five acres of level green grass, free of rocks and power lines, and then you glide back down. It's exhilarating! It's open every day of the year, but they'll take you hang gliding only when the weather permits.

◆ Wallaby Ranch, 1805 Dean Still Road, Davenport, (800) WALLABY, www.wallabyranch.com.

Tampa

Merlin's Books has a wonderful selection of books from around the world on religion and metaphysics, among other things. They stock a lot of hard-to-find books, as well as some first editions and rare hardcovers.

◆ Merlin's Books, 2568 E. Fowler, (813) 972-1766.

I'm not a runner, but I run along the bay in Tampa because it's so beautiful and the breeze off the harbor is exhilarating. There are a lot of beautiful homes, and at every mile marker there is an exercise station. If you run in the early afternoon, you'll avoid the crowd. The cement path is great for biking, too.

People who play golf know to visit Cotton Golf, an out-of-the-way golf shop started by Joe Cotton, who once played in the

PGA. When he first opened the shop they concentrated on club repair and selling used clubs, but now Chris, the current owner, will custom-make any golf club set you want. The high-end copies are priced according to what the customer wants to spend, but the used clubs and knockoff brands tend to be less expensive than usual. You can get a good set of clubs for under $500.

◆ Cotton Golf, 2900 Fourth Street N, Suite B-101, St. Petersburg, (727) 896-4518.

You can camp right on the beach in Fort DeSoto Park, for only $33.30 a night (no reservations, cash only). The West Beach faces the Gulf of Mexico and has white sand with clean, warm water. This place is like the Hilton of camping. Each site has running water, its own picnic bench, a grill, and covered trash cans, and the sites are cleaned after each guest has checked out. There are clean, convenient bathroom facilities and shower locations throughout the grounds. There is also a washer and dryer, candy machines, and a small store (which is a bit expensive, so I recommend stocking up before you get there). The eight-mile-long paved walking/biking/Rollerblading path is gorgeous. A Civil War fort is on the premises, and the camp rangers give guided tours. The park does not allow pets.

◆ Fort DeSoto Park, 3500 Pinellas Bayway, Tierra Verde, (727) 582-2267.

The original Sunshine Skyway Bridge was knocked down in a terrible accident, and instead of rebuilding it, they built a new bridge next to it. Then they built two piers extending from the old bridge, called the North Shore and the South Shore, which have become popular fishing spots. At the North Shore, on the St. Petersburg side of the bridge, you can get all your fishing needs right on the pier, including fishing poles, bait, and food. On any given day, I've caught trout, flounder, yellowtail, and more, but I also go out there to talk to people. Not only do I get a great day of fishing, but I often get a great life story as well. The bridge is only about twenty minutes from the airport, and there is a twenty-four-hour bait shop and information booth.

◆ Sunshine Skyway Bridge, Exit 2-B off I-275, (727) 865-0668.

PHOENIX

This might sound strange, but I was first introduced to Phoenix by the chief pilot from Lufthansa!

How did that happen? For years, that's where Lufthansa trained their pilots. "We have miles and miles of airspace out there," he told me. "We don't have that kind of flying freedom in Frankfurt."

For weeks, German pilots would practice takeoffs and landings at the Sky Harbor Airport, and many confused travelers couldn't understand why so many Lufthansa planes were parked at the airport if they weren't flying to Germany.

Of course, my Lufthansa pilot friend soon fell so in love with the city that he moved there—from the Rhine to the desert—and he never once complained about the heat. In fact, like most folks in Phoenix, he already had the proper spin. "Sure it's hot here," he would say. "But it's a dry heat."

My retort: my oven is a dry heat, but I don't live there!

Well, as I've come to learn, it's not the heat that makes the difference in Phoenix. It's a new wave of lifestyle that celebrates the surprises of the desert.

It's the land. It's the spas. And now it's the restaurants.

You can ride rapids like Rat Trap and White Rock. The intrepid river runners of the Salt River are fearless. Phoenix has now become spa central: not just the typical mud wraps, but Sedona mud wraps, stone treatments, and spas that incorporate Native American culture. At the Biltmore, there's something called Indian Raindrop Therapy—it starts with warm essential oils dropped on your back, followed by a massage. (Don't ask why the oils are essential. Just relax and enjoy it. *That's* essential!)

An America West flight attendant turned me on to the chef's table at the Phoenician, one of the more incredible dining experiences. But be careful: if chef Jimmy Boyce invites you on an early morning hike, better call the paramedics! If anything, Boyce is a living example of what moving to Arizona can do for you. When he was a chef at the Loews Coronado Hotel in Coronado, California, he weighed about eighty pounds more than he does today. He moved to Arizona and embraced a healthy diet and a somewhat demonic exercise program. I've been told never to trust a skinny chef. But in Boyce's case, I'll make an exception.

My flight attendant friend also introduced me to hot air ballooning over Camelback Mountain, jeep tours out in the Sonoran desert, as well as the Phoenix Public Library, as amazing for its architecture as it is for its book collection.

The airport itself works very well. Taxi rides into town usually cost less than $10. And where else but Arizona would an airport feature a bizarre exhibit of giant water bugs for visitors to admire?

AIRPORT TIPS

The Native American exhibit on the second floor in Terminal 3 features black-and-white photographs by local young artists and artifacts made by tribes from northern Arizona.

The architecture of the airport is beautiful, and captures the environment of the city. When you take the escalator down, it's as though you're inside the Grand Canyon.

Oaxaca serves delicious Mexican food. I recommend Chicken Delight—rice, shredded chicken, sauce, and tortillas—for $4. It's a good alternative to fast food.

◆ Oaxaca, Terminal 4, (602) 275-4444.

Lefty's burgers have that backyard barbeque flavor. Although they charge airport prices ($8 to $9), it's worth it because the portions are big and the burgers are grilled right before your eyes.

◆ Lefty's South Rim Restaurant, Concourse B, (602) 273-4837.

CITY TIPS

Although it looks upscale, Alexis Grille, a small restaurant that not many people know about, is very reasonable, and you get home cooking without going far (about a ten-minute drive) from the airport. An average dinner costs $12 to $15, and they offer specials. They have a delicious garlic and pasta dish, and the tiramisu is good, too. The wait staff is helpful and knowledgeable. The place caters to the local theater crowd, and they're only open until 9 P.M., so it's good for lunch and early dinner.

◆ Alexis Grille, 3550 N. Central Avenue, (602) 266-4463.

The Willow House, a private residence in the early 1900s, is now a coffee shop, with nine or ten rooms where you can sit and enjoy your coffee or an inexpensive espresso drink. The house is also a haven for the arts. Local artists showcase their work here, and the place also sells used books. The original garage was turned into a small theater, where poetry readings are held and local bands play. Outside there is a grassy area with picnic tables.

◆ Willow House, 149 W. McDowell Road, (602) 252-0272.

Wink's, a former Taco Bell that retains the signature adobe arches and Spanish tile roof, is now a gay bar and a great place to see drag shows. The crowd includes both gays and straights, who come in droves for the celebrity impersonations. There's no cover charge, and they always seem to offer drink specials. There are two shows a night, on Thursday, Saturday, and Sunday. Get there early!

◆ Wink's, 5707 N. 7th Street, (602) 265-9002.

Sts. Simon and Jude Cathedral is home to Father Mike McCarthy, an Irish priest with an engaging sense of humor. This Roman Catholic church has a congregation of about twenty-five hundred people, and both Pope John-Paul II and Mother Teresa have visited and attended services there.

◆ Sts. Simon and Jude Cathedral, 6351 N. 27th Avenue, (602) 242-1300.

If you have an Imelda-size penchant for shoes but a peasant-size budget, check out Last Chance Bargain Shoes! It's basically a Nordstrom return store with a huge selection of shoes and clothing at bargain prices. I bought $700 worth of shoes for $92—including tax. I found a pair of Isaac Mizrahi ponyhair mules for $17, and a Facconable shirt for $9.97. (The same shirt at a Nordstrom retailer was $110.) Flight attendants are hard on shoes, so we're always on the lookout for a good value. This is the place to find one.

◆ Last Chance Bargain Shoes, 1919 E. Camelback Road #1, (602) 248-2843.

A Touch of Heaven will give you just that in the form of a one-hour body massage. It's $50 for a Swedish massage and $80 for a deep-muscle massage. The place is clean, accommodating, and small (only three rooms). Two locations in Phoenix.

◆ A Touch of Heaven, 9118 N. Cave Creek Road, (602) 395-9957; 524 E. Dunlap Avenue, (602) 944-2699. Hours 11 A.M. to 11 P.M. MasterCard, Visa, and American Express accepted.

The better-known places to hike in Phoenix, such as Squaw Peak and Camelback, are always packed, so I go to North Mountain instead. There's a gorgeous view of the west valley, and you'll see a variety of lizards, rabbits, and birds along the way. The trails are paved, but the incline is a bit difficult in places. It's not a trail for Rollerblading, but it's a good place to run or hike.

◆ North Mountain Recreation Area, north of Peoria Avenue off 7th Street, (602) 262-6696, www.phoenixmountains.org/map.html.

I fly to Phoenix just to have my hair done. Evan Cowden at D.W.E. Hair Design is a very talented artist who just opened a small salon. He hasn't received the attention he deserves, but he does a lot of work for *Arizona* magazine. Evan can suggest the best cut and color to complement your features. He charges $25 to $35.

◆ D.W.E. Hair Design, 10880 N. 32nd Street, (602) 923-6878.

Flight attendants have special skin needs because of the dehydrating effects of flying, and Johnny Kaye at Beauty First, in Scottsdale, understands this. A facial runs about $65, and they also do peels, waxing, and body treatments. It's about twenty miles from the airport, but it's worth the trip.

◆ Beauty First, 8776 E. Shea Boulevard, Suite B2, Scottsdale, (480) 991-4005.

Sarah Jones, my hairdresser at La Femme Salon, cuts my hair just the way I like it, and she's excellent with color. A haircut will run $40 to $45.

◆ La Femme Salon, 7411 E. 6th Avenue #101, Scottsdale, (480) 675-8224.

Interior Fabrics, a well-organized, high-end store, stocks the latest home upholstery fabrics, such as toile and good linen. You can also find pillow fillers, trim, and all kinds of home decorating accessories.

◆ Interior Fabrics, 6925 E. Indian School Road, Scottsdale, (480) 423-0174.

In Celebration of Golf lives up to its name, with an incredible selection of golf memorabilia, books, clothing, silverware, glassware, and custom golf carts. Their collection of golf photographs is unmatched, including close-ups of special holes, autographed portraits of golfers, and shots of famous courses like St. Andrew's.

◆ In Celebration of Golf, 7001 N. Scottsdale Road #172, Scottsdale, (480) 951-4444.

If you want a quick-fix, no-frills massage, visit Rainstar University, a massage school in Old Town Scottsdale. The first hour and a half will cost $43.50, and subsequent one-hour sessions are $29, but no tip is expected. Call ahead for an appointment.

◆ Rainstar University, 4110-4130 N. Goldwater Boulevard, Scottsdale, (480) 423-0375, (888) RAINSTAR.

Cathy's Rum Cake Caterers, in Old Town Scottsdale, is known for its special-occasion cakes. Most of them are yellow cakes with beautiful whipped-cream icing and a wide variety of fillings. The strawberry banana and amaretto peach cakes are especially scrumptious. You can request any size you want; the smallest size would serve about six people and costs $20 or more. The cakes come frozen, which makes them easy to take home. They usually have cakes in stock, so you may not need to special order. I loved these cakes so much that I ordered one for my wedding! Two locations in Scottsdale.

◆ Cathy's Rum Cake Caterers, 4807 E. Greenway Road #5, Scottsdale, (602) 996-9099; 4200 N. Marshall Way #7 (Old Town), Scottsdale, (480) 945-9205.

The Scottsdale Culinary Institute offers single-session classes, workshops, and seminars.

◆ Scottsdale Culinary Institute, 8100 E. Camelback Road, Scottsdale, (800) 848-2433, www.scichefs.com.

I fell in love with the Author's Café and its owner, Nick Ligidakis, a charming Greek man. Nick is passionate about helping aspiring writers get published, and, in fact, is himself the author of *A Man's Journey into Culinary Exploration,* a cookbook that includes recipes from the café. All of the food at the Author's Café is fresh and delicious—for example, the mixed chicken salad with toasted pita bread for $9.95.

◆ Author's Café, 4014 N. Goldwater Boulevard, Suite 104, Scottsdale, (480) 481-3998.

Karyn Smith, at the Arizona Studio of Electrolysis and Permanent Makeup, will put you at ease with her professionalism. She charges $40 for thirty minutes.

◆ Arizona Studio of Electrolysis and Permanent Makeup, 3080 N. Civic Center #29, Scottsdale, (480) 941-8936.

Floating down a river past a beautiful desert on an inner tube is a very relaxing way to spend a layover. You can rent tubes at Salt River Tubing for about $10 each, including the shuttle—they will deliver you to the launch site and pick you up at the end of your trip. They supply coolers, so you can bring drinks. The tubes themselves get very hot, so bring big towels to cover them. You can bring dogs, kids, whoever and whatever you want. A trip down the river can take one to four hours.

◆ Salt River Tubing, 15 miles north of Highway 16, on Power Road, Mesa, (480) 984-3305, www.saltrivertubing.com. Open May through September.

I play a lot of golf, but I don't want to pay $100 per game, so I go to Pepperwood. Carts are available, but you can walk, too. It's a nine-hole executive course, which means it's a par 3 and 4. Basically, you work on your short game. Prices range from $7 to $15, depending on the time of year, and there is no dress code. The clubhouse is pretty basic, but they still have the cart service selling beer. On Sundays during the winter it gets full, so make a reservation.

◆ Pepperwood Public Golf Course, 647 W. Baseline Road, Tempe, (480) 831-9457.

When I'm not flying, I'm an interior designer, and I've found Mercado Mexico–Artesanias Mexicanas, a mom-and-pop pottery store about fifteen minutes from the airport, to be a good source of decorating items. They sell hand-painted and hand-fired serving platters for $10 to $25. You can also find painted tiles for your kitchen and countertops for 25¢ to $5, depending on the amount of detail. The store includes a huge outdoor area, where terra-cotta containers and patio furniture are sold.

◆ Mercado Mexico–Artesanias Mexicanas, 8212 S. Avenue del Yaqui, Guadalupe, (480) 831-5925.

PORTLAND

Imagine my surprise when I boarded my first flight to Portland, Oregon, to see the baggage handlers loading bicycle after bicycle in the hold of the plane. When I mentioned this to the pilot, he simply laughed and said, "You are going to the bicycle capital of America."

Indeed, this is a bike-friendly city, with bike-friendly paths. And one more thing—Portland is home to the world's largest city park.

If that's not enough, Portland is also the microbrew capital of the United States, with more than twenty-five breweries, and at least one flight attendant warned me that she often calls the city "Munich on the Willamette." The Willamette, of course, is the river that winds through the city.

In most cities, you'd have to drive hours outside of town to reach a good hiking trail. Not in Portland. Just hop the city bus to Wildwood Trail, a twenty-eight-mile path that winds through the city's Washington and Forest parks. (My favorite stop along the way is the Japanese Garden.)

Actually, Portland to me is three "*b*'s": bikes, beer, and books. America's twenty-second-largest city is also the home of Powell's City of Books, the world's largest independent bookstore. Imagine a bookstore that occupies an entire city block and even boasts the world's only three-door elevator.

Many of my flight crew friends love Portland because it is also home to other great independent bookstores, like Hawthorne Boulevard Books, which specializes in out-of-print tomes, and the Great Northwest Bookstore.

Portland is perhaps the most manageable city in the Pacific Northwest. It has an efficient streetcar system that travels through downtown Portland, the Pearl District, and some wonderful art galleries. Of course, there's also the Saturday market—the nation's largest continuously operating open-air handicrafts market. (Many flight crews love late-Friday layovers so they can hit the market the next day before their return flight.) It's open every Saturday and Sunday from March through December, with more than 250 crafts booths.

I'm one of those who appreciate the thought that went into redesigning the Portland (PDX) airport. I even like the airport's website (www.flypdx.com), but the best thing about the airport is the light-rail system that takes you right downtown.

The Redline service from the airport runs every fifteen minutes from 4:37 A.M. until 11:35 P.M., 365 days a year. The trip takes just thirty-eight minutes and costs only $1.55.

CITY TIPS

Right on the river with great views, the multilevel Harborside Restaurant is perfect for a romantic dinner in downtown Portland. It is particularly nice at Christmas because many of the boats are decorated with lights, and you can watch them float up and down the river or dock right at the restaurant. They specialize in fresh, local seafood, such as cioppino, but other entrées are tasty, too. Main courses are priced from $12 to $22, and there's a full bar. Reservations are preferred.

◆ Harborside Restaurant, 0309 S.W. Montgomery, (503) 220-1865.

Known more for its historical significance than its food, Dan and Louie's Oyster Bar is located about a block from the water. Since 1877, its specialty has been oysters. When you walk in, you can watch them shuck the oysters right in front of you. Their oyster stew is excellent, and they serve fresh seafood such as clams, salmon, and crab as well. The average price for a dinner there is $12.

◆ Dan and Louie's Oyster Bar, 208 S.W. Ankery, (503) 227-5906.

Huber's, on 3rd Street, is the oldest restaurant in Portland. The Portland Trailblazers basketball team hangs out there after games. The place is famous for its Spanish coffee—Kahlua, Bailey's, and a float of 151 rum, which is then lit on fire. They make it in front of you, and it's quite a production.

◆ Huber's, 411 S.W. 3rd, (503) 228-5686.

For fabulous Vietnamese food, I recommend Pho Van. This place is nothing fancy—just a pleasant, clean restaurant with delicious food. *Pho* means soup in Vietnamese, and this spot has wonderful soups—more in the tradition of Japanese Udon. You pick the kind of noodles you want in your soup, and it also comes with lots of goodies. You can have your choice of vegetarian soup or soups based on seafood, chicken, or other stocks. Soup portions are generous and run $4 to $5; main courses average $6.50. Pho Van serves both lunch and dinner.

◆ Pho Van, 1919 S.E. 82nd Avenue near Division, (503) 788-5244.

Tryon Creek State Park is the largest metropolitan park in the United States. It borders Lake Oswego, which is about twenty miles south of downtown Portland. The park has fourteen miles of well-maintained trails that wind in and out of a canyon. There are deer, fox, hawks, and other wildlife. Look for the trail maps at the entrance. Unfortunately, there are no camping or picnic facilities.

◆ Tryon Creek State Park, from Portland, take I-5 south and exit at Terwilliger Road; 11321 S.W. Terwilliger Boulevard, (503) 636-9886.

Christine's is located in an intimate 1940s-style bungalow on the way to Vancouver (Washington) from Portland and serves breakfast and lunch, with big portions and reasonable prices. They make huge blueberry pancakes—so large that they caution you from ordering more than one at a time. A single pancake is $2.75, and most other breakfast items cost $3 to $4. The place is popular among locals and businesspeople, and on weekend mornings, there's a long line, so call about reservations.

◆ Christine's Restaurant, 2626 E. Evergreen Boulevard, Vancouver, WA.

Giant Drive-In in Lake Oswego, a family business that has been making burgers for around thirty years, wins awards every year for their burgers. It's not an actual drive-in, so you have to go inside, but you can order a burger with virtually anything you want on top, plus homemade milk shakes and both spicy and regular fries. If you are really hungry, order the Giant Filler, topped with an egg, bacon, lettuce, tomato, and just about anything else you could think of. The garlic burger is out of this world. Regular burgers cost around $4; the Giant Filler is about $5. The fries cost extra but are made fresh daily. This is a far cry from the food you get at the fast-food chains.

◆ Giant Drive-In, 15840 Boones Ferry Road, Lake Oswego, (503) 636-0255.

Gubanc's Pub in Lake Oswego is renowned for its homemade soups and its cozy atmosphere.

◆ Gubanc's Pub, 16008 Boones Ferry Road, Lake Oswego, (503) 635-2102.

Hot Locks, a small salon owned and operated by Debbie Perrine, caters to people in their thirties.

◆ Hot Locks, 250 A Avenue, Lake Oswego, (503) 635-9199.

SAN FRANCISCO

It is small, it is manageable, and the pace is dramatically different.

I was lucky enough to live in San Francisco when I was a west coast correspondent for *Newsweek*. I bought a beautiful 1896 Victorian in Noe Valley. And my realtor, who handled the deal, fell in love with the seller; they moved about three blocks away from me, and we all became friends. A few years later, when I decided to sell the house, I sold it to a couple that had rented it from me. They got married in that house.

That's San Francisco. It's a real community. And, many years later, when I was walking down 24th Street to get something to eat and to revisit the old neighborhood, I heard my name being called out. It was the dry cleaner. "Greenberg," she shouted, "get in here. Do you realize you've had some shirts here for six years?"

Where else would that have happened? Only in San Francisco. And where else would this have happened: when I lived there, I was the only straight guy on my block. Am I complaining? Not in the least. Why? As one of my gay neighbors once joked, "Don't worry about locking your door. If we ever break in, all we're going to do is dust and rearrange the furniture!"

He was right. I never felt happier, or safer, than when I was living in San Francisco.

If New York likes to think of itself as the center of America's universe, then San Francisco is America's boutique city. People don't live here because of work. They work here in order to live here. Lifestyle choices dictate San Francisco's reason for being.

Many of my flight attendant friends are based in Los Angeles, but they live in San Francisco. And I thoroughly understand why.

Mark Twain once wrote that the coldest winter he ever spent was summer in San Francisco, but that is more than a slight exaggeration. The fog does roll in, but it's not a hindrance—it's a confirmation of the charm that helps define this city.

But it's more than weather that shapes San Francisco as America's favorite city—it's character. And, of course, the many characters that make up the city. Head out to Polk Street on Halloween, or Fillmore or Castro on any day, and enjoy some of the best people watching in the world. Or just head up to Broadway and stop by Tosca, and if Jeanette likes you, she'll open the back room and let you play pool while you listen to the entire score from every conceivable opera.

It's the one city in America where I don't mind being a tourist. Nob Hill, Russian Hill, the Embarcadero all have special meaning for me now. And, of course, Noe Valley, where I lived, and where I hope to return one day. My fantasy, of course, is Sea Cliff. People in Southern California don't understand Sea Cliff, because it is almost always foggy for a few hours each day. Again, it's not about the sun, it's about the mood.

About the only detraction for me in San Francisco is SFO, which despite its new international terminal hasn't been able to effectively manage its growth. But there's a simple solution to this problem. It's called the Oakland Airport. I now do everything possible to fly to Oakland instead of San Francisco. The airport hardly closes, there are virtually no delays, and you get a major head start out of—or into—San Francisco. It's so much better, and so much faster into the city over the Bay Bridge. Yes, the restaurants and the shopping are better at SFO, but think about it—they have to be. Trust me, you'll be spending a lot more time there, waiting.

AIRPORT TIPS

A flight attendant who's been flying for thirty-two years told me to try the Golden Gate Snack Bar, a little place in the American Airlines Domestic Terminal. Look for the sign that says "Snack Bar." I recommend the wonderful pork fried rice, which they make fresh. The California rolls are also delicious.

◆ Golden Gate Snack Bar, Gates 60 and 62 A, (650) 583-6378.

You can get Noah's Bagels, Peet's Coffee, and Jamba Juice in the United Terminal. They also have one of the best airport bookstores in the country, with hundreds of hardcover and softcover books to choose from.

Draeger's, a gourmet grocery store, is just south of the airport. The second floor of this store is filled with fabulous things for your kitchen and bath. The deli sells delicious sandwiches and other prepared foods, and there's also a sushi bar, bakery, and coffee bar. Viognier, the restaurant on the second floor, is pricey but good.

◆ Draeger's, 222 E. Fourth Avenue, San Mateo, (650) 685-3700.

CITY TIPS

San Francisco has terrific ethnic restaurants. If you like dim sum, don't miss Ton Kiang, which serves tasty dumplings. A favorite is the bol choy gao, which is steamed shrimp and spinach. The restaurant also features excellent Hakka cuisine. One of the specialties, salt-baked chicken, is not to be missed, and I also recommend the vegetarian pot stickers. Try to sit in a downstairs booth.

◆ Ton Kiang, 5821 Geary Boulevard, (415) 387-8273.

The Marina Green is a good place to run, bike, or just relax. There are usually people playing football, volleyball, or Frisbee. Plus it's got a great view of the harbor and is only minutes from cool shops on Chestnut and Union streets.

Be sure to stop by Needlepoint Inc. on Union Square, where they have the largest inventory of beautiful canvases that I have seen anywhere in the world. They will also custom-paint anything you'd like on a canvas, and they do incredible finishing work for your project at their workroom several blocks away. Their silk thread, imported from China, gets shipped to needlepoint shops all over the country.

◆ Needlepoint Inc., 275 Post Street, (800) 345-1622, www. needlepointinc.com.

I go to a secret place called Rodeo Beach. You have to cross the Golden Gate Bridge and do a little easy hiking, but it's worth it. A lot of locals go there, and it's never crowded. The beach itself is like a little cove, but be warned: the water is cold, even in the summer. There's a horse stable where you can rent horses and ride along the beach.

◆ Rodeo Beach, take Highway 101 north, cross the Golden Gate Bridge, and exit at Alexander (the first exit past the viewpoint). After 0.3 miles, turn left onto Bunker Road. There is a one-way tunnel, which cuts under 101. From the other side of the tunnel, drive three miles on Bunker Drive to the trailhead at the end of the road.

The best breakfast is Mama's. It's in North Beach. Expect an extremely long line during the weekends, but it's worth the wait. The smoked bacon is a half inch thick, and it's delicious. It's a really small place—not more than fifteen tables—and when you stand in line, you pass by a glass case that has fresh fruit, pastries, and a view of the cooks. When you get to the front, you place your order and scramble for a table. It's excellent, but a little pricey and touristy.

◆ Mama's, 1701 Stockton Street, (415) 362-6421.

Right across the street from Mama's is a little hole in the wall called Liguria Bakery, where they make one thing: focaccia. They've been at it forever, and if you look in the back you'll see where they do the baking in brick ovens. For next to nothing, you can buy one piece or a whole sheet of four different kinds of bread. The owners wrap it in white butcher paper and tie it with a plain old string. But get there early—it's usually sold out by midday. They also supply a lot of restaurants in the city.

◆ Liguria Bakery, 1700 Stockton Street, (415) 421-3786.

Frascati's is my favorite neighborhood restaurant. They have about thirty tables with excellent food and service, a great wine list, and moderate prices. A typical entrée is about $22. I recommend the coriander-dusted sugar salmon, cooked with a brown sugar rub.

◆ Frascati's, 1901 Hyde Street, (415) 928-1406.

Café Sport on Green is a restaurant unlike any other. The decorations are funky, and they've got some picnic-bench seating were you sit family-style with strangers. The walls are decorated with tchotchkes. The servers bring you plates of great-tasting food loaded with garlic. They have a pesto pasta dish that's out of this world.

◆ Café Sport on Green, 574 Columbus Street, (415) 981-1251.

The city has a new museum—SF MOMA—and the architecture alone is worth a visit. So is the café. And the bookshop. And there's always at least one terrific show.

◆ San Francisco Museum of Modern Art, 151 Third Street, (415) 357-4000.

The Embarcadero has an organic vegetable market several times a week, where you meet a variety of people buying and selling. The organic raspberries are a real treat because you don't see them that often. The market is open year-round, rain or shine.

◆ Tuesday, 10:30 A.M. to 12:30 P.M., foot of Market Street; Saturday, 8 A.M. to 1:30 P.M., at Embarcadero and Green Street; (415) 353-5650.

The Red Room in the Commodore Hotel is, well, red—*really* red. It's a very cool lounge. We go late at night for excellent martinis and people watching. It's just a few blocks from Union Square.

◆ Red Room, Commodore Hotel, 827 Sutter Street, (415) 346-7666.

My favorite place to go with the crew is the Eastern Oriental Trading Company in the Financial District. It's somewhere in between dressy and casual, with a slight yuppyish vibe. They have a microbrewery, and the place is decorated with the symbols of the Chinese zodiac and descriptions of each sign. They serve a shrimp appetizer that's very tasty but a little expensive at $11.95.

◆ Eastern Oriental Trading Company, 314 Sutter Street, (415) 693-0300.

The Swedish pancakes at Sears' Fine Foods are a must during any San Francisco stay. You get eighteen silver-dollar-size pancakes per order at this family-owned restaurant, which has been in business more than sixty years. There's an extensive menu, but I recommend that you stick to the tiny pancakes and maple syrup. Expect lines on the weekend, but the tables turn fast. Wait.

◆ Sears' Fine Foods, 439 Powell Street, (415) 986-1160.

Polaris is a cute shop on Powell Street selling knickknacks and interesting jewelry. They have great antique imitations and unusual marcasite. I bought a necklace-bracelet-earrings set for around $125.

◆ Polaris, 200 Powell Street, (415) 983-0888.

The crew has a favorite place in San Francisco for seafood, although I probably shouldn't give this one away, because it's already crowded. Pacific Café, near the ocean, is a local place—pretty small inside, very down-home. They don't take reservations, so get there right at 5 P.M. when it opens. But while you wait, they serve free glasses of wine from their own label. They serve a wide variety of grilled, broiled, and poached fresh fish every night, including a delicious salmon and swordfish. They also have crab bisque. Prices range from $12 to $25. The decor is warm, with booths and cranberry-colored walls. There is a picture on the wall that we always admire that was crooked after the 1989 earthquake, and I don't think they've straightened it yet.

◆ Pacific Café, 7000 Geary Boulevard, (415) 387-7091.

Take the ferry from Pier 41 to Tiburon and have lunch at Sam's Anchor Café, an outdoor restaurant on the water. Be sure to order the open-face shrimp sandwich. If you're still hungry for dessert, walk down the street to the Swedish bakery, where they have incredible chocolate-covered bananas and good pastries. After lunch and dessert, take a smaller ferry to Angel Island, where there are no cars, just biking and hiking trails. This is California's version of Ellis Island, where the Chinese immigrants came when they were brought here to build the railroad. You can rent a bike and ride to the top of the island, and you'll get one of the most beautiful views of the city. Then ride your bike back, catch the little ferry back to Tiburon, and then the big ferry back to San Francisco.

◆ Sam's Anchor Café, 27 Main Street, Belvedere Tiburon, (415) 435-4527.

When we land from Geneva, we are dying for some exercise. So we head to the Market Street Gym. It's a big place with excellent facilities—cardiovascular equipment, Nautilus, kayak machine, free weights, Jacuzzi, and aerobics. It costs $15 for a one-day pass.

◆ Market Street Gym, 2301 Market Street, (415) 626-4488. Hours 6 A.M. to 10 P.M., Monday through Friday; 8 A.M. to 8 P.M., Saturday and Sunday.

I schedule my flights for midweek to take advantage of lower prices at the Presidio Golf Course. Arnold Palmer's company has just taken over the management there. For about $25 you can get in eighteen holes at a great course during Super Twilight. A driving range and rental clubs are available if you prefer that. Afterward, have a satisfying lunch at the clubhouse and bar. For an $8 fee you can book in advance.

◆ Presidio Golf Course, 300 Finley Road, Arguello, (415) 561-4653; café (415) 561-4661. Super Twilight rates $25 after 4 P.M., Monday through Thursday; $30 after 4 P.M., Friday through Sunday.

Whenever we have a layover and rent a car, I like to take the crew to my favorite view of San Francisco. Drive over the Golden Gate Bridge toward Marin County. Take the second exit and then a left underneath the highway. Follow the road to the southwest part of the Golden Gate Bridge. Go up the hill, where you'll see discarded army batteries from years ago. Then follow the road to the scenic overlook. Better yet, rent a bike and enjoy the spectacular scenery the whole way.

Ambassador Toys is a children's store with a wonderful selection of books and toys. The prices are average, but it's international and multiethnic, so you'll find toys and books from places like France, Israel, and Africa.

◆ Ambassador Toys, 1981 Union Street, (415) 345-8697.

Betelnut is a place you'll want to return to again and again. The food is a mixture of Japanese, Indian, Chinese, and other Asian cuisines. You get small plates, and you can come up with creative combinations for yourself. For example, you might have Nan with Japanese noodles. Everything is so good, and I haven't had the same thing twice. Entrées cost between $15 and $25, and the portions are huge. It's a good idea to go with a group of people because you can share everything. The restaurant has an extensive beer, wine, and sake list, and they also serve tropical drinks.

◆ Betelnut, 2030 Union Street, (415) 929-8855.

SAN JUAN

The real beauty of San Juan is how little most travelers know about it. Most folks only travel through the airport on their way to other parts of the Caribbean. They have no idea what they're missing.

I was one of those travelers until, about ten years ago, one of my flights to St. Marten had a mechanical problem. It took so long to fix the problem that we were forced to overnight in San Juan along with the flight crew, which had exceeded their legal flight time for the day.

And that's when I discovered San Juan—the pilot and two flight attendants were my guides. Until they took me around, I had no idea how great San Juan could be.

From the airport, you're only minutes to the beach. Then there's Old San Juan, a UNESCO World Heritage site. There's gambling, there's a rain forest—El Yunque—and the world's largest rum distillery (for those really long layovers!). But one of the strong attractions for me is the food—crispy pork, plantains (the salty kind), and cod fritters.

For most flight crews, the off season is the time to go. Since most flight crews fly space that's available, it stands to reason that flying to San Juan between April and October is the thing to do. But it also makes sense to me because, in my book, the off season is more or less a myth. As one flight attendant once asked me, "Why would you want to fly somewhere with five thousand escaped *garmentos* in January and February, have to stand in long lines, and get bad service? In the off season, the thermometer is only about eight degrees hotter, prices are lower, service is better, and there are no crowds.

And then, my favorite—and coincidentally the flash point for recent political activity—is the beautiful island of Vieques, which moves to the gentle rhythms of the Antilles. Most people know about Vieques for the protests against the U.S. Navy's use of part of the island as a nine-hundred-acre bombing target. Vieques lies just seven miles east of Puerto Rico—but it's an island roughly twice the size of Manhattan, with some of the best secret beaches in the Caribbean—and they are accessible. This is where some Miami-based flight crews go for two-to-three-day escapes. But a word of caution: no day spas here; no waiters to serve you piña coladas. Pack your own lunch, but at the same time don't worry—even the remote beaches are only twenty minutes from the nearest restaurant.

The nice thing about Vieques is that you don't have to fly out of the main international airport in San Juan. You can fly from the Isla Grande Airport in San Juan—far less of a hassle.

As with most airports in the Caribbean, the Luis Muñoz Marín International Airport leaves a lot to be desired. The good news is that the airport is so close to town that it doesn't take that long to get there, and once there, there's not much to do.

AIRPORT TIPS

San Juan is the major hub for the Caribbean. Almost every airline flies there, although American virtually owns the place. You'll see everything at this airport, from old DC-3s to the latest-generation aircraft. Because it's the big hub, lots of crews overnight here.

One of the crew favorites is the balcony on the second floor of a restaurant called Aeroparque. The balcony seats fifty to sixty people, and it's a fun place for plane watching and spotting the really old birds.

◆ Aeroparque, (787) 253-1515.

Surprisingly, there are no decent, sit-down restaurants in the airport—only snack stands and fast food. (They just opened a Subway there, so people line up for that.) We eat at the Metropol III restaurant in Isla Verde. It's a busy local place, close to the airport. (You can get there by bus in ten to twenty minutes, or take a cab.) They serve mostly local dishes, as well as a really good garlic chicken and great garlic bread. The ambience here is nothing special, but it's pretty popular with the locals. Prices start at about $8.

◆ Metropol III, Isla Verde Avenue, (787) 791-4046.

CITY TIPS

If you have only one night, then go to Piñones. This is a hot tip because when Puerto Ricans come home, this is where they want to go—I never would have known about this place if one of our Puerto Rican flight attendants hadn't taken me there. It's on the ocean, east of San Juan, about ten minutes from the airport. The place is a bunch of little shacks lined up on the beach, where they fry food on wood-burning brick stoves. They serve amarillos, monfongo, pinchos, and acupulria. Each piece is about $1 to $1.50. The best time to go is a couple of hours before sunset. But be careful: if you're by yourself, it's not safe late at night unless you speak Spanish.

◆ Piñones Beach, Avenida Loiza, Isla Verde.

I used to surf around Piñones with another flight attendant, so that's how I discovered Aviones. You can park among the homes and pay a local guy $1 to watch your car (it's worth it). The surf is highest from November through February. Warning: this is not a beginner's surf spot.

◆ Aviones, from San Juan, go to the east coast by the beach, and ask for Piñones.

Music is everywhere in Puerto Rico. Soleil Beach Club & Bistro, a local nightspot, features a variety of music on different nights. This open-air restaurant, with a palm-leaf roof and a great view of the ocean, is a safe place to go at night if you're with a group of people. There isn't really a floor, just sand. Lunch is about $10, and I recommend the monfongo because the seafood is so good here.

◆ Soleil Beach Club & Bistro, 187 Street, Loiza, (787) 253-1033.

La Gran Discoteca, a used-CD store, features new and old Latin music, although they don't carry much in English. One particular CD from there has become a personal favorite: *Rooster's Songbirds*, by Robi Rosa. I've also found selections by Mana, El Enanitos Verdes, Shakira, and Carlos Ponce. Prices range from about $10 to $13.

◆ La Gran Discoteca, Cruz Street, El Viejo, (787) 723-4000.

I like surfing just out of San Juan at Aguadilla because it's away from the crowds, it's more challenging, and things are cheaper. It's about three minutes from the surf break, and since you're on the northwest part of the island, you get more consistent waves off the Atlantic-northwesterly winds. The biggest waves are in January and February. There's also a good surf shop nearby, which stocks wax, T-shirts, and flip-flops.

◆ From San Juan take Highway 22 west to Arecibo, then Highway 2 to Aguadilla; Surf Zone, Cliff Road, Building 704, Aguadilla, (787) 890-5080. Call Surf Zone for surf reports in Aguadilla and directions.

Vieques, the little island right off the eastern coast of Puerto Rico, has a bioluminous bay, where some of the ocean creatures glow in the dark. There's a boat tour of the bay, in which you'll learn about the ecosystem, including the mangroves, and get to see for yourself the little yellowish-green streaks of light as the fish get scared and swim away from the boat. You can also jump out and swim along with them.

From the San Juan Airport, you can take a twenty-minute plane ride to Vieques. La Casa de Frances, a bed-and-breakfast that was once part of a sugar plantation, can organize a tour for you (you don't have to be a guest). A cab ride anywhere on the island won't cost more than $3 to $5. Try to avoid going during hurricane season, especially in September and October, because that's when Puerto Rico always seems to get hit.

◆ For a tour of Vieques, contact Island Adventures, (787) 741-2544, www.biobay.com. Tours depart from Esperanza (City).

SEATTLE

It's entirely possible to be sleepless in Seattle—and not be in love. And no, that's not the result of overdosing on the caffe lattes. My first trip there was spent with my friends Cliff and Nancy. She was a flight attendant for the now-defunct Wien Air Alaska and her father had flown for Western. She knew the Pacific Northwest better than anyone.

The first thing she did was disabuse me of my notion about precipitation. "It doesn't constantly rain here," she insisted. And she was—and still is—more or less correct. But then she introduced me to a lot of water—Puget Sound, locally brewed beer, salmon, coffee, Lake Washington, and the Chittendon locks.

Nancy and Cliff took me everywhere, from Lake Union to the Pike Place Market, then out to Boeing Field (and a wonderful museum), and over to the magical Vashon Island—one of my great real estate regrets (I should have bought there years ago), and then up to Capitol Hill. Many of their friends flew for Alaska Airlines, and they showed me their Seattle secrets when we weren't swapping fishing stories about the king salmon that didn't get away up near Ketchikan.

Nancy introduced me to great Thai food, an incredible Italian place, and funky bars in Pioneer Square; then out to Ray's Boathouse on Puget Sound with stunning views of the Olympic Mountains; and one of my favorite bookstores, Elliott Bay Books—a Seattle institution. In recent years, although I remain a die-hard New York Mets fan, I have to hand it to the folks in

Seattle for the Mariners, a world-class team that plays inside an incredibly well-designed stadium.

But the enduring charm of this city for me remains the water. The ferry system allows the opportunity to take a boat just about anywhere—from Bainbridge Island over to Vashon. Washington State Ferries is the nation's largest ferry system, serving ten routes with twenty-five boats.

Sea-Tac, about thirteen miles south of town, is an airport that tends to work better than others in the region. And, yes, you can find about five Starbucks there. One nice touch (that other airports should follow): there are two ATM machines in the baggage claim area, not just in the upper-level departure area.

AIRPORT TIPS

Northwest Passage sells glass from local artists in the Northwest and Canada. I bought a puffed-out, heart-shaped glass piece for under $20, which is very reasonable.
◆ Northwest Passage, in North Satellite behind Delta, (206) 433-6063.

South Satellite Bar serves the freshest clam chowder—full of clams and really thick and hot—for $3 to $4 a bowl. This is the only bar in the South Terminal in the middle section.
◆ South Satellite Bar, South Satellite in Northwest Terminal, (206) 433-6700.

I discovered 13 Coins restaurant, across the street from the airport and open twenty-four hours a day, seven days a week, when I woke up hungry at four o'clock one morning. I walked into the place and said, "Wow, when did you open?" To which the cook replied, "1967!" And they haven't closed for even a single day since then. Their entire menu, including Pacific pan-fried oysters, creamed crab legs, and outstanding eggs Benedict with warm smoked salmon, is available all the time. You can sit in the high-back leather chairs at the Chef's Bar, where you can watch them prepare the food and interact with the cooks.

◆ 13 Coins, 18000 International Boulevard, (206) 243-9500.

CITY TIPS

Falling into one of the Heavenly Beds at the Seattle Westin hotel is the best thing after a long day. There is also a really good Japanese restaurant downstairs with an excellent sushi bar. I recommend the rainbow rolls.

◆ Westin, 1900 5th Avenue, (206) 728-1000.
Nikko's Restaurant, (206) 322-4641.

Take a walk around the pier area off Market Square, where you can watch the fish throwers and browse the florist stands full of beautiful and affordable blooms. At the fish market, you can have your selection freeze-dried and shipped wherever you want. Go during the day, before they close shop, and then have dinner at Cutter's Bayhouse, where you can sit overlooking the bay and watch the ferries. The food is a little pricey, but they serve a parmesan-crusted halibut in lemon butter wine sauce that is awesome.

◆ Cutter's Bayhouse, 2001 Western Avenue #100, (206) 448-4884.

Gig Harbor is an artist's community outside Seattle that has a New England feel. Tides Tavern, a fun local hangout right on the water, is the Northwest Cheers. It's a forty-five-minute drive from the Seattle Airport, but it's worth it. A lot of people drive their boats right up to the dock. There's outdoor dining, with a view of Mount Rainier, which is nice when the weather permits. I recommend trying one of the four home-brewed beers, which go great with the food, including excellent fries ($3 a pound during happy hour), fish and chips, and clam chowder. The menu is on the website, and you can order clothes with the Tides Tavern logo there, too. Check out their bargain bin, a big tub where everything is fifty percent off.

◆ Tides Tavern in Gig Harbor, 2925 Harbor View Drive, (253) 858-3982, www.TidesTavern.com; www.GigHarbor.com.

The Crabpot on the waterfront serves a seafood dinner—crab legs, clams, corn on the cob, and little potatoes—in a bucket. They put down butcher paper and dump the dinner bucket out on the table in front of you. You get a hammer for the crabs and eat everything with your fingers. It's fun to go with a group and get a big bucket.

◆ Crabpot, 1301 Alaskan Way, (206) 624-1890.

The best bakery in town is Borracchini's. They made our wedding cake and even though we had enough cake for 120 people, we didn't have any leftovers because everyone went back for seconds. The icing was very light. They also sell Italian biscotti and other desserts, and they can make a rush-order birthday cake right then and there. Try their homemade ice cream, too.

◆ Borracchini's, 2307 Rainer Avenue S, (206) 325-1550.

Oberto's Outlet is the place to go for beef jerky. They sell odd-sized pieces and flavors such as honey that aren't sold at stores. Prices range from $4.95 to $16.95.

◆ Oberto's Outlet, 1715 Rainer Avenue S, (206) 322-7524.

The Virginia Inn, once a dive, is now a trendy little bar around the corner from Stewart Bros. that usually features funky blues music.

◆ Virginia Inn, 1937 First Street, (206) 728-1937.

Pike Place Market has beautiful dried flowers that draw raves as home decorations. Small bouquets are eight to ten inches in diameter and cost about $5; large arrangements are twelve to fifteen inches in diameter and cost $8 to $10. The dried flower vendors are located on the street level of the market.

◆ Pike Place Market, www.pikeplacemarket.org.

Angle Lake is a small, serene lake hidden from the road and surrounded by huge evergreens. On a clear day, you can see the Cascade Mountains in the background. There's a little pier for fishing, but virtually no boats, and a family of ducks resides there. This wonderfully laid-back retreat is just two or three minutes from the airport.

◆ Angle Lake, when you exit the airport in the back, facing the Windham Hotel, make a right and go about six blocks until you see the sign for the lake, which is tucked back in the trees, away from the road.

I once saw someone come out of Rudy's with a pink mohawk, so I wouldn't tell the stylists to "do whatever you want." But if you are looking for the latest trend, Rudy's does great modern and up-to-date haircuts. They will make you look stylish. It's also a tattoo/piercing parlor and a coffee shop. Men's haircuts cost about $13, including a shampoo and blow-dry. They have five locations in Seattle.

◆ Rudy's, 89 Wall Street, (206) 448-8900, www.rudysbarbershop.com.

Sit and Spin, in Queen Anne, is much more than a Laundromat. It's also a bar/restaurant and arts center, with a stage where they do poetry and scene readings and have local bands play. Local artists display their work on the walls.

◆ Sit and Spin, 2219 4th Avenue, (206) 441-9484.

Because of their schedules, many flight crews need to eat dinner early, which is a good thing when we go to San Carlos, a small, one-story house in Winslow that has been converted into a Mexican restaurant. The place opens at 5 P.M. every day and is usually empty when we get there, but by 6:30 there's always a waiting line. In the Northwest, Mexican food is made mostly with fish instead of the traditional pork, chicken, or beef, so San Carlos serves things like smoked salmon tacos and crab chimichangas. An average entrée is about $15.

◆ San Carlos, take the Winslow ferry to Bainbridge Island, climb the hill to Winslow Way, and turn left; 279 Madison Avenue, Bainbridge Island, (206) 842-1999.

TORONTO

A United Airlines pilot took me around Toronto on my first trip there. I will always remember my initial impressions of the city: clean, manageable, friendly.

Many years later I reunited with that pilot, who had tickets for us to a Blue Jays game at the new Skydome. I can never forget that game either, for I saw something that night I had never seen before, and will most probably never see again. The game itself was not memorable—a weak outing by both the Blue Jays and the Milwaukee Brewers. I can't even tell you who won. But that's not the point.

We had seats down the left-field line, about one hundred feet beyond third base. One of the fans, a man in his early thirties, sat down in front of me. He had brought his baseball mitt with him. How cute and silly, I thought. This guy actually thinks he's going to catch a ball way out here.

In the third inning, the Toronto pitcher threw a high-inside fastball to a right-handed hitter, and he pulled it hard and fouled down the left-field line. The ball was rocketing straight for me. At the last possible second, the man in front of me stuck up his mitt and caught it.

Not impressed yet? Three innings later, it was the same pitcher, same batter, and same pitch. The ball was slammed straight at us again, and the same fan caught it. Now, *that* was impressive. He looked at me, smiled, and said, "Season tickets," as if he knew exactly where to be. Something tells me he *did* know.

Since then, I've been to three Blue Jays games. I always bring my mitt. But nothing is ever hit even remotely close to me.

Peter Ustinov once said, "Toronto is New York run by the Swiss." I don't know which city would be more insulted by that statement. I like everything about this city, even in winter. I discovered my favorite steak house in North America here. A flight attendant directed me to the most unlikely of places, the House of Chan—that's right, a Chinese restaurant. They have the obligatory (and expected) Chinese menu, but no one ever orders the Chinese food there, except an occasional and errant egg roll. Instead, Toronto insiders know it as the home of the best rib-eye in town. (Order the queen's cut. The king's cut is simply way too much meat, although my flight attendant friends always order one and share.) The House of Chan is at 876 Eglinton Avenue W, (416) 781-5575.

Another favorite of mine, and one of the most special restaurants in terms of service and consistent quality, is called Joso's, an amazing restaurant out on Davenport Road specializing in the freshest fish. It's always crowded, and they serve late, which is even better. Ask for Shirley Spralja, the owner.

The airport also works very well. In fact, with the strength of the U.S. dollar, it's actually affordable to take a limo into town. And they're right outside the baggage claim area.

The other nice touch about Toronto is that the baggage carts only require a deposit—one "looney," or Canadian dollar—which you get back when you return them. Very decent. Very civilized. The way baggage carts should work at all airports.

CITY TIPS

Whenever we go to Toronto, we like hanging out at the Pier: Toronto's Waterfront Museum. It's located in a restored 1930s shipping warehouse where you can pull the steam whistles and visit the Discovery Gallery, which is set up inside the hull of a ship. You can watch artisans constructing traditional wooden boats, or you can sign up for a course in shipbuilding, but the best thing about the place is that you can take one of their boats out for a tour of the harbor. Don't want to go out on the water? Not a problem, since the museum also offers waterfront walking tours.

◆ The Pier, 245 Queen's Quay W, (888) 675-PIER.

The Royal York Hotel is worth seeing, just to experience a huge hotel. We sometimes stay there on layovers, and we never get the same room twice. Sometimes we're given rooms that are so small you can get hurt getting out of bed; other times we're given suites—it's the luck of the draw. But it's right across from Union Station, and the Canadian Pacific Store, in the basement of the hotel, sells unusual railroad memorabilia and beautiful leather jackets.

◆ Royal York Hotel, 100 Front Street W, (416) 863-6333, (800) 828-7447.

When it comes to shoes there's Imelda Marcos and then there's me. A lot of flight attendants tease me about it. I'm not much for museums, but the Bata Shoe Museum, the first museum of its kind in North America, is where I get my ideas before I hit the shops. The building, which looks like a shoebox, holds ten thousand shoes, including the space boots of the Apollo astronauts and patent leather originals once worn by Elvis.

◆ Bata Shoe Museum, 327 Bloor Street W, (416) 979-7799. Admission $6 Canadian.

I like Toronto for the Gay Village. I'm gay and I really feel at home in this city, which happens to have the largest population of gays and lesbians in Canada. Toronto may have had a conservative reputation in the past, but I always feel welcome here now. On the weekends, and especially in summer, we love to go out to Hanlan's Point on the Toronto Islands. Here's a piece of esoterica: even Babe Ruth scored here . . . OK, it's a joke, but the truth is that in 1914 Babe Ruth hit the first home run of his professional career out on Hanlan's Point.

◆ Hanlan's Point, head to the corner of Church and Wellesley Streets.

Acqua is a water-themed restaurant where the seafood is always great.

◆ Acqua, BCE Place, 10 Front Street W, (416) 368-7171.

If the weather is nice, take a walk along Yonge Street. When a flight attendant first suggested we walk there, I had no idea what I was in for—she neglected to tell me that Yonge Street is the longest street in the world! If you're on Yonge Street, you will be near anything that matters in Toronto.

A humorous rite of passage for newcomers on our flights is a visit to Ed's Market of the Absurd, the Unusual, and the Ridiculous, which is actually the collection of a theater impresario, containing costumes from the Old Vic and props from stage and film productions—and it's all for sale.

◆ Ed's Market of the Absurd, the Unusual, and the Ridiculous, 276 King Street W, (416) 977-3935.

St. Anne's Anglican Church was built in 1907 in the Byzantine style. In addition to the services, the murals, bronze reliefs, and interesting mosaics will satisfy your need for the spiritual.

◆ St. Anne's Anglican Church, 270 Gladstone Avenue, (416) 536-1202.

Sometimes when we're in Toronto, we like to just chill at Flo's diner. It's right in the middle of all the upscale stores in the

Yorkville district. Nothing fancy here, just a great spot for hamburgers. And in the summer, head upstairs to the terrace on the roof.

◆ Flo's, 70 Yorkville, Second Floor, (416) 961-4333.

Toronto greets me with its sense of humor every time I land there. The city has some of the most off-the-wall museums—for example, the Arthur Conan Doyle Collection, which is part museum and part library. They actually take themselves pretty seriously there. But the museum that really cracks me up is the History of Contraception Museum, with nearly six hundred exhibits, ranging from ancient membrane condoms to things like dried beaver testicles.

◆ Arthur Conan Doyle Collection, 789 Yonge Street, (416) 393-7000.
History of Contraception Museum, 19 Greenbelt Drive, North York, (416) 449-9444.

The House of Spice, in the Kensington Market, has a wide selection of coffee and tea, and the prices are always cheaper than in the States. It's right next to Perola's, which sells rare chilies and dried herbs.

◆ House of Spice, 190 Augusta Avenue, (416) 595-9724.
Perola's, 247 Augusta Avenue, (416) 593-9728.

VANCOUVER

My first trip to Vancouver, British Columbia, was on Canadian Pacific, and I will always remember the flight. Although it was only a two and a half hour trip from Los Angeles on a small 737, the airline served a three-course dinner on china service . . . in coach!

The flight attendant didn't hesitate to explain her love for her city. "It just happens to be the most gorgeous city on the continent," she beamed. "And you'll see it for yourself," she promised. "Think about it. We have ocean, mountains, and a city. We have whales and coyote and, of course, a few ships."

I was there to catch one of those ships up to Alaska, but my one day in Vancouver convinced me that it was, absolutely, worth a return trip, and I've been going back ever since.

A few years later, I sat next to a San Francisco–based flight attendant for Pan Am who was flying up to Vancouver. "It's our little secret. It's where San Franciscans go for the weekend."

Imagine a city with nearly two million well-mannered people, giant parks, beautiful gardens, and terrific Chinese food—not to mention a Canadian dollar that hovers at sixty-two U.S. cents. Do you need any more reasons to go?

Flight crews love it for the bargains. And I don't blame them. Even basic services are inexpensive. A cab ride from the airport to downtown is just about $20, compared to $50 in Los Angeles.

And then there are the other boats—not the cruise ships, but the B.C. (British Columbia) ferryboats that sail to Victoria and Vancouver Island, and provide some of the more incredible whale watching I have ever experienced.

My flight crew friends like to hike Stanley Park. At one thousand acres, it's the largest city park in Canada. Then they head over to Granville, a hip, energetic island of bars and restaurants, where you can sit and watch the boats leave the harbor.

My first time there, I stayed at the venerable Hotel Vancouver, the grand dame of the city's hotels. Now, thanks to an American Airlines pilot, I stay at the Westin Bayshore, which has its own marina, where you can rent boats and eat at Tojo's, arguably one of the best sushi places in the city. The restaurant is in an office tower, but don't let that mislead you. Tojo's is a bit expensive by Canadian standards, but manageable by those of the United States.

Canadian Pacific is now gone and many of us miss it terribly, but a number of smart travelers from New York now fly on Cathay Pacific (the flight makes a stop in Vancouver on the way to Hong Kong, and the service is dramatically better than on American or Air Canada).

CITY TIPS

Liliget Feast House, in the West End area of the city, is an American Indian restaurant like no other. It's in the style of the coastal Northwestern tribes, and they play "laughing water" and chants for ambience. The lighting is low (there are no windows), and the seating is arranged on raised gravel beds. They serve wild game such as elk, duck, buffalo sausage, and rabbit, with vegetables like sea asparagus and sweet potatoes with nuts. An entrée goes for $18 to $49 Canadian.
◆ Liliget Feast House, 1724 Davie Street, (604) 681-7044.

Cardero's is built on a pier and has a pub on one side and fine dining on the other. I go to the pub in jeans but might feel a lit-

tle underdressed on the other side. They serve excellent planked salmon for $18, as well as local beers for $5.25 Canadian.
◆ Cardero's, 583 Coal Harbor Quay, (604) 669-7666.

If you're looking for somewhere to exercise in Vancouver, Stanley Park is the place. A system of one-way trails goes through the park, and they never really get crowded. Several places around the park rent mountain bikes for about $12 Canadian a day.
◆ Stanley Park, (604) 257-8400.

You can't leave Vancouver without trying the maple-leaf-shaped candy—so rich it melts in your mouth. The hotels and duty-free shops sell it throughout Canada, usually six or twelve in a box, for about $5 Canadian and up.

For a good time, try five-pin bowling at North Shore Bowl. It's like regular bowling, except there are only five pins instead of ten and everything is smaller—including the bowling ball, which has no finger holes so it's very hard to control.
◆ North Shore Bowl, 141 W. 3rd, (604) 985-1212.

I am a marathoner and if I can save fifteen minutes in my day by not shaving, then I'm all over it. So when I found out about Advance Laser Clinics laser hair removal, I investigated. I now pick up Vancouver trips so I can fly out there to have this procedure done. It's cheaper than most places because of the rate exchange, it's virtually painless, and it permanently removes hair.
◆ Advance Laser Clinics, 805 W. Broadway #103, (604) 874-1100; 4250 Kingsway #211, Burnaby, (604) 434-0200; www. advancedlaserclinics.com.

You won't find the Only Café in the guidebooks. It's Vancouver's oldest restaurant, serving affordable seafood for more than eighty years, and it's open for lunch only. The place seats only about twenty people at the counter, but it's worth the wait. The decor is very 1950s, with two U-shaped counters, two worn booths, and no bathrooms, but the food is always fresh and cooked to perfection. The fish is stacked in the front near the window, and you pick what you want. They serve excellent halibut, salmon, snapper, fish and chips, and clam chowder, for $8.50 to $10.

◆ Only Café, 20 E. Hastings Street, (604) 681-6546.

At Zulu Records, the independent record store in town, you can score CDs that you can't get in the United States, including European releases and quality artists you've probably never heard of. Half the store has vinyl records, and the other half is all CDs. They just expanded and took over the space next door, so it is bigger than ever. There's also a Pong video game table that must date back to 1981.

◆ Zulu Records, 1972 W. 4th Avenue, just west of Burrard Street, (604) 738-3232.

Harbour Dance Centre in downtown Vancouver lets us drop in for ballet, jazz, modern, and other dance classes.

◆ Harbour Dance Centre, 927 Granville Street, Third Floor, (604) 684-9542, www.harbourdance.bc.ca.

Wreck Beach is Vancouver's clothing-optional beach. If you can stomach the middle-aged, somewhat flabby die-hards who hang out there, it is a beautiful beach. Not so much sun, sand, and surf here, but rocks, pebbles, crags, driftwood, and cliffs.

◆ Wreck Beach, make a right on 16th Avenue. After about twenty minutes, make a right on S.W. Marine Drive. The trail to the beach is off S.W. Marine Drive, near the Gate 6 entrance into the University of British Columbia campus.

Tucked away beside the Asian Centre is the tiny Nitobe Japanese Garden, an oasis of calm and quiet. It's perfect for a sudden and blissful break from stressful sights, sounds, and thoughts.
◆ Nitobe Japanese Garden, main entrance of the UBC Botanical Garden is located at 6804 S.W. Marine Drive.

Main Street is one of my favorite neighborhoods and shopping areas. Make sure you stop by Pulpfiction, a great used bookstore, on the corner of Main and Broadway.
◆ Pulpfiction, 2418 Main Street, (604) 876-4311.

Bo-Kong Vegetarian Restaurant is a Chinese Buddhist vegetarian restaurant that's so good I take my nonvegetarian friends there.
◆ Bo-Kong Vegetarian Restaurant, 3068 Main Street, (604) 876-3088.

Punjabi Market has beautiful sari fabric and jewelry, plus a great (and cheap) all-you-can-eat Indian vegetarian buffet at All India Sweets Restaurant, offering a selection of desserts, fruit, salad items, chutneys, pickles, papadums, naan, rice, and hot lentil dishes for just $4 U.S. If that's full, try Himalaya down the block.
◆ Punjabi Market, located between three blocks, from 48th Avenue to 51st Avenue, 6400–6600 block, www.punjabimarket.bc.ca.
All India Sweets Restaurant, 6507 Main Street, (604) 327-0891.

I always make a dash for La Casa Gelato because I'm an ice cream junkie. They make Italian gelato in 115 different flavors, including wasabi, curry, durian, garlic, tiramisu, plus the standards, of course.
◆ La Casa Gelato, 1033 Venables, (604) 251-3211.

A pretty standard tourist attraction is the Capilano Suspension Bridge in the suburb of North Vancouver—to which you have to pay admission. However, there is a suspension bridge at Lynn Valley, also in North Vancouver, which is much nicer and costs nothing. The setting is a local park, with a gentle hike all the way down into Lynn Canyon, where you can look up from the creek bed and see the bridge swinging high above you.

◆ Lynn Valley Road, (604) 981-3103.

WASHINGTON, D.C.

I was not introduced to our nation's capital by a flight attendant or a pilot. Like thousands of other thirteen-year-olds, I first went to Washington with my junior high school class on a field trip.

My memories of that trip: the Smithsonian (vague), the Washington Monument (tall), and the agent who fired a gun during the FBI tour (loud).

Thankfully, I wasn't destroyed by that first tour, and my work as a journalist has taken me back dozens of times since.

Thanks to Pierre Charles L'Enfant, an army engineer who fought for the Americans in the War of Independence and who designed the city of Washington, this is a city that goes around in circles.

At first glance, Washington, D.C., seems an area devoid of a sense of humor, a place that all too often takes itself too seriously. However, Watergate ended the notion of the imperial presidency in this country, and since then, the place has loosened up a bit.

With the important things like ground transportation, it's good that D.C. takes itself that seriously. It has one of the best subway systems in the world. And its museums and monuments—both the well known and the obscure—are worth a visit.

I could spend hours at the National Air and Space Museum, and often do, usually with pilot friends who give me a new perspective on the displays and lectures. There are must-stops, like the Vietnam Veterans Memorial as well as the U.S. Memorial

Holocaust Museum. But if you can, stop by the Organization of American States building just to admire its architecture. Also visit Union Station, which is my choice for how to arrive in Washington from New York.

If you've never taken the White House tour, you need to— just once. Speaking of tours, there are a few you should do on your own—and early. There are the Lincoln and the Jefferson memorials, but one that is overlooked, and almost hidden, is at the National Academy of Sciences—secluded on the southwest side of the building is an enormous bronze sculpture of Albert Einstein. If you want to visit Arlington National Cemetery, get there when it opens or you'll be in a long line, especially at JFK's grave site.

And just as D.C. has loosened up about taking itself too seriously, dining in the nation's capital has also improved dramatically. It's no longer just a meat-and-potatoes town.

For drinks before dinner, head to the Mayflower Bar, and ask for Mal.

For dinner, go to Sushi Ko on Wisconsin Avenue. Don't let the fact that it's located next to one of the city's more notorious strip clubs frighten you. Ask for Daisuke, the owner, and if he's in the mood, he will amaze you with his sushi (sesame-oil-seasoned trout) coupled with some of the finest burgundy from France.

Want more traditional fare? Head to 1789 Restaurant, on N Street. If you like a country-inn atmosphere and a very serious wine list, this is the place.

But two of the newest flight crew favorites are DC Coast and TenPenh. Check out the roasted butternut squash soup or the pecan-crusted rainbow trout at DC Coast. My favorite is the roasted garlic corn pudding. Over at TenPenh, the soup is Thai-style coconut and chicken soup with portobello mushrooms. Whatever you do, don't forget the wasabi mashed potatoes. For an appetizer, the pork and shrimp spring rolls with Chinese black vinegar dipping sauce are a must.

I don't know a flight attendant or pilot who is in love with Dulles. It takes a long time to get there, and, once there, it still takes a long time to get there! Reagan is more convenient, especially now that it is back up to full operations. But the sleeper airport (where you'll get the best airfares) is Baltimore-Washington International (BWI). You can thank Southwest for that. When Southwest started serving Baltimore, average fares dropped for all airlines by about thirty-five percent.

AIRPORT TIPS

Dulles Airport

Dulles Airport is a nightmare. The airplane taxies to one terminal, then you deplane at another terminal and hop on a bus that takes you to a different terminal, where you're crammed like sardines with all the people from your flight. You finally get to the main terminal, where you get your car and your bags. The whole operation is antiquated and a real nuisance. As far as I know, there's no way to get around it. You just have to follow the crowd.

Ronald Reagan Airport

People stuck on a layover in D.C. ought to check out the Taxi Café down by the taxi stand. Any airport personnel can point it out. The food has an Indian or Middle Eastern flavor, but whatever it is, it's fantastic. Indian beans and rice and the chickpeas-and-rice special are particular favorites. As soon as we get to the airport, the flight crew starts asking, "Who's going for the beans and rice?"

◆ Taxi Café, (703) 419-9530.

BWI

Go to the lower-level baggage claim ground transportation booth and take the bus to the train station. It is a three-minute ride, and then you can take the Marc train to D.C. Weekdays it costs about $5, and weekends, it's $10 on Amtrak.

◆ www.bwiairport.com/ground_transportation/marc_train.html.

CITY TIPS

Rock Creek Park is a good place for jogging. The ring goes from D.C. to the Potomac River, and you can catch the path at many locations, including at 28th Street and M Street.

◆ Rock Creek Park, www.nps.gov/rocr/.

Thai Luang, owned by Muttika and his family, serves excellent Thai food and is about ten minutes away from Dulles. The place is not superformal (you could go in jeans, but probably not a T-shirt), and it is definitely not touristy. Dinner entrées run about $9.95.

◆ Thai Luang, 171 Eldon Street, (703) 478-2233.

Even from the farthest spot in the room, you're close enough to see the faces of the musicians featured at the 9:30 Club, an intimate live-music venue that attracts a raw but eclectic crowd for its diverse shows. Well-known groups like Blues Traveler play there, as well as less famous acts, with cover charges adjusted accordingly. Although the club is in a less desirable section of D.C., there is a secure parking area close by.

◆ 9:30 Club, 815 V Street NW, concert line (202) 393-0930.

Modern Nails in the Fashion Center at Pentagon Mall gave me the best manicure I've ever had. The staff is friendly and efficient, and the place is clean. The acrylic nails last for three to four weeks. At lunchtime and in the late afternoon it gets busy, but mornings are quiet. You can schedule an appointment, but they do accept walk-ins.

◆ Modern Nails, 1100 S. Hayes Street, Arlington, VA, (703) 413-3404. Hours 10 A.M. to 9 P.M., Monday through Saturday; 11 A.M. to 6 P.M. Sunday.

During the summer, people sit on the Capitol steps for free outdoor concerts given by the U.S. Air Force Band and their spin-off groups, like the Singing Sergeants. They play all kinds of music, including classical, pop, jazz, and Latin. Few people seem to know about these concerts, because they're never full, but the performers look very sharp in their uniforms, and they give star-quality performances. It is beautiful to sit under the stars and listen to the music. Bring a pillow to sit on, though, because the Capitol steps get very hard. Concerts start around 7 P.M. and usually last about two hours.

◆ U.S. Air Force Band, (202) 767-4310, www.bolling.af.mil/band.

We like to rent a car and drive to a lovely old farm called Field of Flowers, near Leesburg, Virginia, about forty-five minutes from the Maryland suburbs. The owner has planted beautiful flowers, such as delphiniums, bachelor's buttons, chrysanthemums, cockscombs, and hyacinths, around five acres of her home that she lets people come and pick. The flowers are much cheaper than in a grocery store or at a florist. The owner also offers classes in flower arrangement, as well as various seminars around the holidays. She can teach you how to make table arrangements, and she sells decorative pieces that either she has made or people have given to her on consignment. She also has local crafts and sometimes even fresh-baked pies.

◆ Field of Flowers, (540) 338-7131. Opens May 1, 2002.

Sometimes you go to a consignment shop and think: This is a lot of junk! But not at the White Elephant, on Route 15 in Leesburg, with branches in Middleburg, in horse country, and in Warrenton, an upscale, rural neighborhood, as well as in Indian Head, Maryland. The attraction of these shops is that they're in areas where people have disposable income, so that the items being sold are generally of excellent quality, with a great selection and good prices. They have clothes, furniture, mirrors, candelabra, antique books, children's items, and decorative items such as prints. In the summer, they often have garden furniture, they might have pillowcases or duvet covers by Ralph Lauren, and they always have shabby chic.

◆ White Elephant, 1045 Edward Ferry Road NE #G9, Leesburg, VA, (703) 771-2060; 103 W. Federal Street, Middleburg, VA, (540) 687-8800; 601 Frost Avenue, Warrenton, VA, (540) 349-0666; 6015 Port Tobacco Road, Indian Head, MD, (301) 752-1053.

Parkway Custom Drycleaning in Chevy Chase, Maryland, is expensive, but they have saved several very good outfits for me. And I am not the only one who recommends them—on the wall is a letter of thanks from Supreme Court Justice Ruth Bader Ginsburg!

◆ Parkway Custom Drycleaning, 8402 Connecticut Avenue, Chevy Chase, MD, (301) 652-3377.

Tucked away on the main floor of Union Station is a small counter for the U.S. Mint, selling jewelry, uncirculated coin sets, commemorative coins, and other nice things at very reasonable prices. The place has many international clients, and is a good source for gifts, such as the coins of different presidents, which come in presentation boxes.

◆ U.S. Mint, 50 Massachusetts Avenue NW, Washington, D.C., (202) 289-0609.

Washington, D.C., is a great place for antiquing, and my favorite shop is the Brass Knob in the Adams Morgan area, an interesting, bohemian neighborhood about two-and-a-half miles from the White House, with funky stores and fun restaurants.

The Brass Knob salvages parts from historical houses that have been torn down, so they sell some wild stuff—architectural antiques, decorative glass, lighting, iron works, and, in the warehouse, big things like bathtubs and doors. It's a terrific resource if you are fixing up your house or want to find unique decorative items. Merchandise generally dates from the year 1850 to about 1930, though some things are more recent.

◆ Brass Knob, 2311 18th Street NW, (202) 332-3370. There's a companion store at 2329 Champlaine Street NW, (202) 265-0587.

Hillwood Museum and Gardens is a very interesting place that many tourists never see. In fact, most people in D.C. don't even know about it. It is the former mansion estate of Marjorie Merriweather Post—who wasn't just an heiress, she was a collector who had an incredible eye. The museum has the largest collection of Fabergé eggs outside the Soviet Union. The museum was recently redone, for about $7 million dollars. The former carriage house has been converted into a museum shop and a café, and the gardens are currently being redesigned. A dacha built on the grounds displays Native American items, such as headdresses that a chief would have worn. Only about 250 people are permitted to visit the house in a day, guided by a docent, and you must make an appointment. Post's daughter, the actress Dina Merrill, is on the board and runs the museum.

◆ Hillwood Museum and Gardens, 4155 Linnean Avenue NW, (202) 686-8505. Hours 9 A.M. to 5 P.M., Tuesday through Saturday.

The Franciscan Monastery is an actual working monastery, where the monks wear sandals and long robes. It is a beautiful place, with gardens containing replicas of shrines from Jordan, Israel, Syria, and Egypt. There are also replicas of catacombs and monuments to saints.

◆ Franciscan Monastery, 1400 Quincy Street NE, (202) 526-6800.

The Arena Stage is one of the top repertory theaters in the nation. There are actually two theaters there: the Fichandler, a theater in the round, and the Kreeger, neither of which has a bad seat. *The Great White Hope*, with James Earl Jones and Jane Alexander, premiered there thirty years ago. About seven plays a year are performed here. A limited number of half-price tickets are sold ninety minutes before curtain time until thirty minutes before the show starts, but this is a hit-or-miss situation, because you never know whether they will have seats.

◆ Arena Stage, 1101 6th Street SW, (202) 488-4377, www.
arenastage.com.

PR & Partners hair salon attracts a funky clientele, ranging from hip twentysomethings to little old gray-haired ladies. They are known for their skill with coloring, but all the services they offer are excellent. Haircuts cost from $30 to $60; prices may vary depending on the stylist. A manicurist comes in four days a week; prices may vary according to style.

◆ PR & Partners, 7710 Woodmont Avenue, Bethesda, MD, (301) 657-4488.

Secondi is a fabulous consignment shop that carries high-end designer fashion, ranging from Donna Karan to Betsey Johnson, including accessories like Coach handbags and Joan & David shoes. The store's policy is to keep its inventory current; it only accepts items in good condition that are less than two years old. You can find many designer clothes here for a fraction of the original price.

◆ Secondi, 1702 Connecticut Avenue NW, Floor 2, (202) 667-1122.

After shopping at Secondi, head across the street to Kramerbooks on Connecticut Avenue. Kick back, relax, and have a glass of wine at their wine bar. Or better yet, have lunch or dinner on the outside patio. They have a full restaurant with excellent specials, and it's a great place to go if you are dining alone. Visit their incredible travel section—the best place to buy travel books in D.C. Kramer's is a privately owned bookstore whose claim to fame is being the place where Monica Lewinsky bought Walt Whitman's *Leaves of Grass* for President Bill Clinton.

◆ Kramerbooks, 1517 Connecticut Avenue NW, (202) 387-1400.

Overseas

AMSTERDAM

"A lot of people think we're boring," smiled the KLM flight attendant. "We laugh about it, because it just means they haven't figured out how to have fun. It's impossible not to have fun in Amsterdam."

You can say that again. First, let's start with the layout of the city. Amsterdam has more bridges than Paris and more canals than Venice. Add bicycles, boats, an attitude that says there is no reason to rush anywhere, and a café society that is starting to embrace some great food, and you have every reason to visit.

Perhaps the most refreshing aspect of Amsterdam is that the city has resisted gentrification. The rough edges are still there, but they don't frighten you. They are just part of the city's personality. And as many flight attendants tell me, this is a destination you can do in three-day trips. Yes, there are the must-sees, ranging from the Rijksmuseum (it's true what they say about *Nightwatch*—as you look at Rembrandt's incredible painting and walk through the room, the eyes on the canvas seem to follow you) to the sex museum, with perhaps the largest sculpture I've ever seen of a penis. At both museums, you are tempted—perhaps for different reasons—to pose in front of the, uh, art!

This is a city through which you stroll, or pedal slowly, or glide along the canals. I took the advice of my KLM flight attendant the first time I went by renting a "pedalo"—a bicycle—near the Rijksmuseum. And later, I jumped on a canal boat. Coffee? A place called New Deli. And afternoon tea at the Amstel Hotel.

An even better bet: bicycle over to Da Kaaskamer on Runstraat, and load up on Dutch farm cheeses, ham, and some wicked pickles, not to mention a good selection of French wine, and have your own picnic near one of the canals. There's also a great lunchroom called Villa Zeezicht, known for only one thing: apple pie.

I love hanging out at the Art Nouveau Athenaeum bookshop in the late afternoon. After the sun goes down, pick any café. My favorites: Café Americain and Café in de Wildeman.

In the evening, if I have friends with me who have never been to Amsterdam, we make the pilgrimage to the notorious red-light district. But invariably we head for either the traditional Dutch seafood restaurant Osterbar or fabulous Indonesian fusion food at Dynasty.

One note of caution: if you rent a bicycle, be sure to lock it when you're not riding it. In Amsterdam, people don't steal bicycles, but they do like to borrow them without bringing them back.

AIRPORT TIPS

The Aviodome Museum of Aviation, showcasing the history of Dutch aviation during World War II, as well as educational programs for kids, is located in the middle of the airport.
◆ For hours and admission, call 020 406 8000.

There are heavenly bedlike easy chairs in the airport that feel like big pillows. Perfect for a catnap!
◆ Easy chairs, located in D Gate, Floors 1 and 2, and E and F Gates.

Food Village, a great supermarket at Schiphol Plaza, opens early in the morning and stays open until late at night. They stock everything from wine to fresh sandwiches (in the deli) to dessert. They bake fresh bread every morning, so if you're in the airport around 6 or 7 A.M. you can smell that delicious yeasty aroma!

◆ Food Village, 0900-Schiphol. Open until midnight daily.

The best way to get to the city from the airport is to go to the train station, which is in the airport itself. (There are clear signs to direct you.) Take the Central Station Train, which takes you right to Central Station in the middle of Amsterdam. The stops are announced in both Dutch and English, and it takes about fifteen minutes to get into the city. It costs about $2 to take the train, whereas a taxi ride to the city might cost about $20.

CITY TIPS

I always bring back flowers from Amsterdam, where they are beautiful and fresh year-round. Here I can get two bunches of lovely big pink and white oriental lilies for $7, whereas in the States you would pay about $30. (Of course, you do have to lug them back.) You can find many varieties of tulips for $3. Every street corner in any part of town will have them. When you take them on the plane, don't put them in water; ask the flight attendant to store them somewhere for you in a wet cloth. When you get home, cut the stems and put them in water with some flower enhancer. The lilies generally last for at least two weeks.

Tara jewelry shop is known for its beaded bracelets and necklaces. It's located around the corner from the Victoria Hotel, which is across the street from the Central Train Station. They deal mainly in silver, but have many other kinds of jewelry, including fresh and saltwater pearls. Bracelets are priced from $11 to $40, and necklaces from $20 to $90. The owners are a married couple, both of whom speak perfect English. They accept credit cards and euros.

◆ Tara, Hasselaerssteeg 22, 020 420 7935. Hours 12 noon to 6 P.M., Tuesday through Sunday.

If you need some postflight R&R, go to the Beauty Planning Salon at the Golden Tulip Grand Hotel Krasnapolsky in Dam Square. They do wonderful facials and manicures, and they also have a spa that does great massages. A full-body massage costs about $50, and you get your own private and very comfortable room. The whole place is decorated in pink, and the masseuses wear pink outfits. They're busy, so make an appointment.

◆ Beauty Planning Salon, Golden Tulip Grand Hotel Krasnapolsky, Dam 9, 020 554 9111.

Bijenkorf sells boxes of twenty candles for about 4.52 euros. They're dripless, and they come in lots of colors. They also have lots of nice candleholders.

◆ Bijenkorf, on the Dam Square, right next to the Krasnapolsky Hotel; Dam 1, 020 621 8080.

Although Amsterdam always seems to have great flea markets, two are particularly notable. The first is the Albert-Cuyp Market, named for the street on which it is located. Here the vendors sell mostly household goods and clothing. The other flea market is Waterlooplein, also named for its location, behind Dam Square. This market is a trip back to the 1960s. I've bought scarves, a long skirt, and a retro-'60s jacket there, all for just a few dollars. It's like entering a time warp.

◆ Albert-Cuyp Market, open 9:30 A.M. to 5 P.M., Monday through Saturday; Waterlooplein, open 9 A.M. to 5 P.M., Monday through Saturday.

If you have a group of hungry people, go for a rijsttafel (rice table), which is actually an Indonesian custom. You get a bowl of rice and a box with twelve to forty little compartments full of different foods to try. The more people the better. It's a fun way to spend an evening.

◆ Sarang Mas, Damrak 44, 020 622 2105.

We all like Rum Runners on the Prinsengracht, about fifty meters from the Anne Frank house. They serve delicious Caribbean-style seafood there, along with rice and beans, for reasonable prices.

◆ Rum Runners, Prinsengracht 277, 020 627 4079.

Cirelli's, a great Italian restaurant with a high-tech decor, serves wonderful pasta dishes in good-sized portions. If you want wine, they bring the whole bottle to your table and charge you based on how much you drink, so you can have as much or as little as you like. Dinners cost from 6 to 34 euros, plus drinks.

◆ Cirelli's, Oudezijds Klok 69, 020 624 3512.

When you're in Amsterdam try some of the local treats such as *pannekoeken*, which are big pancakes, and *stroopwafels*, which are little round cookies filled with caramel that you put on top of your coffee cup or teacup. You can get them at grocery stores like Albert Heijn or at stands on the street. There's also a coffee-flavored hard candy called *rademaker hopjes* that you can't get at home, but that sell here for around $2 for a little bag. You can get a discount card for such purchases, for which there's no fee, regardless of whether you live overseas.

◆ Dam Square, 020 421 8344.

Albert Heijn sells Drogheria & Alimentari spices, which come in interesting glass containers with grinders on the bottom.

Each spice costs under $2. These are unique to Europe and attract admiring comments back in the States. Albert Heijn also carries Italian truffle oil, called Olio d'Italia, for only $2 or $3 for a large, square 500-milliliter bottle. Another shop, Douwe Egberts, sells the best coffee I've ever had. I get the gold brand, which comes prepackaged and preground, and costs less than $2 for 250 grams.

It's almost a matter of national pride that there are so many interesting beers brewed in the Netherlands and Belgium. I like to try different ones from shops all over Amsterdam. They even have fruit-flavored beers. Beer may cost anywhere from $1.50 to $4 per bottle, depending on how unusual the brew is.

P. W. Akkerman is not a stationery store, nor is it a place to buy postcards or birthday cards. It only sells pens. The shop is downtown on a street that is closed to traffic and is famous for its boutiques and department stores.
◆ P. W. Akkerman, Kalverstraat, Number 149, 020 623 1649.

The Dorint Hotel, which is actually in The Hague, about one hour from Amsterdam, is the place to stay if you are seeking peace and quiet—and it is probably cheaper than staying in Amsterdam. The train ride to get there from Amsterdam is gorgeous, with fields of tulips blanketing the countryside. The hotel rooms are huge and some face the North Sea. The hotel will loan you a little bicycle if you want to ride around town.
◆ Dorint Hotel, Johan de Wittlaan 4244, 070 416 9111.

If you want a good deal in gold jewelry, go to Stefan Witjes. Not only does he fix jewelry, he also sells very contemporary custom designs.
◆ Stefan Witjes, NZ Voorburgwal 135, 020 622 6522.

I really needed a haircut, so I followed a recommendation and went to Toni and Guy. I was not disappointed. Their shop originally opened in London, but now they even have a few in the States. The stylist I always go to is Marcelo, who speaks English and does a fantastic job with my hair. Everyone who comes out of his chair looks great. I get my color done at the same place by Ingrid.

◆ Toni and Guy, Magna Plaza Shopping Mall, Third Level, Spuistraat 137, 020 620 0662.

AUCKLAND

Twenty-eight years ago, I was a journalist for *Newsweek* and I had amassed nearly thirteen weeks of vacation time, which, if I didn't use them quickly, I'd lose. My best friend, David, at *Time* magazine, was simultaneously confronted with the same vacation dilemma.

We had to leave town. But where would we go? I spun the globe, and David closed his eyes. Wherever his finger landed, we would be there in three days.

New Zealand? Well, that was the deal.

In 1974, you needed a visa to get there, so the next morning the two of us dutifully headed for the New Zealand consulate. A couple days later we were on a 747 100-model plane, which meant a refueling stop in Hawaii and then on to Auckland. On the way, we had plenty of time to talk to the flight crew. An Air New Zealand purser cautioned us, "I think you'll find New Zealand a little slow for your tastes. Stay one night in Auckland, and then go to Takapuna."

When we arrived nineteen hours later and stumbled into the terminal, a band started playing. It was seven in the morning, two days later, thanks to crossing the international date line. Must be someone very important arriving, we thought. About four minutes later we found out who that someone was—us!

When we filled in our visa forms back in Los Angeles and listed our occupations and our employers, apparently all hell had broken loose Down Under. The word spread quickly—*Newsweek* and *Time* were coming to New Zealand!

Not only was there a band, but also someone from the prime minister's office was on hand to officially welcome us. He handed each of us a gold kiwi pin, shook our hands, and told us that our appointment with the prime minister was in three days in Wellington.

We were in too much shock to do anything other than try to find a hotel and recover from jet lag.

After sleeping for about eight hours, I met David in the lobby to explore. That's when we discovered that, at least in 1974, New Zealand closed at 6 P.M. I am not exaggerating when I tell you that we could not find a single restaurant open in the city after 6 P.M. Not even in the hotel. And the pubs closed at 8 P.M.

There was one television channel, and it went off the air at 8:30. Out of desperation, I went back to the lobby and got one of those "What's Happening in Auckland" handouts. Listed for that day: at 11 P.M. the *Royal Viking Star*, an American-based cruise ship, was sailing for Sydney. It was the only listing for that day!

I grabbed David and we went down to the docks and watched the ship sail. I was beginning to worry about a country whose national bird was nocturnal and couldn't fly, and where sheep outnumbered people thirteen to one.

The next morning, dazed and hungry, we headed to Taka-puna. The Air New Zealand purser was right. We had rooms on the water. We swam. We water-skied. I fell madly in love with the receptionist at the restaurant, who, at twenty-four years of age, was already a jet pilot in the New Zealand Air Force and a doctor. Our real New Zealand adventure had begun.

Three days later, we interviewed the prime minister (even though we were not exactly on assignment). David's first question was, "Can you tell me why your country closes at six in the evening?"

The prime minister's answer: the family unit is the most important thing to New Zealanders. He was serious. And he was right. And by that time, we were no longer worried about eating—we were digesting something else: one of the most beautiful countries we had ever experienced, with some of the nicest people.

Today, nearly three decades later, only certain things have changed in New Zealand. The sheep still rule; the family unit is still paramount. And the scenery keeps getting better.

The Travelodge has become the Copthorne Hotel (still one of my least favorite places). But the building is now surrounded by the Maritime Museum and some great bars, and it's also the headquarters for the Americas Cup.

Not only can you now get dinner at 9 P.M.—and later—the food has become world class. Within walking distance of the Copthorne there are places like SeaMart, Euro, Soul, and Stonegrill.

Flying down to Auckland recently, I asked another Air New Zealand purser for advice. This time, he didn't tell me what not to do. He gave me more than enough to do—ranging from fishing in the Bay of Islands and ice climbing, to bungee jumping and sea kayaking.

AIRPORT TIPS

Auckland's airport is a favorite of all crew members. It has showers available to the public and, for a quick snack, the airport has wonderful scones and muffins—perfect with a cup of coffee or tea while waiting for your airplane.
◆ Showers and bathrooms opposite Gate 5 and near Gate 9, 09 256 8845.

This is something new: if you buy goods at the duty-free shops and have an Australian or New Zealand passport, you can get express entry through Customs.

CITY TIPS

None of our trips to Auckland would be complete without a trip to Breen's. The manager, Grant Barlow, has been catering to airline crews for years. They carry all kinds of excellent wool and sheepskin products. They'll also barter if you get creative. ("If I buy this, will you throw in this jar of lanolin or this sheepskin handle cover?") They will ship to your home, for a reasonable fee. A very popular purchase is a wool-filled comforter, which comes in several sizes and weights. Once you have slept under a wool comforter, you won't be satisfied with anything else. The cost varies by size, thickness, and exchange rate, but a queen-size comforter of the lightest weight costs about $100 U.S. (Their bed dimensions are different from ours, so keep this in mind when you buy.) The wool-stuffed pillows are also popular and cost about $42 U.S., depending on the exchange rate. They will custom-make beautiful sheepskin rugs, or you can buy them ready-made. They also carry sheepskin-lined bedroom slippers and some great sheepskin jackets and wool sweaters.

◆ Breen's, 6 Customs Street West, 09 373 2788, bynzmade@xtra.co.nz.

The Hunting Lodge, about thirty-five minutes northwest of central Auckland, is a little pricey by New Zealand standards, but the food is wonderful and they have an excellent wine list. They offer nightly specials, but the regular menu includes superb steaks, seafood, pork, chicken, and pheasant. Entrées cost between $25 and $35 N.Z., including potatoes and vegetables, but salads and desserts are extra. This is a very romantic place; I proposed to my wife while having dinner here. The owner is Justin Wade. Reservations are advised.

◆ Hunting Lodge, Waikoukou Valley Road, Waimauku Auckland, 09 411 8259, www.thehuntinglodge.co.nz.

Little Italy, a great place for Italian food in Auckland, is where all the cops—and, now, quite a few flight crews—hang out. The place is known for its pizza, and they will put anything you want on top. They also have great garlic bread, pasta, steak, chicken, and seafood. This is a B.Y.O.B. spot, but you can also buy a glass of very inexpensive wine. If you want something nicer, there is a liquor store right across the street, and there is no corkage fee. Three men run the restaurant and they spend a lot of time talking to the customers. The walls are covered with postcards sent by happy customers from all over the world.

◆ Little Italy, 43 Victoria Street West, at Victoria and Albert Streets, 09 379 5813.

I insist that everyone go to Lord Nelson's on Victoria, near Sky City. (Look for the sign that says "Dentist," otherwise it's a little hard to find.) Legend has it that this was an old Pan American hangout. They serve full orders and half orders, and they have a full bar that includes a good wine selection. It is not overly expensive, and they have great lamb. Last time I was there, I had shrimp on a skewer, which was delicious!

◆ Lord Nelson's, 37 Victoria Street, 09 379 4564.

Harting's is the store for wool duvets, which are lighter and easier to clean than other kinds. A king-size duvet costs about $200 N.Z. They also sell slippers.

◆ Harting's, 148 Quay Street, 09 366 4739.

A favorite place for those who espouse the virtues of holistic medicine is the Uptown Pharmacy, and the person to see is Trish Joe, who will meet with you for a free consultation. Many crew members go there for health screenings; you can also get cleansings. They offer herbal mixtures for everything from hormone replacement to liver tonics. Flight attendants have a chronic complaint—we're all dehydrated. Trish recommends certain vitamins and adrenaline. Jennie Hyde gives fabulous facials and does micro-dermabrasions at about half of what they cost in the United States—and they're every bit as good. This is a great way to unwind and relax after a long flight, and it will also rehydrate your face.

◆ Uptown Pharmacy, 178 Karanghape Road, 09 373 3552.

Because the British gentry were some of the first to settle in this area, Auckland is a treasure trove of fine English antiques. Antique and Estate Jewelry, a tiny jewelry shop in the Queen's Arcade, contains many wonderful treasures from the Victorian and Edwardian eras. Graeme Thomson, the shop's gracious host, has one of the best antique pocket watch collections to be seen anywhere. Because the U.S. dollar is currently so strong in New Zealand, the prices here are great.

◆ Antique and Estate Jewelry, 34 Queen Street, 09 303 1912.

If you really want to treat yourself, go to Serville's Spa, offering a full range of services in a beautiful atmosphere. The surroundings are intimate and designed to soothe the senses. As you enter, candles light the corridor, there's a floral aroma, and you hear the sound of gently flowing water from a fountain. The treatments are unrushed and will make you feel very special.

◆ Serville's Spa, on the Prince's Wharf, Level 1-Shed 20, 09 309 9086.

Ferg's Café and Kayak on the waterfront is owned by Ian Fergason, a former Olympic kayaker and one of New Zealand's top sporting personalities. He operates a small kayak shop in the front of the cafe. This café is one of the few places where you're actually right on the water. You can watch people shove their kayaks into the sea and take off in Okahu Bay. In addition, Ferg's bacon and eggs are really good, and the coffee is great. In New Zealand most people order a "flat white" (a good Kiwi term to know), which is like a cappuccino without the foamy milk on top.

◆ Ferg's Café and Kayak, 12 Kayak Tamaki Drive, Okahu Bay, 09 529 2230.

In the summer in New Zealand it stays light until 9:30 P.M., which is when the local people like to kayak to Rangitoto Island, a small, extinct volcano about five kilometers (approximately three miles) across the main shipping channel from Auckland. This is usually done in groups of about twelve people, with a guide. Once you get to this wild, beautiful green island, covered with bush, you hike for about an hour to the top of the volcano—a medium-to-difficult hike—where you have a picnic and watch the sun set. On the return trip, of course, it's dark, so you wear miner's lamps. It's an amazing adventure!

All the local people know that when you want to dance, you go to the Spy Bar, in the Viaduct part of town. The place features the best music in town—techno and funk—and even though it's not a particularly attractive place, there's usually a line to get in (it helps to be a well-dressed, attractive woman). They also have a great wine selection—try Daniel Le Brun, a New Zealand sparkling wine.

◆ Spy Bar, 204 Quay Street, 09 377 7811.

Marlborough, in the northern part of South Island, is known for its sauvignon blanc wines, with their fresh, grassy, sharp bite, and Glen Garry wine shop in Auckland is a good place to get them. The 2001 Kim Crawford sauvignon blanc is fabulous and costs the equivalent of only $7 U.S. This chain of wine shops puts out an interesting newsletter containing details about their specials; you can sign up for the mailing list.

◆ Glen Garry wine shop, 118 Wellesley Street, 09 379 3740.

Since our layovers tend to be about two days, we have a chance to really see part of the country. We discovered the Twin Pines, a fabulous restaurant in the town of Paihia on the Bay of Islands. From the outside, the place looks like an old farmhouse with twin pine trees in the front, but their presentation of meals rivals that of any of the finest restaurants in the United States. The waiters are attentive and will recommend the freshest fish and seasonal specialties. The restaurant specializes in seafood dishes, with seafood soup being a particular standout. There is also a very nice wine list. Two complete dinners with cocktails and wine was $40 U.S. Call ahead for reservations. Bay of Islands is quite a drive from Auckland, so you should plan to spend the night. There are many small hotels in the area, and the prices generally run around $50 U.S. per night.

◆ Twin Pines, Puketona Road, Road 1, Bay of Islands, 09 402 7195.

In the town of Opua, about three and a half hours out of Auckland on the Bay of Islands, you can catch the ferry to Russell, which was the first capital of New Zealand. At that time Russell was a rough-and-tumble whaling town, where all the sailors came to drink and party. Now it is a quaint old village with lots of antique houses. Just as you leave the ferry dock going into Russell there is a place called Omata Estates, on the grounds of which is a wonderful restaurant that very few tourists know about. This romantic restaurant is in a large circular building constructed of old beams and looking out over the Bay of Islands and the vineyards. You can go outside and visit with the chef, who cooks your meal in a covered alcove. The food is served on long glass dishes, and they have a wonderful wine list. Main courses start at about $25 N.Z., which is quite reasonable for Americans. The last ferry back to Opua leaves at 9 P.M., so arrange to stay someplace in Russell for the night because you will have a long drive back if you miss the ferry.

◆ Omata Estates, Aucks Road 1, Russell, 09 403 8007.

BANGKOK AND CHIANG MAI

I first flew to Bangkok on a Cathay Pacific L-1011 from Hong Kong in the late 1970s. The Hong Kong–based Cathay pilots assured us we were about to have an incredible time in Thailand. "This is where we go when we have a few days off," they said. "Great people, great food, great style, culture, shopping. And, of course, great women."

One of the pilots was married to a Thai. The other was, let's say, not exactly opposed to the idea for himself.

The pilots told us where to eat, where to watch wild Thai kickboxing events, and where they always shop. They each had a favorite tailor; they each had a favorite place to buy silk and antiques. One of them had furnished his entire flat in Hong Kong from Thailand.

We took notes.

And from the moment we landed in Bangkok, I couldn't help but remember the famous Groucho Marx line, "I don't want to belong to any club that will accept me as a member." I couldn't help thinking that people were nice to me because they had been expecting another guy named Greenberg. But, as I soon discovered, it had nothing to do with me at all. It's how the Thais treat everyone. And just as quickly, I was spoiled.

A few hours later we bumped into those same pilots at Narayapan, which is not exactly a store but a series of stores and stalls within walking distance of the Regent Hotel. We also saw flight crews from Air France, SAS, and Qantas shopping there. I soon learned why. Not only were the prices cheap, but the workmanship, especially on wooden items and silk, was excellent. "Let me give you some help," one of the SAS flight attendants recommended. "If you see something you like, buy ten of them."

Ten?

"That's right. They pack everything beautifully, and if it's too big you can buy inexpensive luggage here as well. And then, when you get home, you have presents for birthdays, Christmas, baby showers, weddings." Spot-on advice, which I have been following for years. By the way, the stores will eagerly deliver your purchases right to your hotel. There's a very good reason why Bangkok (and also Chiang Mai, up north) is a favorite crew layover. In many cases, since so many flights are a long haul to Thailand, the crews get at least two days' rest—plenty of time for shopping and/or day trips to the magical mystery tour that is Chiang Mai and indulgences at the Regent there, or down south to Phuket and R&R in the Andaman Sea.

With the Thai baht at about forty-seven to the dollar, it is also one of the best bargains in the world. It is impossible to find a bad hotel in Thailand. Or a bad meal. One of the great experiences is to get up very early in the morning and hire one of the long boats to take you down the klongs of the river—not to the floating markets frequented by tourists, but to the local floating markets. Breakfast of Thai noodles at 5:30 in the morning, floating on the river, is definitely the way to go.

After the 1994 earthquake in Los Angeles destroyed my house, I went back to Bangkok and, while my new house was being constructed in Los Angeles, virtually every piece of wood for it—from the built-in cabinets, to doors, window moldings, bookshelves, and even my beds—was being shipped over from Bangkok.

Yes, Bangkok has terrible traffic. Yes, it is polluted. And yes, if I ever somehow fell into the Chao Phraya River I'd probably die just from the bacteria and the chemicals that have become the river. But it doesn't keep me from returning all the time. In fact, I love Bangkok so much I bought a place there ten years ago. That should tell you something. Latter-day Grouchos are more than welcome here. They're encouraged to come . . . and to return.

AIRPORT TIPS

The best airports in Asia for shopping are in Singapore and Bangkok. In Bangkok, you can get beautiful long-stem or-chids—a dozen of them and they are *heavenly*—for less than a quarter of what you would pay in the States. They're long-lasting and perfect for decorating back home. They're packed individually in a box with cubes of water to preserve them. It's not a problem bringing them through customs, either—you just declare them and get a stamp.

◆ Bangkokgreen Company, Third Floor, Departure Hall,
02 535 2516 and 02 535 2517, bkkgreen@a-net.net.th.

CITY TIPS

Bangkok

The Central Plaza Hotel in Bangkok has an incredible buffet, although you might not know how to pronounce the names of any of the dishes. It doesn't matter—this is the place to go!

◆ Central Plaza Hotel, 1695 Phaholyothin Road, Chatuchak,
02 541 1234.

In Panthip Plaza you can find black-market computer software at great prices. There's software and hardware on display at every store on every floor, but nothing is well organized. Take a taxi to get there; however, remember that every taxi in Bangkok

has a meter, but these meters are purely ornamental—they are almost never turned on. Negotiate in advance.
◆ 604/3 Panthip Plaza Building, Petchchburi Road, 02 254 9797.

Thai massage is notorious as a result of tales told by men boasting of some sort of sexual conquest in the process. But if you really want authentic Thai massage, go to Baan Sawasdee Thai Massage, run by two Thais who are former flight attendants, and located near Central Plaza, halfway between the airport and the World Trade Center in the city. During a Thai massage, you wear thin pajamas so you're not naked, and the masseuses don't touch your skin directly. They apply pressure with their thumbs or their hands, or by standing on you. The massages are cheap—$10 for two hours or $13 for two-and-a-half hours—and you can walk in or call to make a booking, depending on the day. Their herbal massage is really worth trying—you get a one-hour Thai massage and a one-hour herbal massage for $10, and it's totally clean.
◆ Baan Sawasdee Thai Massage, 16-53 Soi Horwang 3,
Vipawadee Rangsit Road, 02 513 2299. Hours 10 A.M. to 10 P.M. daily, including weekends.

The Suda Restaurant is very cheap and the portions are huge—for $10 to $12, your belly is full. I recommend the fried rice and Thai soups. The restaurant is on the street level away from the traffic, and you can sit outside. Take the Sky Train during rush hour—it saves a lot of time (get off at Asok). Take it back, too, because it's always safe. Trains stop running at 12:30 A.M.
◆ Suda Restaurant, 571 Sukhumvit Soi 14, 02 229 4536.

At Cabbage and Condoms you sit up on the roof surrounded by trees that are so big, you think you are actually sitting in one. There are mango and papaya trees, but they also put fake fruits on the trees, which look so real and juicy that the place resembles the Garden of Eden, right in the middle of the busy city.

There's a lot of room on the roof; it seats about one hundred. The menu is extensive, with a wide selection of curries; they also have an English menu. A typical entrée, Pad Thai, is only $5, and the portions are large. I thought "condoms" was short for "condiments" until I went downstairs after lunch and saw that the souvenir shop sells lots and lots of condoms! In fact, at the end of the meal you'll get a condom instead of an after-dinner mint.

◆ Cabbage and Condoms, 10 Sukhumvit Soi 12, 02 252 7349.

At Premier Tailors, within walking distance of the legendary Oriental Hotel, the man to see is the owner, Lek. He can take any item of designer clothing—DKNY, Armani, Joseph Abboud—ask you what color, fabric, and style of buttons you want, and within twenty-four hours, he has copied the garment and delivered it to your hotel. It's superior craftsmanship, at a fraction of the price of an original. The last three outfits he copied for me cost $90. And the same outfits—well, you know what they would have cost back in the States.

◆ Premier Tailors, 123 New Road, 02 235 9090.

Peter, of Peter Furniture, did such a great job making the furniture for the Regent Hotel that they built him his own workshop and showroom right behind the hotel. He can custom-make any kind of furniture from any type of wood to the specifications you provide. Since he has catalogues and design books from furniture makers in the United States and Europe, he can reproduce nearly anything you might want. He also does excellent leather work. He will ship it to you in the States when it is finished; shipping is charged by the cubic foot rather than by weight, and you pay no duty charges because Thailand is considered a developing country. My order for a dining table, six chairs, a china cabinet, two bookcases, and a small coffee table took about three months and saved me at least $4,000.

◆ Peter Furniture, 157/2 Soi Mahadlek 2, Rajdamri Road, Lumpini, Pathumwan, 02 251 7668 or 02 252 5236, petersf@ksc.th.com.

I go to Alex Fashions so frequently that Alex has my measurements on file. I can call and ask him for a green suit, and he will send swatches to my hotel; later, he will send the finished garment to my home. He can make you whatever you want for a very reasonable price. For example, he custom-made me a two-piece suit for under $100—and it arrived completely wrinkle free. The store is located in the Rembrandt Hotel.
◆ Alex Fashions, 19 Sukhumvit Soi 18, Klong Toei, 02 261 7100, cellular 01 837 9920.

When I go to another country I like to experience it as local people do—eat where they eat, shop where they shop, and really immerse myself in the culture. I often stay at the Landmark Hotel on Sukhumvit Road, a major street in Bangkok, and right across the road is a Foodland market with a small lunch counter, called Took La Dea, that seems to always be open. It's a great place to eat and people watch after a long day of shopping or an evening of nightclubbing. The food, always very fresh, is a combination of Thai and Chinese, and they prepare it right in front of you. I recommend the fried glass noodles with pork, but their prawn red curry is also delicious. A lime squash or watermelon juice makes an excellent accompaniment. Above the Foodland is the nicer version of the Took La Dea, a regular restaurant with tables and chairs. The food is just as good, but the local color is not quite so . . . colorful. There are two Foodlands in the Sukhumvit neighborhood.
◆ Landmark Bangkok, 138 Sukhumvit Road, 02 254 0404.
Foodland Supermarkets, on Sukhumvit opposite Soi 63 aka Ekami and at Sukhumvit Soi 5.
Foodland Supermarket Co. Ltd. Head Office, Ladprao Road, Wang Thong Larng, 02 530 0220, 02 530 0222.

Exit Foodland through the front door, turn left, and then take the very first right to a little massage parlor called Buathib, where you can get an excellent Thai massage. As you enter you are handed a cotton shirt and drawstring pants, then you are led to a private booth, where you lie down on a wide mattress. There the receptionist will introduce you to your masseur or masseuse, or you can request someone in particular. A full-body massage takes two hours and costs only 200 baht. You feel like you are walking on a cloud when you're done!

◆ Buathib, 4/1-2 Sukhumvit Soi 5, 02 251 2627. Hours 1 A.M. to midnight daily.

If you don't want to hire one of the long boats, and you're feeling bold, then jump—and I'm not kidding about the jump—on a water taxi. These taxis slow up at the dock just long enough for you to jump in. And whatever you do, time the jump well—you *never* want to fall into that river! They make scheduled stops up and down the river, but only during certain hours. Our return trip to the point of origin took seventeen stops, but by the time we got back, we were all soaking wet and laughing hard. It was a harrowing experience, but quite commonplace for the local people and something that shouldn't be missed. (Don't dress up!)

◆ Water Taxi Service, 076 219391-2.

Chiang Mai

Some of our flights allow us a three-day layover in Thailand, and if you plan it just right, you can take the overnight train trip from Bangkok to Chiang Mai on the State Railway of Thailand. The train leaves at 8 or 9 P.M., and the trip takes about thirteen hours. Go first class because it's not expensive—it will cost you about $38 for one person, one way. You travel in a sleeper car, in an individual room with bunk beds and a safe, as well as a little fold-down table where you can eat the meal they serve you.

When you wake up in the morning, you can watch the sun rise over the countryside, or you can get out and stand in between the train cars for some fresh air. The trains are very safe. From Chiang Mai, you fly back—it's about a one-hour flight. Buy your plane ticket from a travel agent, otherwise you'll pay full price. Our travel agent, believe it or not, is also our tailor, and he gets us our tickets for just $100.

◆ State Railway of Thailand, 1 Rongmuang Road, Rongmuang Pathumwan, Bangkok, (662) 225-0300, www.srt.motc.go.th/ httpEng/, based in Bangkok but service to Chiang Mai.

If you enjoy a culturally and internationally mixed crowd and want to hear some great live blues and R&B, then visit the Riverside Pub and Restaurant. This is also the perfect place to observe Loy Krathong, the floating lanterns festival held on the river. An extra dock is built for the event and it is a thrilling experience to watch the regatta of beautiful floating krathongs under a light-filled sky while dining on delectable Thai food. This is a popular event, so be sure to make a reservation.

◆ Riverside Pub and Restaurant, 9-11 Charoenrat Road, 053 243239.

All world travelers know that the best food is found where the locals dine, and that means economical, but good-quality, meals. The old part of Chiang Mai is still squared off by four gates. The Than Phi Gate, in the east, is where you will find the very cheap guest houses that cater to the numerous trekkers. Vegetarians will find ample nourishment in that area. My favorite restaurant, Aron Rai, is near the Than Phase Gate. It offers an immense menu, but don't expect ambience—just a cement floor and great food. It's an open-air place with a "deli counter" that is at least worth a look, even if you don't want to take out a bag of grubs or fried grasshoppers. (Don't knock it until you try it . . . tastes like chicken!) But please don't let those exotic options scare you off. You will not be the only tourists there, but you will meet other adventurous travelers!

◆ Aron Rai, #45 Kotchasarn Road, Muang, 053 276 947.

Even if you're not a shopper, the Night Bazaar is fun. Bring a photo of a loved one to the basement of the main building (most stands are outside, lining the street, and you are sure to find this huge building). Here you will find talented artists who will do a charcoal drawing in just a day or two from a photo, for about $25. Of course, you can sit for one, too.

◆ Night Bazaar, Changklan Road.

The Galare (pronounced "Ga-lay") Guest House is not four-star, but it's a very peaceful place with carved wooden ceilings and roof; tables and chairs in a large, cool, shady yard; and a restaurant that will make you want to stay all day. If you really want to unwind, they will arrange for a masseuse to come to your room for a minimum of two hours, which will cost you only $18. However, this place is only two blocks away from the hustle and bustle of the Night Bazaar, the busy nighttime shopping area. To get there, walk out to the main road from the airport and take a songtaew (the back of a pickup) or splurge and take a taxi for about $5. Rooms run about $25.

◆ Galare Guest House, 7 Chareonprathet Road, Soi 2, 053 818887 and 053 821011, www.galare.com.

You will be encouraged to visit the cottage industries on the outskirts of town, but don't shop there—it's a tourist trap. A lot of tourists go there thinking they'll get better prices at the factories, but they don't because the vendors raised their prices in anticipation of the tourist traffic. If you do go, visit the umbrella "suburb," where you can watch men and women in an ancient art of twirling umbrellas with their toes while painting exquisite designs. Massages are always very cheap here—less than $8 an hour. A masseuse will come to your hotel room for a minimum of two hours for $18.

◆ Cottage Industries, located nine kilometers from Chiang Mai on Highway 1006.

The Warorot Market is not your typical upscale American mall. It's a bit dark and dingy, but you will find a wealth of indigenous crafts and local fabrics. On the lower levels the local people buy their household items, on the second and third floors you can hang out on the balcony and get a good view of the scene, but in the upstairs, which is a lot less crowded, you can find good deals on clothing. Sarongs, if you barter well, will cost only about $2 or $3 each. You can also find affordably priced raw Thai silk, as well as rubies, sapphires, emeralds, some diamonds, and 18-karat gold. The merchandise at Fancy Fabrics is mostly Indonesian, but that's what the country people in Thailand wear. The men use these fabrics in their traditional costumes, but the fabrics also make great tablecloths, sarongs for the beach, or beach towels. Taxi drivers know how to get to Warorot Market, but you might need to know how to ask in Thai because a lot of the drivers don't know English. And when we're talking taxis, we're really talking tuk-tuks—motorized rickshaws we've nicknamed "little iron death machines." Hold on tight!

◆ Warorot Market, corner of Wichayanon and Chiang Mai Road, 053 251458 (ask for Kay; she speaks English).

It's not a bad idea to hire the services of one of those tuk-tuk drivers because they act as tour guides, too. Instead of going on a bus tour, it's acceptable, affordable, and comfortable to hire the services of one of these men for the day. Some have photo albums that show where they can take you—for example, to see waterfalls and orchid farms or to do elephant riding. We hired the same guy every day because each morning when we walked out of our hotel, he was parked in the same place, waiting for us.

His services cost about $20 for the whole day. (Don't pay the first price you're offered for anything other than restaurant food.)

Rented clubs, golf cart, and eighteen holes of golf will cost you only $30 to $35. At Chiang Mai Lamphun Golf Club, the course is beautiful with lots of trees, hills, and water. When we went, our driver actually stayed with us and drove the golf cart.
◆ Chiang Mai Lamphun Golf Club, San Kamphaeng-Ban Thi Near, 053 8808804, www.chiangmaigolf.com.

BARCELONA

Barcelona is a city that truly benefits from its location, lying snugly between the foothills of the Pyrenees and the Mediterranean. Because of its position and design, Barcelona is best experienced on foot. "Anytime we can walk a city it's one of our favorites," one flight attendant told me.

It also means that Barcelona is just a few hours' drive from southern France and the seduction of northern Costa Brava. If you want something close to perfection in the western Mediterranean, Barcelona is it. Speaking of local transportation, don't knock it—Barcelona is the only city I know where there's an underground train to the local beach.

But Barcelona isn't just the capital of Catalonia; this two-thousand-year-old city has finally gotten its well-deserved recognition as one of the most artistic and stylish cities in Europe. Credit the 1992 Olympics, when Barcelona was officially reintroduced to the world.

All you really have to do is walk around to see it. Start with La Rambla, the mile-long walkway that takes you down to the port. Don't miss the large pavement mosaic by Joan Miró. Want to know how serious they are about walking in Barcelona? On La Rambla, if you want to sit, you rent a seat!

You could begin at the Arc del Triomf, which was the main gateway to the universal exhibition in 1888. If you head due south from there, you'll be at the Parc de la Ciutadella, one of the nicer city parks I've ever seen. It's got a large boating lake and the Cascada Fountain, which was designed by a famous architect—Josep Fontserè—who was helped by his even more famous student, Antonio Gaudí.

If you're not careful, you might be tempted to think Gaudí built most of Barcelona. He didn't, of course, but so much of the city bears his trademark design. Seeing the dreamlike designs of Gaudí in Barcelona is not only unavoidable, it's essential to understanding the level of tolerance that exists in this city—think about an art and design movement that poked fun at (or perhaps made fun of) traditionalism, whereby buildings were constructed without a single straight line or right-angled corner. You look, you admire, and, often, you chuckle.

CITY TIPS

The attraction of La Rambla is the nonstop activity. This is a pedestrian boulevard at its most interesting, with a circuslike atmosphere. Everywhere you walk, you'll see cafés and flower stalls, bird sellers and fortune tellers, jugglers and tarot card readers. It's in your face, but it's not oppressive. This is free theater!

If Gaudí isn't your style, then check out the work of Basque architect Luis Pena Ganchegui at the Parc de L'Espanya Industrial. This is postmodernism at its best, if not its most intense. This park includes ten strange-looking towers, giant steel ramps, and overhangs that make the place look like a playground for monsters and giants.

The old part of the city is called the Barri Gotic. Restaurant Siete Portes has been there since 1836 and has delicious seafood, including, of course, paella. It is on the formal side, but we were admitted in casual dress. I had grilled merluza (hake) and a special dish made of spinach, pine nuts, and raisins. Dinner was about $25, with a glass of wine.

◆ Siete Portes, Passeig Isabel number 11, 14, 093 319 3033.

The Christmas Fair is also located in the Barri Gotic, where the streets are narrow and winding. Located in front of the Catedral de Barcelona, the fair begins around December 5 and runs through December 23. Hundreds of vendors sell a fascinating assortment of mass-produced and handcrafted nativity scenes, some of which form entire miniature villages, like those made for model railroad sets. The prices vary according to the elaborateness of the scene, but all vendors accept only cash in payment.

◆ Catedral de Barcelona, Pla de la Seu, 093 315 1554.

In the park behind the Fira Palace, the hotel staff had set up an elaborate nativity scene at Christmastime. The concierge pointed out a comical little figure in the scene, explaining that every nativity scene in Barcelona, including those sold at the fair, would display him. Usually, he is depicted as a farmhand or a shepherd, in the squatting position, with his breeches down. In Catalan, they call him *Cacaner*.

◆ Fira Palace Hotel, Av. Rius I Taulet, 1-3, 093 426 2223.

Yes, some flight attendants still smoke. Cigarettes are dirt cheap at the tobacco stores (*tabacs*) in Barcelona. I'll pay $4.89 for a pack of cigarettes in New York state. I paid $1.80 for them in Barcelona.

BEIJING

When I first flew to Beijing, shortly after Richard Nixon's first visit to China, it wasn't exactly on the hit parade of great layover cities for flight crews—terrible food, nothing to buy, and few places to go. "I know it sounds blasé," a pilot once shrugged, "but how many times can you eat Peking duck or go to Tiananmen Square or the Great Wall?"

Answer: more than you think!

There are limits to duck consumption, but the flight crews got smart. As more and more of China opened up, and within a year or two of Nixon's visit, the same pilots and flight attendants who dreaded going to Beijing began to covet the flights. They went beyond the original "friendship" stores and found great bargains on everything from silk to fine china. They also found hidden corners of the once forbidden city—temples, pavilions, parks, and museums.

Then they found the floating TGIF parties held at either the British, the American, or the Canadian Embassy—and got themselves invited on Friday nights.

They also learned the best hours to sneak into the Summer Palace and that you should go early to the Great Wall. If pressed, they could tell you which Peking duck restaurant was tolerable. (Ordering Peking duck in the former Peking is not always advisable. You actually get better duck in cities other than Beijing.)

Many flight attendants and pilots I know who regularly fly to Beijing keep a bicycle at their hotel (or they just rent one) because that's how the city moves. Other than for a trek out to the Great Wall (for which you should hire a cab), the bicycle is the way to go. You'll see more of the city, and even though you have presumably mastered the fine art of two-wheel travel, you will be constantly amazed at the Chinese who use bicycles to transport loads of cargo that we would reserve for—at the very least—a pickup truck. It is a never-ending acrobatic ballet to watch bicycles—often obscuring their drivers from any possible view of their direction or position—maneuver through the streets. If you've ever wondered how so many of the Cirque du Soleil acrobats got so good, it is arguable that at least some of them got their training as bicyclists on the streets of Beijing. Of course, part of that maneuvering includes the obstacle course of phlegm. Spitting in Beijing is about as close to a national sport as you can get. And everyone does it, even though, technically, spitting is illegal in Beijing. But that's like saying jaywalking is illegal in New York City. So be aware, and try not to get caught in the crossfire.

One fashion note: virtually everything in Beijing is powered by coal. Flight crews don't like going there in the winter—not because the city can get very very cold (it can), but because so many coal-fired heaters are used that white shirts (often worn by pilots and flight attendants) don't stay white very long.

CITY TIPS

The first thing many of us do when we hit Beijing is serious pearl shopping at the Hongqiao Market, aka the Pearl Market. Everyone knows where it is, and it's free to get in. Just be prepared to bargain with the vendors. The cost of the pearls is based on how large or round they are. You have to be persistent and assertive because the competition in the market is fierce. The third floor contains innumerable pearl booths; on the fourth floor, ask for a woman named Mey. She can copy anything. Just bring in a picture of a piece of jewelry that you like, and she will make it for you. She works with crystals, beads, pearls, turquoise, and all kinds of stones such as aquamarine and topaz. Mey copied the necklace Madonna had made for her daughter, Lourdes, for my own daughter. It's made of sea pearls and crystals, with a crystal heart hanging from the front. Mey also made a bracelet to match, and I paid only $20.

◆ Hongqiao Market, 16 Hongqiao Lu (across from the east gate of the Temple of Heaven), Chongwen District.

Across from Mey in the Pearl Market, there's a shop that sells beautiful globes made from lapis lazuli, turquoise, mother-of-pearl, and jade. They cost about an eighth of their price in the States, so, although they're a little awkward to bring home, it's definitely worth the effort.

◆ Hongqiao Market #4310, Fourth Floor, 010 67114231.

The price range at Sharon's Store is astounding: $1 to $10,000—and there is no bargaining. However, she sells a huge variety of wonderful jewelry, and she is very reputable.

◆ Sharon's Store, Hongqiao Market #4201, Fourth Floor, 010 671718888, www.sharonpearl.com, sharon@sharonpearl.com.

The Chinese make a special seaweed soap called Soft, which is wonderful but hard to locate. You can buy it in the States, where it costs $50 for four bars, but in China it's only 50¢ a bar. You can usually find this soap on the first floor of the Pearl Market, among the cosmetics and the wigs and the bathing suits. It's not prominently displayed, but it's worth the search. Don't let the soap's packaging scare you. Along with the many misspellings, it reads: "Cleans the dirtiness out of capillary holes."

At the Pearl Market, vendors sell everything from knockoff North Face jackets to Coach bags. Some of them look quite au-

thentic. If you ski, they also have excellent Gore-tex material that they make into ski jackets and pants, for a very affordable price.
◆ Hongqiao Market #4313, Fourth Floor, 010 67112508, cell 13910321378, fax 010 67112508, Maelmd@263.net.

China can get very cold, so it's fortunate that one of the best deals in Beijing is on down jackets. You can find name brands such as Gore-tex, Columbia, and Jantzen for only $20 to $40. Usually the jackets have two layers that you can separate with snaps or a zipper. You can buy these jackets in the Hongqiao Market on the second floor or at the night market across the street from the Holiday Inn Lido, where you can also buy good-quality cashmere sweaters for about $40.

Want to have fun and meet a lot of flight attendants at the same time? Head for the bowling alley at the Holiday Inn Lido. We almost always go there when we're in Beijing. They have fluorescent bowling balls and wild colors everywhere, and it's always really lively. It's like an American bowling alley, but all the scoring is in Chinese, so you have to figure out how to work the board. The attendants are very friendly and usually will help you out. An evening of bowling costs under $5, including shoes.
◆ Beijing Lido Holiday Inn, Jichang Road, Jiang Tai Road, 800 810 0019 or 010 64376688.

Gallery Bar in the Holiday Inn Lido serves an excellent cabernet wine from a company called Dragon Wine. A glass of it will cost $3 to $4. You can also find this wine throughout Beijing in the markets and stores.
◆ Beijing Lido Holiday Inn, Jichang Road, Jiang Tai Road, 010 64376688, Ext. 1956, and 800 810 0019.

Silk Alley, or Xiu Shui, near the embassies and the huge McDonald's, is the place to find anything you've ever wanted from a Victoria's Secret catalogue. There are leather pants, shoes, cashmere sweaters, silk shirts for men, Abercrombie & Fitch apparel, and other clothing. The quality of the merchandise varies; also, be careful about sizes because the Chinese tend to be small and their large size is equivalent to our small.

◆ Silk Alley, Jianguomen Wai, Chanoyang District.

There are duck restaurants everywhere in Beijing, so you would think that the thing to order would be Peking duck. Problem is, most of the ducks are too greasy when cooked and often they're not properly cooked at all, so you're eating a lot of fat. As an alternative, we've discovered A Fun Ti, a Mongolian type of restaurant featuring a burlesque show that gets wilder as the night goes on. The performers throw their hats and various other things into the audience, and by the end of the night everyone's dancing on the tables. We stayed there all night eating and drinking, and it cost us only $10 per person.

◆ A Fun Ti, 2 Houguaibang Hutong, Chaoyangmennei, 010 65251071.

Berena's Bistro, in the city hotel complex, serves typical Chinese fare, but the food is delicious and the price is right. Try the sweet-and-sour chicken and the shredded potato—they are unlike anything you've ever had. Berena's serves beer and wine, and has clean rest rooms—a rarity in Beijing. Another bonus is the black-market CD vendor who's always sitting in the corner. CDs are $1 each.

◆ Berena's Bistro, 6 Gongti East Road, 010 65922628.

The Lufthansa Center, a multilevel shopping mall, is like a regular department store, with quality goods at set prices. They have a really nice grocery store in the basement. If you are looking for a good wine, try Great Wall chardonnay or sauvignon blanc, which you will find there for about $8 a bottle. You can buy cashmere there, too.

◆ Lufthansa Center, 52 Liangmaqiao Lu, Chaoyang District, 010 64651188.

Whenever I fly into Beijing, I get a haircut outside of the Forbidden City by the Great Wall. You can't miss this guy—he's the only man with a barber chair in the middle of the street. He does a good job and he's fast, but the best part is the price. It costs just $1, which is a lot of money to some Chinese, but make sure you negotiate for that price.

BERLIN

Late one November night in 1989 the phone rang in my London hotel room. It was a flight attendant friend from British Airways. "Be at Gatwick tomorrow at 5 A.M.," she insisted. "The wall is going down."

I knew exactly what she meant. She and a group of pilots knew about one of the early flights into Berlin and had booked me a seat. When I got to the airport the next morning, she was already waiting for me with a shopping bag. Inside were a hammer and a chisel. "Thought you might need these," she laughed. And we did.

Four hours later, we were both standing at the wall, hammering away, as the big party in Berlin started. It was almost a rave that night at the Brandenburg Gate—not a single person was older than thirty-five.

Berlin is a city that has become youthful again. There's a rhythm here that just doesn't quit.

Today, I still have those pieces of the wall framed in my office. And I will always remember the big party that was, and that continues to define, Berlin. In fact, I think it's still going on!

The best way to see Germany's wildest and most notorious city is on foot. Berlin is no longer divided (except by the River Spree and dozens of canals). Start your tour at the Brandenburg Gate—the symbol of the city's reunification. Then head over to the Hotel Adlon, a charming, historic building that was rebuilt in 1997, and on toward Friedrichstrasse. Make a left turn at the Galeries Lafayette and continue until you end up at the Gendarmenmarkt, which still ranks as one of the more vibrant, beautiful squares in Europe. Along the way you'll find new-wave galleries and old-style museums, triumphant tributes to German classicism.

There are two events you should remember. First is the Love Parade in July each year, which comes as close to Woodstock as you can get, with a million young people taking over the streets. The second is the Christmas Markets, which open in early December and last until right before Christmas. There are some eighty markets with stalls selling just about everything. Do what the flight crews do and go the very first week of December. (Remember, you've been *encouraged*!)

Of course, you cannot go to Berlin without making the pilgrimage to the Paris Bar. Is the food great? Hardly. The decor? Depressing. The service? Good luck. "This is not a place you go to," one flight attendant from Lufthansa once told me, "this is a place you end up." And, invariably, that's what happens every time you go to Berlin.

There are other spots, ranging from Chez Maurice Bistro, another chaotic crowd scene (warning: no credit cards), to the 808 Bar and Lounge, where the crowd is friendlier (at least you can hear yourself when you order something). Want a quieter place? Adermann is the choice—climb a flight of stairs and you'll discover an elegant bistro.

And in the summer, go to the Strandbad Wannsee, the largest inland beach in Europe. Don't be surprised to find about twenty-five thousand sun worshippers there on a good day.

CITY TIPS

After the Kaiser-Wilhelm-Gedächtniskirche (Memorial Church) was damaged in World War II, a new church was built next to it, which makes it look even worse from the outside. But when you go inside, you realize that the walls consist of little windows made with colored glass that gleams all around you. You can still see the damage from the war on the roof, and it's a miracle that the church is still standing at all. Today the church is a meeting place for locals, and it's a good spot for people watching—you might see teenagers with skateboards, elderly couples, artists. From the airport, it takes fifteen minutes to get there.

◆ Kaiser-Wilhelm-Gedächtniskirche (Memorial Church), Breit-scheidplatz, 030 2185023.

Aviation buffs will find the Luftwaffe Museum in Gatow, a suburb of Berlin, to be very interesting. It houses an extensive collection of East German aviation artifacts, including uniforms and static displays of aircraft, as well as old Soviet aircraft from the Cold War. Admission is free, but donations are encouraged. Public transportation is available.

◆ Luftwaffe Museum, Berlin/Gatow, General Steinhoff-Kaserne, Flugplatz Gatow Kladower Damm, Gatow, 182–188, 030 3651 052. Open Thursday through Sunday.

For an interesting experience you will not soon forget, visit the Thermen in the Europa Center, a completely au naturel, coed public swimming pool and sauna. When you enter you are given a card with your time on it. Inside you will find three saunas and an indoor/outdoor pool. You can rent a towel, but I recommend bringing your own bathrobe for lounging around poolside. A three-hour stay costs $15 to $18.

◆ Europa Center, Nürnbergerstrasse 7, 030 257576-0.

CAIRO

My first flight to Cairo was on an aging EgyptAir 707. How old was this plane? Let's just say the seat belts were frayed and the buckles still had the Pan Am logo! "This is one of the great planes," the captain told me at one point during the flight, when he emerged from the cockpit. "It is strong. It is a battleship."

On the outside, perhaps. When we made a somewhat rough landing, the seat in front of me literally disintegrated, dropping the passenger on the floor in a cloud of particles and dust.

Welcome to Cairo. Welcome to dust. And welcome to one of the great travel experiences of your life. Once on the ground, the captain caught up with me and in true Cairene style invited me over to his house for dinner and to meet his family. Of course, I accepted.

"To understand Cairo is to understand that we are a city out of control," he told me. "Too many people, too many cars. Too crazy. We even have people living in cemeteries!" (Indeed, he later took me to visit the City of the Dead, where hundreds of people live inside abandoned crypts. We had tea.)

"To truly enjoy this city you have to beat the sun at both ends of the day," he advised. Meaning? "Start two hours before the sun comes up and get back. Then start again two hours after the sun goes down."

He was right. Cairo traffic is legendary, and as long as you embrace the notion that you're not getting anywhere fast, you can enjoy the ride. My first taxi experience was funny. My driver, like all the other drivers, had developed a habit of honking the horn even when we were trapped within a mass of vehicles going absolutely nowhere. At one point, when we approached a red light and stopped, the driver continued to honk, even though we were right at the light and no one was in front of us. "Excuse me," I asked, "why are you honking your horn? There's no one here."

He turned to me and smiled. "I am not honking at the other drivers," he laughed. "I am honking at the light. The light will hear me, and the light will change." Just then, the light switched to green. He smiled again. "You see?"

The captain was also right about beating the sun. Want to see the pyramids? Hire a driver at four in the morning to take you out to Giza. You'll be there for the sunrise. And you'll miss all the postcard hawkers.

Or, at two in the morning, hit the bakeries, or the small shops selling freshly made rice pudding.

The Egyptian Museum is best seen first thing in the morning, as is the famed bazaar.

One more thing: EgyptAir finally retired the last of its 707s about nine years ago—they had been using the planes to shuttle tourists from Cairo down to Luxor. The airline now proudly flies a fleet of 767s and 777s. One thing hasn't changed: the pilot or a flight attendant may still invite you to his or her house for dinner. And if the invitation is extended, by all means, accept.

AIRPORT TIPS

When flying into Cairo, request a seat toward the front of the aircraft, so that you can disembark quickly and be one of the first in the many lines for immigration, for cabs, and so forth, because there are lines for everything.

Don't get a cab from in front of the hotel. Rather, walk around to the back—it will save you half the time. Also, never take the first one; compare fares and negotiate the best deal. As with anything you barter for in Egypt, always negotiate to half, and then go back up to an amount that is satisfactory to both parties.

A cab from the airport to the Nile Hilton should take approximately forty minutes and should not cost you more than $15. Don't let anyone tell you otherwise! A cab from the Hilton to the bazaar is £E10, not £E20! As you leave the hotels and catch cabs farther out, you'll see that the fares to the bazaar for the locals are cheaper by about £E2 ($29).

CITY TIPS

For safety purposes, make a deal with a taxi driver to wait for you or pick you up again when you are out and about in Cairo. Four of us can take a taxi to the bazaar and back for $4 or $5, about a twenty-minute ride.

If you need a tour guide, Samy is your man. He operates out of the American Express office at the Nile Hilton Hotel. He speaks English very well, and his prices are reasonable compared with others. You can always try to barter anywhere in Egypt— there is nothing wrong with that—but with Samy you don't need to.
◆ Samy, Nile Hilton Hotel, 02 385 8368 or 02 578 5001.

The first time I went to Cairo the whole crew went to see the pyramids, and it was quite a mob scene—people hawking postcards, folks on camels offering rides, and, of course, the pyramids themselves and the Sphinx. We thought it was a great experience until we returned to the hotel and bumped into another crew member, who said, "Let me show you the real way to see the pyramids. Be in the lobby of the hotel tomorrow morning at 3:30, and bring your cameras." The next morning, we met her there. She said a few words to the driver, who spoke English, and the next thing we knew, someone appeared with horses for the six of us. We were led out, in the darkness, into the desert. And then we witnessed the most magical scene. Shortly after six in the morning, as we sat on the horses, alone and freezing, the sun began to rise over the pyramids. As we finally left the area around 8 A.M. to return to the city, we saw all the tourist buses heading for the circus that we had avoided. The hotels will tell you the pyramids are closed at that hour and that you can't make such a trip. But you can—just tip the cab drivers, who know exactly what to do. One important note. If you try to arrange for horses yourself, you will get whatever they want to give you—many of the horses look mistreated and malnourished. Do research to find more reputable stables that will have healthier horses.

If you make the trip to the pyramids and want to stay for lunch, head to the legendary Mena House. Instead of going to the regular restaurant, however, visit their Indian restaurant, the Mughal Room.

◆ Mena House, Pyramids Road, Giza, 02 383 3222, www. oberoihotels.com/mena/menamain.htm.

You never have to take an organized tour in Cairo—just hire a car and driver, and you'll have the best time. If two or three people share the cost, it's very affordable. Most Egyptian drivers treat traffic lights as nothing more than ornamental fixtures, so just sit back and hold on tight! Direct your driver to Paprika for great barbeque chicken to go. Pick up some beer, and have a wonderful picnic on board the feluccas on the river. But try to get there right at midday; if you go later in the afternoon, the flies and the mosquitoes can be serious pests. A group of four

can buy lunch and charter the sailboats for under $20 a person. It's a great way to spend an afternoon.
◆ Paprika, 1129 Corniche El Nile, 02 578 9447.

Jacques Dessaux is an excellent hairdresser in the Swissotel who gives good value for the money. Go to him, and you won't have to wear a hat for the rest of your holiday!
◆ Abdel Hamid, Badawi Street, Heliopolis, 02 297 4000.

After one of the crew took me to the Old Cairo Bazaar, I needed to buy more suitcases. We found three or four adjacent shops, specializing in gold, jewelry, and Oriental gifts. You can watch owner Adel Iskandar Abd Allah and his son Karem making the jewelry. You can find wooden jewelry boxes overlaid with mother-of-pearl for $10 to $40 each, depending on the detail and the size.
◆ Old Cairo Bazaar, opposite St. Sargehos Church, 02 363 8228 or 02 363 9592, www.OldCairoBazaar.com.eg.

Hesham El Tahlawey mass-produces silver and gold for jewelry in his shop Al Risaie Gohar (which means "jewelry"). He does specialized pieces, such as bracelets and cartouches. His shop is located not far from the Old Cairo Bazaar.
◆ Al Risaie Gohar, 02 365 3720.

The Old Cairo Papyrus Museum sells unframed artwork done on papyrus. It's a little touristy, but the workmanship is excellent, and if you go first thing in the morning, you can get there before the tour buses arrive. You can buy an $8\frac{1}{2}$-by-11 picture of the Sphinx for about $15. Larger ones cost $50 to $60. Ask for Ayman Kamel.
◆ Old Cairo Papyrus Museum, 4 Salah Salem Road, 02 363 0357.

Cairo is a great place to buy perfume bottles, which come in beautiful colors, some with gold on them. Many people use them simply as decorative pieces; others fill them with perfume. This store is close to the Old Cairo Bazaar.

◆ Mohammed Hassan Company, Way 12, Khan el Khalili, 02 592 7510.

The Thousand and One Nights shop inside the Khan El Khalili Bazaar makes a variety of essential oils from various flowers. You can dilute the oils with alcohol to make perfume. I spent $75 for twelve six-ounce bottles. Ask for Khalid.

◆ Thousand and One Nights, Gamal El Helw at 59 Gohar El-Kaed Street, Cairo, 02 590 5111.

Although he speaks English, you don't really negotiate with Said, but he usually gives you a good deal on gold cartouches at Gouzlan. He will ship merchandise anywhere in the United States, and he is reliable. If you have trouble finding his store, anyone in the bazaar can direct you. Right across from Said in the bazaar is a safe and intriguing restaurant, with beautiful dark oak paneling, where you can smoke your hubbly-bubbly (tobacco in water pipes) and look at all the interesting ethnic things.

◆ Gouzlan, 6 Khan el Khalili, 02 593 1064 or 02 590 4721, www.gouzlan.com.

Pharmacist Sirag al Halsawi has been widely known in the industry for over forty years. Dr. al Halsawi is intelligent and trustworthy, speaks perfect English, and will diagnose you and arrange to conveniently deliver the remedy right to your hotel. If you wish to continue consulting him, he can keep in touch with you by e-mail. He has even helped us get seats to the whirling dervishes performance in a Catholic church near his office.

◆ Dr. Sirag al Halsawi, 02 590 2168, fax 02 240 2720, sirag@intouch.com.

If you're looking for belly dancing equipment or trinkets, go to Yasser's little shop in the Khan El Khalili Bazaar, the shopping Mecca in the center of the city. The shop is small, but it has everything you'll ever need—beaded scarves, clips for the fingers, outfits, you name it. The rule of thumb in Egypt is to barter everywhere, but you can rely on Yasser to be trustworthy and honest—he won't trick you and he doesn't play games.

◆ Yasser, Khan El Khalili Bazaar, 02 593 2481.

The Nile Hilton Hotel may not be the most state-of-the-art, up-to-date hotel, but you'll be very comfortable there. Located across the street from the Egyptian Museum, the hotel has a huge, gorgeous pool, as well as good clay tennis courts and a tennis pro on staff. Try to get a room above the ninth floor in the main section overlooking the Nile, where the VIPs tend to stay. Egyptians are generally heavy smokers, so request a nonsmoking room if you are sensitive to that. The service here is wonderful; leave a tip for the housekeepers on your pillow each day, and they will treat you well. If you smile first, you're likely to receive an ear-to-ear grin in return.

◆ Nile Hilton Hotel, Tahrir Square, 02 578 0444.

Rotisserie/Belvedere is a terrific restaurant on the rooftop of the Hilton. Request a table with a view of the Nile, and go for a late dinner when they have a band and dancing—it's fabulous. A typical dinner will cost around $30, all inclusive (I recommend the lamb). Reservations are necessary. In the hotel lobby there is a lively disco called Jackie's Joint. It's on the ground floor—you can't miss it.

◆ Nile Hilton Hotel, Tahrir Square, 02 578 0444.
Jackie's Joint, 02 578 0666.

If a flight schedule allows us a three-day layover in Cairo, we'll make the ten-hour train journey to Luxor and go to Baraka Carpets, under the Alsay Bazaar, where they make hand-sewn quilts. They also sell kilim rugs, Bedouin silk, patchwork, and appliqués. The quilts are somewhat pricey, but they cost a whole lot less than in Cairo—and outrageously less than in the United States. The manager is Mourad Mahsoz.

◆ Baraka Carpets, across from the Meridian Hotel and close to the Isis Hotel, 02 12 227 2363.

At Luxor, avoid the modern American Hiltons and such places, and stay in the old section at the Winter Palace Hotel. The old section is absolutely beautiful. You have a choice of garden or Nile view. There are tennis courts, gardens, and a heated swimming pool.

◆ Winter Palace Hotel, Corniche El Nile, Luxor, 095 380 422.

CAPE TOWN AND JOHANNESBURG

The flight to Johannesburg can be one of the longest in the world. And in bad weather, planes have to land at Cape Verde, an archipelago of ten islands and five islets 385 miles west of Senegal. If you befriend some pilots, they'll let you in on a layover secret: fishing.

The real destination, of course, is Cape Town. It's one of my favorite foreign cities—great climate, great wine, and a great seacoast. Not to mention great history.

I've got Cape Town down to a two-minute drill. Actually, it's a two-day drill that includes the scotch bar at the Cape Grace Hotel and a walk along the Victoria and Albert Waterfront. There's afternoon tea at the Mount Nelson, trips to the Noon Gun Café, and then it's over to Robben Island, where Nelson Mandela was imprisoned. Then there are the incredible South African wineries, all within a three-hour drive of the city.

A lot of tourists take the cruise from Cape Town to Table Bay, but my flight attendant friends head for Hout Bay, a much better boat trip, with great beaches and surfing. You get both gentle shorebreaks and monster curls, so beginners and experts have a choice. (Hint: first-timers, head for the beaches of False Bay; those with a death wish go directly toward the Cape of Good Hope.)

I take friends on helicopter rides down to the Cape of Good Hope. Cape Town is the South African equivalent of San Francisco, Sydney, and Key West all rolled into one. And with the South African rand hovering at about twelve to each U.S. dollar, it is the best luxury discount destination in the world. A high-end hotel room costs about $160 U.S.

Johannesburg is a different story. To me, it's essentially a place to change planes, with a terrible crime rate. But if you have to go, head to Sandton, a manageable suburb with decent hotels and better shopping. Or drive about forty-five minutes to Pretoria, for Rovos Rail, an adventure not to be missed. Rohan Vos has devoted the last twenty years to restoring the old trains of South African Rail, turning them into a luxury two-day trip to Victoria Falls. From there, it's a short drive into Botswana and the Chobe River, and some of the best safari/game watching in the world.

AIRPORT TIP

Johannesburg

The airport has just been renovated. If you're a frequent flyer or a business or first-class traveler, it's nice because it's attached to a hotel that has an arrivals lounge and a gym. You can get your clothes pressed, shower, get breakfast. Like many of the airports in Africa, it's very slow because they don't have as many flights. Cape Town and Johannesburg tend to be the end of the line, so there's a relative ease of transfer.

◆ Fitness Center, Airport Sun Inter-Continental Johannesburg, 011 961 5400.

CITY TIPS

Johannesburg

The Linger Longer is what I call an Internet restaurant: a great place to download . . . and unload.

◆ Linger Longer, 58 Wierda Road West, Wierda Valley, Sandton, 011 884-0465.

We avoid downtown Johannesburg because it's just not safe. Rosebank is quite nice, but it's risky to wander around on your own anywhere in Jo'burg at night, even on the outskirts. Sandton, however, is a relatively safe area.

Gatrile, Son & Co. 5, in Sandton, is one of the best restaurants in the Johannesburg area. Even Bill Clinton has eaten here. They serve exceptional and unusual dishes that vary with the season, such as ostrich tartare and venison fillet. For dessert, their crème brûlée is excellent. Depending on the wine you order, you won't pay more than $30 or $40. (I recommend the '96 Shiraz.) The restaurant is divided in two, with wine cellars in one section and a big fireplace in the main restaurant area. (Try to sit by the fire.) The service is excellent, too. Make sure you call for dinner reservations.

◆ Gatrile, Son & Co. 5, 5 Esterhuyzen Road, off Grayston Drive, Sandton, 011 883-7398/9.

In South Africa, everything is much cheaper than in the United States or the United Kingdom—for example, a facial can start at R220, compared to £40 in England. So I always get a pedicure and facial at the Sabine Salon in the Protea Midrand Hotel, a quaint place built around a courtyard. It's convenient, it's cheap, and they know what British people like.

◆ Sabine Salon, 14th Street Noordwyk, Halfway House 1687, 011 318 1868.

CITY TIPS

Cape Town

Typically, on a Sunday we'll head out to La Petite Ferme, at the top of a valley with a superb view of the entire valley below. It's a wonderful place for a day-long outing.

Our favorite South African wine is Vergelegen, from the fabulous vineyard on Rondekop Hill. I recommend the wine, the tour that follows, and the food, which consists mostly of salads and couscous with amazing desserts.

◆ La Petite Ferme, Franschhoek Pass Road, 021 876 3016.

I have yet to have a disappointing meal at Bukhara, an Indian restaurant on the second floor, off Church Street, a promenade where they have antique stalls and antique shops during the day. The place has a wonderful atmosphere, with candlelight and a well-stocked bar. I recommend the fish *tikka,* which melts in your mouth; the *dal makhani,* which is spicier and more flavorful than anywhere else; and *saag paneer.* The butter chicken is so good that even I dip into the sauce. Their wine selection is superb, and at South African prices, it can't be beat. Try the Meerlust Rubicon. Be sure to make a reservation well in advance—at least two days ahead. The place is packed by 8:30 P.M.

◆ Bukhara, City Centre, 33 Church Street, 021 424 0000.

African Image, at the famous Greenmarket Square, is the place you should go if you want to make sure you are buying authentic wares. Ask for Tracy, one of the partners, who will spend time explaining anything you want to know. She has great taste and a great eye for helping you purchase gifts. The last time I saw her, she had just finished advising David Bowie. With our exchange rate, this place is a bargain.

◆ African Image, corner of Church and Burg Streets, www.greenmarket.co.za.

Without a car in this city, you're lost. But dealing with driving on the left side of the road and the high crime rate can be a burden. Cape Town is not as bad as Johannesburg, but cars do get broken into and hijacked. With the great exchange rate, a chauffeur service is an affordable alternative. A chauffeur can take you wherever you need to go and may even advise you about fun things to do.

Hospitable, classy, accommodating, and just plain nice, chauffeur Mark Bayly worked for years as a manager at Ellerman House, an exquisite Relais Chateau hotel in Bantry Bay, Cape Town. Because he has spent his whole life in Cape Town, he knows most of the hideaway spots and avoids the commercial and touristy places. For example, Mark knows many of the winemakers at the vineyards and can arrange private visits. All of Mark's tours are tailor-made—you guide yourself, instead of going with a busload of tourists. Most transport is provided in VW vans, but more luxurious transport can be arranged at a higher rate, of course. A day tour around Cape Town will cost between R1,200 and R1,500.

◆ Mark Bayly, 083 270-2446, markbayly@yahoo.com.

The menu selection at ColCacchio, a great pizza place at the bottom of Bree Street near the Waterfront, is huge, with a wide range of healthy options and exotic toppings. All the crusts are thin and baked right there in an open pizza oven. Their salads are phenomenal, too. They don't take reservations, so you may have to wait for a table. If they offer you a table outside, be careful—it can get windy, and pizzas have been known to become airborne!

◆ ColCacchio, Shop #2, 42 Hans Strijdom Avenue, 021 419 4848.

Nando's Tasca serves wonderful Portuguese-style chicken takeout. It's fast food that's both healthy and delicious.

◆ Nando's Tasca, 154 Victoria and Albert Waterfront, 021 419 3009.

If you are interested in fishing, Kalk Bay is a fascinating place. The big wooden fishing boats are directed by men who stand on the nearby cliffs and shine lights and mirrors to signal where the schools of fish can be found. The boats then drop their nets. Excitement runs high over the catch, which ranges from snoek (a very popular Cape Town fish) to small species of shark. When the boats approach the beach, people come running from all around to look and buy fresh fish. Whether or not you like fishing, this is a good excuse to be up at the crack of dawn to watch the sunrise at Cape Point. Check in advance to find out the exact time, and bring a sweater. You could start your day of sightseeing there, then proceed to Simonstown to see the navy fleet, and on to Boulder's Beach to see the jackass penguins, so named because they sound like donkeys.

◆ Boulder's Beach and Simonstown, from Cape Town, take M Street straight to Tokai Street; when you reach the T-junction at Tokai, turn left; go straight until you reach Tokai again, and turn right; www.sunsetbeach.co.za/penguins.htm.

Want to get really crazy? Out near the airport, a guy named Andy Cluver runs a helicopter business called CivAir. He operates all over the Cape area, and it's the best way to go down to the Cape. Ask Andy if the Strykemaster is available—this is his very own fighter jet, flown in the Botswana Air Force and returned to the Brits. With the exchange rate so favorable, a ninety-minute ride of a lifetime is about $400. You strap on your pressure suit, and off you go over Table Mountain, down to the Cape, and back, in eight minutes. You fly over islands full of penguins, get an aerial tour of wineries, and, if you're in the mood, they might even let you buzz the pool at the Mount Nelson Hotel. You definitely can't do that in the United States!

◆ CivAir, Victoria and Albert Waterfront, 021 419 5182.

FLORENCE

Long before jet travel became a way of life for so many of us, Florence was one of the great hub cities. On one level, it's a giant museum. It has more museums and exhibits per person than any other city in Italy. "Ask Florentines what they are," a flight attendant told me, "and they will tell you what they once were."

Perhaps the best piece of flight crew advice about Florence is logistical. "Think of a visit to Florence as going through O'Hare to get to where you really want to go: all of Tuscany."

Indeed, Florence is the hub of Tuscany. First-time visitors go to Florence and then explore places like San Gimignano, Pisa, Siena, or Fiesole. But repeat visitors reverse the process, preferring to enjoy the treasures of Florence by staying in other parts of Tuscany and driving in.

The first time I visited Florence, I went with my family, and like most tourists, we went to the Duomo to view the incredible bronze doors of the Baptistery of San Giovanni. The doors facing south are known as the Doors of Paradise, and I will always have a special feeling for these doors, and for the memory of the welcome we received there. On our first visit there, while we were admiring the doors and their depiction of the life of Jesus and scenes from the Old Testament, about seven pigeons got together and flew over my younger sister, pooling, uh, their resources and scoring a direct hit. It was, and still is, the largest single amount of bird droppings I have ever seen on any one person's head. With my sister howling in front of the Doors of

Paradise and my mother yelling, "It's not funny," at both my father and me, we hurriedly retreated to our hotel.

Not surprisingly, my sister has never returned to Florence, but I have been back many times.

I go to the Uffizi Gallery, to view some of the earliest identified work of Leonardo da Vinci. Most people who go think they'll be seeing a lot of Michelangelo's work. Actually, there's only one in the Uffizi—and it's his earliest painting. If you want to see Michelangelo's work, just look around you in Florence. It's everywhere.

But the real treasures of the region—at least for me—are outside Florence. Rent a car, share the costs, and see Tuscany on day trips. Just five miles northeast of the city, you can find Fiesole and the winding side road (Via Vecchia Fiesolana). But Fiesole is just the appetizer. My favorite is San Gimignano and its unexpected skyline. At certain times of the year, you can balloon over Siena, even during the horse races in July and August. Manageable day trips are perfect for flight attendants on a layover. Perfect for you if you only have a few days.

CITY TIPS

To get to Florence from the Milan Airport you have to get to the Stazione Centrale (Central Station) in the center of Milan and take a train called the Malpensa Express. When you walk out of the Milan Airport, you'll see a sign that says "Treni" (Trains). Follow that sign, walk straight through a little overpass, and end up in the train station. Look for the signs that say Malpensa Express, indicated by a little red, green, and white streak, with the international train sign.

When you get to the train station, buy a ticket from an agent or use an express machine. A one-way ticket from Milan Malpensa Airport to the downtown Cadorna Station costs 7.75

euros. The train leaves about every twenty minutes, and the trip takes about forty minutes. At the airport, unlike in the rest of Italy, business hours are continuous from 6:50 A.M. till 8:20 P.M. With the exception of emergencies, you will arrive at the airport between those times. Taking a taxi from the airport to the Central Station will cost about 50 euros. Taking a taxi from the Cadorna Station to the Central Station will cost around 7 euros, plus 2 euros for a bag (and if the driver is good, leave him 2 euros as a tip). From the Central Station, you can catch the Eurostar train to Florence. The Eurostar is a two-class train that makes only two stops between Milan and Florence. Trains leave almost every hour from Milan between 6 A.M. and 8 P.M. Two first-class tickets will cost about $70 one-way to Milan. I suggest you pay extra for first class because it has wider seats, it's quieter, and you can ask for a nonsmoking section.

◆ Eurostar, 02 27763, or for operator, 02 20222, www.eurostar.com.

Florence is a walking city, but if you need to rent a car, book it ahead of time with EuroCar. I recommend Kemwell. The further ahead you book the car, the better the deal you get. All the car rental places are located on Borgo Ogni Santi. Cars are never ready on time, so while you're waiting, you can visit the bakeries or fornaios in the area. I recommend renting a midsize four-door sedan, because anything bigger becomes impossible to park or drive through the busy streets. Keep in mind that only manual transmission is usually available. Getting out of Florence is no problem, but driving into Florence is a huge problem since all the streets are one-way—you have to allow a lot of time. Touring Club Italiano, a service similar to AAA, can provide you with the best map of Tuscany I have ever bought: La Grande Carta Stradale d'Italia, in English, German, French, and Spanish.

◆ Kemwell reservations and customer service (800) 576 1590, www.kemwell.com, www.touringclub.it/english/default.shtml.

Wash-n-Dry (*lavanderia*) is a basic Laundromat you'll find all over Florence. It costs about a dollar to wash clothes yourself, and not much more to have them do it. Five locations.

◆ Wash-n-Dry, Via dei Servi 105/R; Via della Scala 52/54R; Via dei Serragli 87R; Viale Morgagni 21R; and Via Nazionale 129R; (800) 23 11 72.

Italy is known for fine leather shoes, and one of the best shoe stores I've found there is Gilardini. It sells all different kinds of leather shoes and Italian loafers for very reasonable prices. The owner's name is Giuseppe, and everyone there speaks English.

◆ Gilardini, Via Cerretani #8R and Via Cerretani #20R, 055 214 2977.

If you bring your dry cleaning to Elensec Cal-Ni by 8 A.M., they will have it back for you the next afternoon.

◆ Elensec Cal-Ni, Via del Neri 46/R, 055 28 37 47.

You don't need to skip your workout while in Florence. Vivarium is a good gym with a hardwood floor, Nautilus equipment, three treadmills and three bikes, aerobic classes, and more. A day pass will cost you 7 to 10 euros. The staff speak English and are very nice.

◆ Vivarium, Via Accursio #4R, 055 232 0059. Hours 9 A.M. to 9 P.M. daily; 9 A.M. to 1 P.M. Saturdays; closed Sundays.

What could be more unlikely than encountering an Elvis impersonator while dining out in Florence? You had to see it to believe it: "Jailhouse Rock" sung by a gentleman with a full beard, wearing a yarmulke and a big belt that said "Elvis" (in case we had any doubts), gyrating his hips in true King-like fashion. The audience, convulsed with laughter to the point of tears, threw money and distributed tips generously. Such was the entertainment the night we went to Paszkowski, a wonderful restaurant in the Piazza della Republica, near the Duomo. A *delizioso* dinner with wine for three people cost about $80. I recommend that you try a bottle of limoncello, a lemon liqueur served chilled.

◆ Paszkowski, Piazza della Republica 6/R, 055 210236.

FRANKFURT

I'll be honest. Frankfurt is not my favorite city, but the airport really works. And so does the train link to and from the airport. You have to give the Germans credit for efficiency.

Most folks will tell you that Frankfurt is dull and boring. But flight crews know better. Frankfurt is home to the richest collection of museums in Germany. That's a big surprise. (Be sure to check out the Museum of Modern Art, and then, along the Main River, there's the Stadel Museum, which has everything from Rembrandt and Botticelli to Cézanne and Renoir.)

But almost no one who lives in Frankfurt hangs out there. My Lufthansa friends go to Sachsenhausen, which is on the south bank of the Main. That's where you eat, drink, and otherwise be merry—thanks to a large supply of Ebelwei, or apple wine houses.

Since eighty percent of the old city was wiped out by Allied bombing in 1944, Frankfurt is more or less a new city. Lots of people fly to Frankfurt because it's a major port of entry to Germany. But from there, they connect to the trains. Want to go anywhere, from nearby Marburg to Hamburg or Cologne, to Nuremberg—or south to Heidelberg and Stuttgart? Hop the trains. And your bags even connect, in most cases, right to the trains. The main train station in Frankfurt handles more than fifteen hundred trains a day!

AIRPORT TIPS

The airport is very convenient for people with luggage because the carts are free, and they fit on escalators without tipping over.

You'll find wonderful restaurants and a grocery store in the airport. There's a shop for just about everything you need. You could live there for a week, and you wouldn't have to leave to get anything. They also have free recliner seats, so if you want to sleep, it's like you're on a lawn chair. For an international airport, that's an incredible luxury.

CITY TIPS

The real beauty of Frankfurt is in what surrounds the city— places like Aschaffenburg, Mainz, and Wiesbaden. All are accessible and are easy drives. Thus, Frankfurt can easily serve as a day trip hub for all of these locations.

Aschaffenburg

I lived for a part of my childhood in Aschaffenburg, a small town about forty kilometers southwest of Frankfurt. You can drive there by getting on the autobahn right outside the airport or you can take the train from the Central Train Station in downtown Frankfurt. Aschaffenburg has one of Germany's largest castles, Schloss Johannisburg, which was the summer residence of the Archbishop of Mainz, the second most powerful Catholic in Europe. The castle was destroyed during World War II but has since been rebuilt and is open to the public. My brother and I used to play in the ruins when we were children back in the late 1950s. Once we found four heads that had come off statues. We took them home and gave them to our mother.

During the Gulf War, I was flying 747s and we were diverted to Rhein-Main Air Force Base outside of Frankfurt. I decided to look up an old childhood friend of mine. We got together and toured the castle, which had been restored by this time. In the guidebook, it mentioned that the heads from the statues, which depicted four of the most important saints and had come from the archbishop's private chapel, had been destroyed during the war. I told my friend that I thought I had the heads. On my next trip to Frankfurt, I delivered them to the castle. They were ecstatic to have them returned. They gave us a plaque and copies of the heads made out of alabaster. Now the guidebook states that an American returned the heads to the castle.

The castle is full of fantastic art, including works by Rembrandt. Inside there's also a small wine-tasting room—the Schloss Weinstube. It is open in the evenings and features a lovely view of the Main River. You can order snacks, sample wines, and watch the sun set. (See tip below.)

The wines of the Bavarian region are generally of the sweeter variety. I prefer to drink beer in Germany and am particularly fond of the weizen (wheat) beers and weiss (white) beers. They are unfiltered and contain a lot of sediment, but they are smooth and sweet. Most every town has its own brewery, and since some of the beers are not available outside that immediate area, you just have to try them all.

◆ Schloss Johannisburg, Dalbert Hotel, Pfaffengasse 12-14, 06021 3560.

After you have spent your day touring the castle, try the Dalbert Weinstube, across the street from the newspaper office, along the river. It has traditional German food, excellent service, and very reasonable prices. I recommend Ribchen mit Kraut—a boneless pork cutlet, very tender, with a peppercorn sauce on top and a side of sauerkraut. It is a traditional Bavarian dish, and I have it every time I go there. There is also a charming thirty-five-room hotel.

◆ Dalbert Weinstube, Pfaffengasse 12-14, 06021 26782.

Right next to the Schloss Johannisburg in Aschaffenburg is a home called the Pomejanum built by Ludwig II, who was the mad king of Bavaria. During his reign, the style was to build homes resembling those in Pompeii. The home he built was an exact replica of a home in Pompeii and is quite spectacular to see. Your admission ticket to the castle also allows you to tour the Pomejanum. In the courtyard, there is often music to entertain you as you wander the grounds.

Mainz

Don't miss St. Martins Dom, one of the oldest cathedrals in Europe that was not completely destroyed during World War II. There's a big brick square outside the church that has been there for hundreds of years as well. Legend has it that two American pilots were captured in Mainz after their plane went down in World War II. Instead of being taken as POWs, they were taken to the town square and shot. In retaliation, American pilots on bombing missions would purposely fly over Mainz in order to hit there, saying, "Save one for Mainz." Thus, Mainz got bombed mercilessly throughout World War II, and a large part of the town was destroyed.

◆ St. Martins Dom, Mark 10 55116, 06131 253412.

Specht, a restaurant in Mainz, has been operating since 1557. They won't even serve water there because the plumbing is too old. Although it's somewhat expensive (about $40 for an average meal), they serve some of the best German food you'll find. I once asked them to prepare me a beef stroganoff, which was not on the menu. They made it with the finest beef and served it with spaetzle, mushrooms, and a delectable gravy. You won't regret eating here.

◆ Specht, Rotekopfgasse 2, 06131 231770.

You don't very often see take-out places in Europe, but I recommend Restaurant Pepe. They have a delicious tortellini alla panna, as well as perennially popular tiramisu.

◆ Restaurant Pepe, Augustinerstrasse 21, 06131 229986.

Wiesbaden

Wiesbaden, a town about thirty to forty minutes outside of Frankfurt on the #9 S-Bahn train, has one of the best and most exclusive restaurants in Germany—Die Ente, which means "the duck," located inside the exclusive Hotel Nassauer Hof. You will definitely need reservations, but the food is exquisite, as is the wine list. There's a magical piano bar, and in the summer you can eat outside.

◆ Die Ente, Hotel Nassauer Hof, Kaiser Friedrich Platz, 0611 133666.

There are three categories of hotels in Wiesbaden. First is the Ibis Hotel, which is a very inexpensive chain that always offers special rates. It's right in the center of town and is close to everything. Then there's the Hotel Nassauer Hof, which is beautiful and very exclusive. Finally, there's the Schwarzer Bock, a very nice, medium-priced hotel. It is also near all the restaurants in the city. Everything is within walking distance. They also have good service and nice rooms. It belongs to the Radisson SAS Group, so you should be able to find it on the website.

◆ Ibis Hotel, Kranzplatz 10, 0611 36140.

Radisson SAS Schwarzer Bock Hotel, Kranzplatz 12, 0611 155666, www.gabler.de/gmi/hotel/radbock.htm.

Hotel Nassauer Hof, Kaiser Friedrich Platz 34, 0611 1330.

There's an old park in Wiesbaden with a beer garden inside called Käfer, which means "beetle" in German. The historic casino was featured in Dostoevski's *The Gambler*. The Russians used to go there to spend their summers. You are permitted to walk around it without any kind of tour.

◆ Casino Wiesbaden, Kurhausplatz 1, 0611 536100.

Paulaner in Wiesbaden serves typical Bavarian food—very good quality and not too expensive. A good dinner with drinks will cost $15 to $20. I recommend duck with red cabbage and potato dumplings. The service is efficient and very friendly. There's also a beer garden, but without trees because it's in the city. Definitely make a reservation because it's very popular.

◆ Paulaner, Wilhelmstrasse 58, 0611 421527.

Modern-looking Sushi Circle (sometimes referred to as "Fai Sushi"), in Wiesbaden, is a great place to eat in or get take-out. The food is always fresh and good. An individual plate costs about $3. No reservations necessary.

◆ Sushi Circle, Ellenbogengasse 13, 0611 9009827.

HONG KONG

My first trip to Hong Kong was not a pleasant one. I flew in on a Pan Am 747-SP, one that was then billed as the longest non-stop flight in the world—a trip of nearly fourteen hours from San Francisco. The plane had a very bad internal air-conditioning system for such a flight, and passengers and flight attendants alike had trouble breathing.

"You think this is tough?" said one of the Pan Am crew. "Wait for the landing."

The landing? How tough would that be? Was there bad weather in the area? "Oh no," she laughed. "You'll see," she said, "and you'll also smell."

And then, about thirteen hours and forty minutes after leaving the United States, we started our approach to the legendary Kai Tak Airport. I had the pleasure, so to speak, of sitting on the right side of the wide-body, in a window seat, when we made our approach. And I will always remember what I saw in the last two minutes of the flight. We came in low over the water, headed for a hill, and at the last minute, made a sharp twenty-five-degree bank—and dropped down very low, over and through high-rise apartment buildings. Looking out of my window, I found myself suddenly starting to inhale. I could see people in their dining rooms having dinner. Worse, I could make out the labels on the wine they were drinking! We were *that* close.

As we taxied to our gate, the Pan Am flight attendant was laughing as she announced, "For those of you on the right side of the plane, welcome to Hong Kong!"

Two things hit us when we landed. First, it was the smell. In Chinese, Hong Kong means "fragrant harbor." And that is not understating the case.

And the second development? We all came down with the flu.

Eventually I recovered, and for many years I told my friends to always sit on the right side and prepare to inhale during the approach when they flew to Hong Kong.

I have never known a flight attendant who didn't like Hong Kong. In fact, a number of them met their husbands on flights to Asia and now live there as part of a large expat community.

Hong Kong has energy—and a skyline—that can be duplicated only by Manhattan. First-time visitors—especially to the Kowloon side—often find themselves standing at their hotel windows, unable to move.

I took the crew's advice and hit the night market of Temple Street. The next day, some of them took me for afternoon tea at the old Repulse Bay Hotel. And then to the horse races.

A pilot once told me that Hong Kong "is a borrowed place living on borrowed time," a reference to British colonialism. Despite the 1997 handover of Hong Kong from the British back to the Chinese, much of colonial Hong Kong remains, partly because the Chinese are more capitalist than we are!

Hong Kong means great antiquing, incredible restaurants, and a transportation system that works very well. Get yourself invited to the China Club, not just for the food, but for the artwork. Seafood? Try Yu at the Intercontinental (formerly the Regent). And traditional afternoon *yum cha* (tea) at the venerable Peninsula.

Yes, the old airport at Kai Tak closed after seventy-three years, and the wildest final approach in the world went with it. But the stunning new airport at Chek Lap Kok off Lantau Island works, and works very well. And speaking of islands, most visitors don't realize that Hong Kong consists of about 235 separate islands.

Do what many flight crews do: pool your resources, charter a boat, and head out to one of those islands—Lantau, Lamma, or one of many others—for an evening meal.

What's particularly great about Hong Kong is that it seems the place was tailor-made for flight crew layovers—it moves at such speed that you can pack a lot into just a day or two. And then, as in the traditional bad joke about Chinese restaurants, you're hungry for more an hour later. That, to a certain extent, explains why we keep going back.

AIRPORT TIPS

After you pass Immigration on the seventh floor, you can use the Internet for free, without having to buy anything. There are ten computers, and you can check your e-mail with no strings attached.

◆ Intellect Sitting Area, After Immigration, Seventh Floor.

Pilots appreciated the old airport because it was a challenge, but the new one is safer and more secure. The bus ride from the airport over the bridges into the city is slower than the train (about a half hour), but it's cheaper and it's a great ride.

◆ Citybus Ltd., City Flyer, 2873 0818.

CITY TIPS

Every place expects you to barter, so never pay full price. The more you buy, the better the deal you will get, so if there are several of you shopping together and you all want the same things, buy in a group. The more you deal with a particular salesperson, the better the deal as well. One word of caution, however: do not buy electronics from any of the small vendors.

If something goes wrong, you have no recourse and the equipment is not always made to operate in the United States. Most places are open seven days a week, but not all, so it's a good idea to check.

For quality pearls, diamonds, and gold, go to the Pearl Shop and ask for Joyce. Flight attendants have been going there since the Pan American days. They carry Tahitian, South Seas, Japanese, and Chinese pearls. The South Seas pearls are the most expensive and usually the largest. The Tahitian pearls are darker in color and the most prized. Tell them the size of the pearls you want and how long you want the string to be, and they will string it for you on the spot. This business has been around for a long time, and they are very reputable.

◆ Pearl Shop, 54 Nathan Road, T.S.T., Kowloon, 2366-9259.

The place to go for loose, semiprecious stones is King Star Jewellery. Their prices are great, and they have a fabulous selection.

◆ King Star Jewellery, Unit 1216, Floor 12, Block A, Focal Industrial Center, 21st Man Lok Street, Hung Hom, 2356-9598.

If you are in need of new eyeglasses, you might want to wait until you can get to Classy Optical in Hong Kong, where they cost about two-thirds of the price you would pay in the United States and they have the latest technology for vision exams. Their machine actually reads what your eyes see best, so you don't have to determine, lens by lens, what your prescription should be. They also have a wonderful selection of frames, and they have a talent for helping you choose what will look good on you. On top of all this, they offer same-day service. If you go there, ask for Tony.

◆ Classy Optical, Shop #A, G-F (ground floor), 12 Peking Road, T.S.T., Kowloon, 2312-2635. Hours 11 A.M. to 11 P.M. seven days a week.

Bring a picture of what you want to Peter at H.K. Broadway Custom Tailors and he will make it for you, whether it's a tie, shirt, blouse, suit, or dress. He can finish a suit in a day or two, but he prefers to have longer in order to do additional fittings. The shop has a wonderful selection of fabrics, but remember to barter.

◆ H.K. Broadway Custom Tailors, 49 Mirador Arcade G-F (ground floor), 58 Nathan Road, T.S.T., Kowloon, 2723-7427.

Chilli N Spice is a great Thai restaurant in a mall of restaurants. They have an English menu, and almost everyone there speaks English. The Thai papaya salad is excellent, and the green curry pork is very good, but very spicy. Each dish costs $45 H.K., which comes out to about $6 U.S. At most Hong Kong restaurants, a ten percent service charge is added to your check automatically, but customarily you also leave pocket change on the table.

◆ Chilli N Spice, G-F (ground floor), 13-15 Cleveland Street, Causeway Bay, 2504-3930.

The Red Pepper offers Szechuan cooking at its best. Dimly lit, but not romantic, the place is decorated nicely, with lovely melon-colored tablecloths. The clientele is mostly local or in-the-know foreigners. Try the braised eggplant with shredded pork and hot garlic sauce or the sliced beef with green pepper and black bean sauce. The fried bean curd (tofu) with brown sauce is also delicious. But the pièce de résistance is the sizzling prawns—let them cool off a bit first and then dig in boldly. You will not be disappointed. Portions are generous and the prices are reasonable. They offer a fixed-price lunch for $70 H.K. (about $8 U.S.) that includes a choice of four items. Reservations are advisable after 7 P.M.

◆ Red Pepper, 7 Lan Fong Road, Causeway Bay, 2577 3811.

Tott's is on the top floor of the Excelsior Hotel, where you have a gorgeous view of Victoria Harbor. Music begins at 9:30 P.M., and sometimes there is a drink minimum. The wait staff is very friendly.

◆ Tott's, Excelsior Hotel, 281 Gloucester Road, Causeway Bay, 2837-6840.

There is a spectacular view of Hong Kong from the bar on the top floor at the Peak. The best time to go there for the view is a day or two after a typhoon because that is when the skies are clearest. You can get to the Peak either by taxi (which I recommend) or by the tram (which costs more).

◆ Peak Café, 121 Peak Road, the Peak, 2819-7868.

"Going to Shenzhen" is shorthand for the daylong shopping trips to Lo Wu in Shenzhen Province in Mainland China. It is a forty-five-minute train ride from Hong Kong, and you need a visa, which can be purchased at the border. By the time you clear Customs, it will have taken you about two-and-a-half hours. Crossing the footbridge from the Customs hall will bring you to this five-story shopping center with about two hundred shops on each floor, many of which are kiosks. The top three floors are occupied almost completely by drapery shops, which will custom-make draperies at a fraction of the cost for the same service in the United States. Another popular purchase is pashmina, which is very inexpensive here. Be sure to take cash in Hong Kong dollars, as most places will not accept credit cards. Stores open at 10 A.M., but closing times can be arbitrary, so if you are having something custom-made for pickup the same day, make sure you confirm the store's closing time. The temptation is to buy so much here that you will be worried about getting it all home. You can FedEx your purchases yourself (most stores do not ship) or you can bring an extra suitcase along in which to stash your loot.

◆ Lo Wu, Shenzhen Province, if your hotel is on the Kowloon side, go to the Hunghom terminus of the Kowloon Canton Railway (KCR) and stay on all the way to Lo Wu; if you are staying on

Hong Kong Island, catch the MTR, get off at Kowloon Tong, and follow the signs for the KCR.

Horizon Plaza is a giant shopping center, some twenty-six stories high and a city block long. The stores are like showrooms, but with warehouse facilities, and you can find nearly everything here. Some stores take up an entire floor of the building. This is a terrific place to buy furniture, both new and antique. There is an enormous selection, at various stores. The prices will surprise you, especially when compared to those for comparable items in the States—depending on what you buy, you can save thousands of dollars here. The sales staffs are knowledgeable and accommodating; they can help you arrange for reliable shipping overseas (shipping charges are additional).

◆ Horizon Plaza, 2 Lee Wing Street, Ap Lei Chau, Hong Kong.
Dynasty Antiques, Room 2014-2020, 20F, Horizon Plaza, 2554-8861.
Matahari, 11F, Horizon Plaza.
Shambala, 2F, Horizon Plaza, 2555-2997.

One of the crew's favorite outings is to take the ferry from the Queens Pier on the Hong Kong side to Lantau, about a forty-minute boat ride. There's no charge for the ferry, but you have to eat at the restaurant that operates it when you get to Lantau. However, the seafood is very good, so it's worth it.

◆ The ferries from Central District arrive at Silvermine Bay (Mui Wo). You can also take a bus or taxi. The bus terminal is right in front of the ferry pier; there are several buses per day to the bus stop at Po Lin Monastery. Taxis (they are blue) are also available on Lantau Island. Ferry departure time is between 6 and 7 P.M.; it returns at 11 P.M.

If there are enough of you (and our 747 crews might consist of as many as sixteen people), your hotel concierge can charter a boat to take you from the Queens Pier to Lamma Island, which has nothing but seafood restaurants. When you arrive, select a restaurant, sit at the huge round tables, pick out your fish from the tanks, and eat family style. Don't wear good clothing, because it can get messy. And since you're not driving, you can drink. We just divide the tab at the end, and it usually averages about $14 a person. The boat then takes you back. The boat trip costs about $400 U.S., but divided among sixteen people, that is really quite reasonable.

◆ Hong Kong Kowloon Ferry, 2815-6063, www.hkkf.com.hk.
Chuen Kee Ferry, 2375-7883 or 2982-8225, www.ferry.com.hk.

Boh tea, grown in the Cameron Highlands of Malaysia, is a black tea that is very strong but not bitter. You can get it in most grocery stores in Hong Kong, and it comes as loose leaves in a can. In Malaysia, you can find it in the local tea shops.

ISTANBUL

Some cities are capitals, others are transit points, and then there is Istanbul: historically, geographically, and emotionally a city at the crossroads. It straddles Europe and Asia and is the only city in the world that lies on two continents.

One of the best ways to see Istanbul is to sail into it (many cruise ships do just that), but no matter how you get there, it is one of the great layover cities because you can, within a short time and distance, do so much.

Consider this: when John F. Kennedy Jr. got married in 1996, he and his wife didn't honeymoon in a luxurious Parisian hotel or on an upscale Caribbean island or at a fancy Hawaiian resort. They headed to Istanbul. And why not? Sultans and harems have called Istanbul home for centuries, and flight crews love it as a perfect stopover for shopping and food, ranging from rugs to spices, from leather goods to the aromas of exotic herbs, fruits, and vegetables.

Visitors should cross the Galata Bridge over the Golden Horn or take a boat out onto the Bosporus—there are regular ferries. It doesn't even matter where you go, you just need to get out there and experience the water and the views, passing by elegant wooden villas and former palaces.

Also check out (but not necessarily into) the Ciragan Palace Hotel, right on the Bosporus. Originally an Ottoman palace, the hotel constitutes an amazing tour of history and architecture. On the outside, it is a most impressive building in a most impressive location, with a fantastic view of the water. Inside, however, the design and color choices feel like Baskin-Robbins-meets-Sultan-of-Brunei or the result of a commingling of Henry VIII and Michael Jackson.

You don't just see history in Istanbul, it actually confronts you on every corner—from the old, crowded ferryboats steaming along the Bosporus to the covered bazaar, from Topkapi to the Blue Mosque. You also see some reminders of the recent past. The Four Seasons Hotel, for example, was converted from a notorious prison—and in some of the suites, you can still see messages of complaint carved into the walls by prisoners. One of my flight crew friends took me to the bazaar for the first time. "There's a special art to the deal here," she told me. "It's almost like a slow minuet—you do the dance." You walk into a store. You stay a minute. See something you want, then turn and walk out. The storekeeper follows you outside and romances you back. You admire the object of your desire a second time. Flirt with it. Then turn and go back outside. Again, the storekeeper follows—only this time, he makes a proposal. And the dance continues. The price drops. And drops. And then . . . stops.

"This is where it gets interesting," she told me. "At that precise moment, just when you think—and, more important, just when *he* thinks—the deal is done, you use your credit cards to get two additional discounts below his last price, even when you had no intention whatsoever of using those cards."

I told her I didn't understand. "Watch," she said, as she pulled out her leather wallet. She removed her American Express card. A look of horror came over the owner's face. "No!" he pleaded. "No American Express. Too expensive." Translation: the shopkeeper didn't want to pay the credit card commission. She was expecting this. So she withdrew a Visa card. "Okay, how much for Visa card?"

He dropped the price, but then asked, "You can't do cash?"

She smiled. She knew this was coming. "Okay, how much for

cash?" The price dropped again. She was right: two additional discounts after the final price, just for flashing plastic. Not bad.

Speaking of money, remember that Turkish liras are about as close to wallpaper as you can get. Because the government continues to devalue its currency (at last count, more than seventy-one percent in a single year), it also pays to carry lots of single U.S. dollars with you and not wait for change. Why? The exchange rate is absurd—about 1 to 1.5 million Turkish lira per U.S. dollar.

Last but not least, you can't go to Istanbul without experiencing at least one Turkish bath. Public baths are still very much a part of life in Istanbul. Try the Cagaloglu Hamami—this is Ottoman-era bathing at its grandest (and oldest). A bath, body scrub (believe me, they scrub you!), and massage costs about $30. Try to go early in the day because you'll need a three- or four-hour nap afterward; otherwise, you'll never make it through dinner.

CITY TIPS

Be very careful when dealing with the cab drivers because they will try to take advantage of you. Instead of taking you to the front of your hotel, they will pretend that the cab has broken down before they get there. A lot of Turkish people speak English, so my strategy is to talk a local passerby into telling the cab driver that I am not a tourist and that I know what he's trying to do. I also ask the person to tell the cab driver that I want to be dropped off in front of the hotel. You must also understand the money before you go over there because it all looks similar and it is easy to be fooled. In fact, the best thing to do is not to change your money into Turkish liras at all. Instead, before leaving home, go to the bank and get $200 in one-dollar bills—George Washington speaks a universal language.

When we're not shopping, we head to the newer side of the city, where the embassies were before the capital was moved to Ankara. On Istiklal Caddesi, a walking street that begins at Taksim Square, you'll find Sarau, a wonderful shop that has been selling delicious baklava since 1949. Thirty pieces cost around $7 or $8. They also serve sandwiches and thick, sweet, or medium coffee.

◆ Sarau, Istikial Caddesi No. 102 Beyoglu, 0212 292 3434.

If you continue down Istiklal Caddesi, you will come to Ipek, a store selling beautiful silk scarves. You can get hand-painted Christmas scarves with gold accents for around $40.

◆ Ipek, Istikial Caddesi No. 230/7-8 Beyoglu, 0212 249 8207 or 293 7388, www.kapalicarsi.net.

Guler Ocakbasi, a block and a half off Cur Huriyet, the main street, is a local hangout. Downstairs is an oven where they bake the puffy bread that they serve with meals. They also make wonderful hot or cold appetizers—we like to pick out a dozen at a time. Once you finish that, you can order lamb on a stick, ground-up lamb, chicken, or eggplant. All the appetizers you can eat, a portion of meat and bread, and two or three beers might cost you $14 a person. The atmosphere is casual and attracts local people, a lot of couples, some families with children, and Delta crew members.

◆ Guler Ocakbasi, Babil Sok No. 37, 0212 241 1866.

When I took my eighty-nine-year-old father to Turkey, we stayed at the Celal Sultan Hotel, near St. Sophia and the Blue Mosque, where the manager takes wonderful care of everyone. Then we flew to Kayseri on Turkish Airlines and spent time in Kapadokya (Cappadocia) in the central part of the country, where there are unique rock formations that make you feel as if you are on the moon. We spent two mornings taking hot air balloon rides in the area.

◆ Celal Sultan Hotel, Yerebatan Caddesi Salkimsogut Sokak No: 16 34410 Sultanahmet, 0212 520 93 23-520 93 24, www. celalsultan.com.

Cappadocia Balloon Trip Company (Kapadokya Balloons), Goreme, TR-50108 Nevsehir, 0384 271 2442, mobile 0532 436 8008, www.kapadokyaballoons.com.

Centuries ago in Kayseri, the Hittites carved homes and churches into the rocks to avoid persecution. Now, people have turned the places into hotels of twelve or fifteen rooms, with running water, showers, comfortable beds, and individual patio or balcony areas. We stayed at the wonderful Urgup Evi Guest House, run by a Parisian woman named Ana, who also did the cooking. An afternoon pleasure here is to ask for a cup of tea and watch the sun go down.

◆ Urgup Evi Guest House, Esbelli Man, No. 54, 5400 Urgup, Nevsehir, 0384 341 3173 or 341 6269, www.urgupevi.com.tr.

You can only do this in a group, but it's an experience you won't want to miss, even in the winter months. Take a one-hour-and-twenty-minute flight south to Dalaman, or a little farther to Bodrum, and locate Mustafa Nalbantodlu, who operates a small fleet of ninety-foot wooden motor sailers. You can charter them as a group of eight to twelve people, fully provisioned, to cruise the Turkish Mediterranean. You can go for a day, two days, or a week and visit all the islands, swim, and eat incredibly well. The boat rental costs $1,000 to $1,500 a day, but divided among ten people, it's affordable.

◆ Kumbahce Mahallesi, Imren Sokak No. 8, 48400 — Bodrum, 0252 316 37 64, fax 0252 316 49 86, www.adamvoyages.com, e-mail adamvoyages@turk.net.

Fatih Falman will give you a good deal on carpets. He will also talk with you about carpets, explaining the different cities they came from, the various thread counts, and how to distinguish a good carpet from a bad carpet. His prices are good—I paid $500 for a five-by-six carpet. In the States, a comparable carpet would go for at least twice that. After a sale, Fatih will wrap the carpet tight and put it in a canvas tote bag so that you can just carry the rug right onto the plane. But he will ship them, too, and that should be negotiated into the price.

◆ Fatih Falman, #135 Sultanahmet, Arasta Bazaar, 0212 516 7948, galerifatih@yahoo.com.

Kahraman is the place to find cultured, freshwater, and dark pearls. They also do excellent repairs, such as restringing or replacing clasps, at very reasonable prices.

◆ Kahraman, head to the bazaar, and you will be let off at Nuruosmaniye; don't go through the gate, but turn right and walk to the end of the street; then take the first left, which looks like an uneven alley, and look for the big blue sign; Kilicilar Sok, #23 Nuruosmaniye, 0212 526 8803.

The three brothers who own the Flamingo Bar Restaurant try hard to speak English and will make you feel at home. They offer the crew a prix fixe menu with tons of food for $15 each, not including the tip (and we do tip). *Cankaya* (white wine), *Doluca* (white wine), and *Yakut* (red wine) flow freely during our meal. We start with a meze platter, an appetizer plate consisting of stuffed grape leaves, eggplant dip, and a small Turkish pizza (flatbread with ground-up lamb on it). They also serve a fabulous potato salad, which is a little more spicy than what we are used to in the States, and chopped cucumbers with a yogurt sauce. Next, they bring salads. For the main course, we choose lamb, beef, or chicken. The chicken is stuffed with spinach and is simply delicious. Dessert is fruit. This is a very clean and attractive restaurant, near Taksim Square and the Divan Hotel. On Mondays, Tuesdays, Fridays, and Saturdays they feature live music.

◆ Flamingo Bar Restaurant, Receppas, a Caddesi No. 15/B, Talimhane, Taksim, 0212 250 63 22 or 0212 235 7854.

Erkan Yilmaz sells big, beautiful towels that are the fluffiest I have ever seen. Two enormous towels and two smaller ones might cost about $20. They also carry unprocessed cotton towels, as well as bathrobes priced from $6 to $20. This store is located in the bazaar.

◆ Erkan Yilmaz, Kapalicarsi Yorgancilar, Caddesi store Nos. 5, 7, 8, 9/11, and 24, 0212 512 0789.

LONDON

I first flew to London when I was twelve. I had just read Charles Dickens for the first time and London seemed like everything Dickens had said it was. Gray. Cold. Formal. Stiff. Oh yes, the British pound was equivalent to something like $2.40. Ouch.

Bette Midler once said, "When it's three o'clock in New York, it's still 1938 in London." In a way, she's right, but only if you want it to be 1938 in London.

The good news is that London has changed. In fact, it rocks. Many of my flight attendant friends choose London as their most desired layover city. It's manageable, the people speak the same language, and lately the British pound has been kinder to Uncle Sam.

I now find myself in London at least once every six weeks, and I look forward to the visit to Europe's biggest city every time.

It was a TWA flight attendant who first introduced me to the great flea market at Camden Locks. It was an American flight crew that insisted I take the train from Paddington Station down to Bath for lunch on the Royal Crescent. And a United flight attendant took me to a little trend-setting noodle canteen called Wagamama for lunch and to a great Thai place called Tui for dinner.

My aunt and uncle and my cousins have lived in London for as long as I can remember, and, through them, I return the flight crew favors by introducing friends to Halepi, an incredible Greek taverna near Lancaster Gate, or to the Blue Print Café, right on the Thames River.

Or I take them to the park near Hampstead Heath for long walks, which invariably pass by the Highgate Cemetery. Talk about tributes to the dead—this is an outdoor museum of gravestones and catacombs. And for drinks you'll find me at the bar at Dukes Hotel or more often than not sitting with my friend Sally Bulloch, who runs the Athenaeum and has turned the bar into a legendary watering hole for single malt aficionados.

Twenty years ago, the food was bordering on inedible in London. On my current trips, I find myself in conflict over a choice of excellent restaurants—fabulous Lebanese places in Shepherd Market, tapas bars, the China House, located in the former Barclays Bank building on Piccadilly. And then there's Red Fort, on Dean Street—good Indian food, but even better nan bread of every variety and flavor.

First-timers always go for afternoon tea at the Ritz Hotel on Piccadilly or a shopping excursion at Harrods and the changing of the guard at Buckingham Palace. And I must admit that if I'm passing by the palace and the soldiers are marching, I always find myself stopping. Let's face it, nobody does pomp and ceremony like the Brits.

But if you want a new experience on weekends, head for a different sort of ritual in the Palm Court of the Waldorf Hotel—afternoon tea, with fox-trots and waltzes.

I still prefer the Fifth Floor, which, as its name suggests, is where you'll find it at Harvey Nichols, the still trendy Knightsbridge department store. Yes, it's a restaurant. Or, within walking distance from a hotel that used to be the definition of stodgy—the Berkeley—you'll find Vong, an expensive but memorable dining experience.

My favorite hangout is around the back of the National Gallery, where you'll find the National Portrait Gallery—a sort of who's who, not to mention who *was* who.

On Sundays we take boats to Greenwich, in southeast London.

Thanks to the Heathrow Express, as long as you have manageable luggage, it's about eighteen minutes from Paddington Station to the airport. For any other kind of travel within London, I love the cabs. Why? They never get lost, they're clean, and I am constantly amazed by their narrow turning radius. But for the airport, and unless you're the poster child for the excess baggage telethon, it's the train, hands down. It's a considerable savings of time and money. London remains my favorite airport hub for seeing all of Europe, and for day trips to Paris and Amsterdam or for heading north to Ireland and Scotland, the express train to the airport has become my friend. Who would have guessed?

AIRPORT TIPS

There are a variety of shopping opportunities at the airport. Harrods is duty free here, but my favorite shop is Lush, a bath store that sells the giant bath bombs that fizz when you put them in the tub. After they dissolve, the rose petals float in the water. Lush also sells wonderful homemade soaps. Boots pharmacy is a great place to pick up last-minute treats for the flight home.
◆ Harrods, Terminal 4, 020 8745 6724.
Lush, Terminal 3, 020 8745 0652.
Boots, Terminal 4, 020 8897, 1893.

Thomas Cook runs Terminal 4, and Cook's is the place you go to exchange money. But if you're stuck at the airport for an extended period of time, I recommend Cook's little rest area. There are fully reclining chairs, and blankets are available. They also have showers and will provide you with towels, shampoo, and soap. They offer snacks and beverages as well.
◆ The Business Centre, Queen's Building, between Terminals 1 and 2, (0)20 8759 2434. Rates £20 for lounge; £10 pounds for shower; £25 for both.

CITY TIPS

As a flight attendant, I don't want to spend money to get a theater ticket ahead of time because if the flight is delayed, I'll miss the show. So I get tickets at the half-price theater ticket booth, which is about a ten-minute walk from the theaters in Trafalgar Square. It's almost exactly like the TKTS booth in New York, except the people here are much more helpful. I saw the musical *Buddy* for £12 (about $18).
◆ Leicester Square Theatre Ticket Booth on the south side; tube stops are Leicester Square or Piccadilly Circus.

I go to Boots, the chemist (pharmacy), for nail polish because their brand doesn't have formaldehyde to make the polish last longer like the American brands do. A bottle of polish costs $3 to $6, and it comes in a wide variety of colors. Boots has locations all over London.
◆ Boots, 285-289 Oxford Street, 020 7629 2105.

Biagi's is a really small place (only about eight to ten tables) in the Marble Arch. It doesn't get excessively crowded, except on Saturday nights, but the food is terrific. I recommend the mouthwatering spinach salad for only £3 ($5.50) or the grilled chicken with asparagus for £8 (about $12). Pasta dishes go for $7 to $12, and fish for $13 to $15. Ask for Dino; he'll take care of you.
◆ Biagi's, Upper Berkeley, 020 7723 0394.

The food at Sofra is healthier and lighter than what you usually find in London (English food tends to be heavy and high in fat), and although the portions are a little smaller than average, the meals here are completely satisfying. The cuisine is Middle Eastern, and they offer a special that comes with pita bread, hummus, olives, a starter, and an entrée. I recommend the basmati rice and grilled vegetables, but everything is good here. If you go between 4:30 and 7 P.M. or after 10 P.M., there is a special prix fixe theater menu for about $10. You can come early for dinner and go to the theater afterward.

◆ Sofra, no. 1, Christopher Place; no. 18, Shepherd Market, Mayfair; 020 7493 3320.

Belgo, in the Covent Garden area, is a bustling restaurant where the waiters dress like Druids. The place specializes in mussels from various regions, prepared in different ways; you can also order them by the kilo, served in a bucket. They offer chicken, fish and chips, and a few other dishes as well. On Monday through Thursday nights, the price of your meal is based on your arrival time—if you get there at 5:30, your meal will cost £5.30, to a maximum of £10. They have an extensive beer list, from which you are welcome to try samples. You may have to share a table with other diners, so it's definitely not the place for a romantic dinner, but it's lots of fun.

◆ Belgo, 9 Belgo Centraal, 50 Earlham Street, 020 7813 2233.

Café Montpeliano, an Italian restaurant in the Knightsbridge area, is not in the brochures and is not frequented by tourists—that's why we like it. This is the place to hang with the locals. The food is excellent and moderately priced, and it's located close to good shopping.

◆ Café Montpeliano, 144 Brompton Road, 020 7225 2926.

The Wagamama Noodle Bar serves a large selection of healthy, light, tasty food. I recommend the salmon ramen, a giant bowl of noodles and vegetables with a big slab of real salmon floating in it. The restaurant does not permit smoking, which is unusual for Europe, and the prices are reasonable.

◆ Wagamama Noodle Bar, Streatham Street, 020 7323 9223.

Camden Market is an ongoing giant flea market and bazaar where you can find all kinds of leather goods, antiques, knick-knacks, and collectibles—everything you can imagine. The best time to go is on weekends—a sunny day will really bring out a crowd. Prices are reasonable, and you can bargain for stuff. There's no admission charge.

◆ Camden Market, from Camden Town Station, take right-hand exit, and turn right onto Camden High Street, which becomes Chalk Farm Road.

If you know someone who is hard to shop for, try the gift store at the Victoria and Albert Museum. You can find wonderful stuff that's typically British, such as William Morris prints and cutwork cream ware. Much of the merchandise is museum quality, and you will find things that you can't find anyplace else.

◆ Victoria and Albert Museum, Cromwell Road, South Kensington, 020 7942 2000.

Often during layovers I sleep only sporadically and wake up feeling as if I hadn't been to bed at all. But then I discovered Molton Brown's Sea Moss Stress-Relieving Soak Therapy. After bathing in it, I am so relaxed I can sleep through the entire night. Now I never travel without it. It's unscented, but it turns your bathwater aqua blue. It comes with soap, too. Perfect for those long, deep British bathtubs!

◆ Molton Brown Cosmetics, 58 S. Molton Street, 020 7499 6474; also available at Selfridges, 400 Oxford Street, 020 7629 1234.

I discovered Jo Malone perfume when Jo was on Walton Street in London. She's since moved to Sloane Street and become quite the big name in the perfume industry. Neiman Marcus, in the United States, now carries her products. She has some wonderful, subtle perfumes.

◆ Jo Malone, 150 Sloane Street, 020 7730 2100.

After a long flight, one of our flight attendants insisted that we go for after-dinner drinks. I'm glad she did. Now one of our must-stops is the ground-floor bar of the very old-style Leonard Hotel, near Marble Arch. This quiet bar is typically British and is set up with sofas around a fireplace. You keep expecting someone from World War II to walk in.

◆ Leonard Hotel, 21 Longmoore Street, 020 7834 2765.

Here's a surprise: a pub that serves really good Thai food. Forget the menu at Churchill Thai Kitchen. Just ask them to do it family style. The food is good, cheap, and hot! Meals, with beer, go for £10 to £15.

◆ Churchill Thai Kitchen, 119, Kensington Church Street, 020 7792 1246.

If you are on your own in London and don't know where to eat, grab a good book and head for the nearest Pret A Manger. These are a group of sandwich/salad shops where the food comes prepared—they have salads, sandwiches, and little packaged cakes. Their chicken-and-avocado sandwich is wonderful, and it costs only about £2.50. This is a great place to duck in for a quick bite or for something to take back to your room with you.

◆ Pret A Manger, 556 Oxford Street, 020 7723 9004.

Most of us refuse to shop at Harrods because it's too expensive and too crowded. But we love that neighborhood for two things: window-shopping and eating. The Stock Pot offers nothing more than soups and stews, but they are very inexpensive and very good. You know when you go there that you're going to find something you like.

◆ Stock Pot, 273 Kings Road, Chelsea, 020 7823 3175.

Once a year there is a good reason to shop at Harrods—for their Christmas teddy bears with the date embroidered on the foot.

They cost about $37, depending on the exchange rate, and they are really cute. Each year's bear has a different personality. You can find them downstairs in the basement with the souvenirs and upstairs in the toy department.

◆ Harrods, Brompton Road, Knightsbridge, 020 7730 1234.

Tapisserie, a needlepoint store, is a real find—almost hidden among all the expensive designer stores. They have some unique and beautiful pieces, including lots of floral work and summery, traditional, European-looking items. They also have some of the cutest teddy bears I've ever seen.

◆ Tapisserie, 54 Walton Street, 020 7581 2715.

Every once in a while flight attendants splurge—and it's not just on shoes. We also like to buy jewelry, and for that we go to Elizabeth Gage. She uses some very unusual Roman and Greek coin designs and her settings are old-fashioned hammered gold—Renaissance or Byzantine in appearance. I spotted a particular amber and gold piece in her window that almost made me pound the glass and say, "I need you." Since it cost about half a year's salary, I settled for a little gold and sapphire ring, which I love dearly.

◆ Elizabeth Gage, 20 Albermarle Street, 020 7499 2879.

My Old Dutch serves crepes the size of large pizzas. You can go vegetarian or order a combination of veggies and different meat or chicken toppings, for £4 to £6. The dessert crepes are decadent and as large as the dinner crepes, so take friends along to help you eat them. The light-pine decor accentuates the casual atmosphere—this is a good place to go when you want to save some money but try something new at the same time.

◆ My Old Dutch, 221 Kings Road, 020 7376 5650.

Glaister's Garden Bistro, on Hollywood Road off of Fulham Road, is where the local people go. The interior is a pleasant mix of casual and formal, and the waiters are friendly and eager to please. The excellent food is artfully arranged and reasonably priced. I especially liked the fact they serve chocolates with a *big* cup of full-bodied decaffeinated coffee. (I am always reluctant to order decaf in London, as many times it is instant coffee. Not here. It is as good as the real stuff.) You might even spot Margaret Thatcher here, since she lives nearby.

◆ Glaister's Garden Bistro, 4 Hollywood Road, 020 7352 0352.

I am not usually a fan of pubs, but Jim Thompson is not like most pubs. It is one of the prettiest pubs you will ever come across—and lacks the omnipresent pinball machines you find everywhere else. They have Lowenbrau on tap, which is reason enough to come here, sit by the fireplace, and quaff a wonderful Münchner brew. The Thai/Malaysian restaurant in the back is lovely, with artifacts on the walls from the Spice Islands, which meld with the pastel color scheme and candlelight to create an Asian mood. The tasty entrées cost about £6 for generous portions.

◆ Jim Thompson, 617 King's Road, Fulham, 020 7731 0999.

I find myself avoiding Indian restaurants because the servings are often minuscule and the waiters are not always friendly. I changed my mind with Loofs, which is more like bistro dining. The restaurant is stylish and the food matches the ambience, with a bit of flair in the preparation. The portions are large and cost £6 to £8. The wait staff is very cordial, and the manager is on hand to make sure you have a pleasant experience. Its Earls Court location makes it easy to find.

◆ Loofs, 234 Old Brompton Road, 020 7370 1188.

Try the biriani deluxe, a mixture of meat, vegetables, and rice in a spicy sauce, at the Grand Indian restaurant, in Soho, on New Row. Meals range from £15 to £30, and they serve a variety of good imported Indian beers.

◆ Grand Indian, 6 New Row, Soho, 020 7240 0785.

MADRID

My first flight to Madrid was, to say the least, unforgettable. "The city will surprise you," the flight attendant told me. "It's no longer a dark and dirty city." But first, I had to survive the flight, which was divided into two distinct sections: smoking, and more smoking.

Indeed, Madrid was a whole lot less smoky than the flight. But the noise was deafening. We're talking serious noise pollution. Today, Iberia has thankfully banned smoking, but Madrid is still very loud.

The good news is that Madrid has always had something to be noisy about. Yes, Barcelona is known for its architecture, but Madrid is known for simply ignoring the clock and offering some of the best restaurants in the world. *Madrileños* enjoy a sophisticated cultural scene and pay no attention whatsoever to the notion that, for everyone else, the workday starts at eight or nine in the morning.

Many flight attendants tell me they schedule their flights to Madrid in order to slowly take in the Prado, one of the world's great museums, one room per flight. Others have graduated to the relatively new Thyssen-Bornemisza Museum, opened in 1992, which houses an impressive collection of old masters, impressionists, and even some modern art.

Go to Madrid in spring and summer to experience the bullfight. Hemingway romanticized the ritual in *Death in the Afternoon*, but it is essential to see the matadors in action at the corrida. You can visit the huge Plaza de Toros Monumental de las Ventas, but be sure to avoid the cheap seats, because you will be scorched by *el sol*. Instead, buy the more expensive *sombra* (shaded) seats.

You also go to Madrid to eat. As in most Spanish cities, showing up before 9 P.M. is considered decidedly unhip. There are few chain restaurants for a city this big, and, refreshingly, most are individually run. I have yet to have a bad meal in Madrid. There are even some good Japanese restaurants in town, although you hardly go to Madrid for sushi. Instead, if you can afford it, try La Broche, a two-star Michelin restaurant (located inside the Hotel Miguel Angel). The restaurant features a world-class tasting menu, which the chef changes every two weeks and which runs about $60 without wine. (The place seats only about fifty, so make reservations and be prepared to wait anyway.)

You can also go for the hot and cold tapas and *callos* (tripe), not to mention the *patatas bravas* (potatoes in a spicy tomato sauce) and my favorite, the prawns in garlic, or, if you're really bold, anchovies in vinegar. Head to the Café Commercial (it's the Bilbao stop on the metro) and do nothing but sit, people-watch, and sip a coffee. Or at the Chocolateria San Gines, order a plate of *churros* (the twisted doughnuts) and a huge cup of hot chocolate designed not just for drinking but for dipping the doughnuts.

The Palace Hotel, restored at an astronomical cost a few years ago, is worth it just to view the painted ceilings. And the Ritz, also renovated, retains much of its charm from when it was first opened in 1910 by King Alfonso XIII.

But you don't have to spend a lot of money to enjoy Madrid, which is why so many flight crews love the city. Taxis are everywhere, and you won't pay more than $4 for a trip to the city center. The metro system is also excellent—a ten-ticket carte will also cost you $4.

CITY TIPS

Madrid is a city of music lovers! At El Corte Inglés, Spain's largest department store chain, you will find an enormous world music selection. They stock a wide range of Latin American, Flamenco, Spanish, and Italian recordings, and much more. It's not necessarily cheap, but it's comprehensive, and there are listening stations, too. You can also find good-quality Spanish classical guitars for $150 to $200 in Madrid. Union Musical Española specializes in guitars, but they carry many other instruments as well.

◆ El Corte Inglés, Preciados 1-4, 091 556 2300.

Union Musical Española, Carrera San Geronimo 26, 091 429 3877.

El Corte Inglés is also a good place to buy seafood. You can find such delicacies as canned tuna fish in a delicious vinaigrette, mussels and clams with sauces flavored with garlic and onions, and del sol calamari in salsa picanta (cuttlefish in hot sauce). They sell a wide variety of olives stuffed with such things as red peppers, onions, and anchovies. The olives are canned, but they will sell them to you too in little bags so that you can try them out first. The store also carries a wonderful selection of olive oils at half the price they sell for in the United States. Many of the things you find here are things you can't get in the States, but if you buy something to bring back, pack it well. The last thing you want is to break the glass or have the tin leak.

Another find at El Corte Inglés is Picchis—knee-high nylons that never slip off and rarely run. The elasticity is really good, and they don't hurt you or cut off your circulation. They come in many colors, and there are two to three pairs per package, for around $4.

My favorite local place is the low-key Restaurante Platero, run by Ramon and his wife, who does the cooking, and their daughter. His personal touch pays off in the good quality of both the service and the food. The prices are also reasonable—about 7 euros per person for a meal that includes salad, entrée, dessert, wine, and bread. The place seats about forty people, and if you go around 8 P.M. you will certainly get a table (but remember, that's early by Madrid standards).

◆ Restaurante Platero, Espoz y mina, 20, near Puerta del Sol, 091 521 2337.

Champagneria Gala offers a fixed-price menu, including salad, entrée, wine, bread, and dessert, all for $30. But you really go there for the paella. It's a fun and busy place—especially around 10 or 11 P.M.—with a young and trendy ambience. Inside there's a garden with lots of round tables because people tend to come here in large groups. Make a reservation because it gets crowded.

◆ Champagneria Gala, Moratin, 22, 091 429 2562.

Although officially it's called the Restaurante Alvar, this great little restaurant, near the Hotel Husa Princesa, is known among the airline crowd as "the Garlic Place." The owner, Ovidio Alvarez, does it all—he waits on the tables, does the cooking, and greets his guests. Ovidio speaks very little English, but he does have an English menu. The dinners include your choice of starters (I recommend the lentil soup), a mixed salad, and an entrée. The chicken dishes are delicious and include potatoes, a vegetable, and rice. In addition, you get dessert, bread, all the wine and/or beer you can drink, and coffee and a liqueur. All this for 2,100 pesetas (about $11). Most of us give him a little extra if we drink more than a glass or two of wine, and sometimes, if we are there late, we help Ovidio do the dishes. This is a home away from home for flight crews, as you can tell from the pictures of crews and airplanes on the walls. The place is small, and they don't take reservations, but don't let that stop you!

◆ Restaurante Alvar, San Bernardino, 13, 091 541 2026.

Typically in Madrid you finish dinner around 1 A.M., and then you go out for coffee. Around 2 A.M., it's off to the clubs. A new disco opens every day—each one different and very creative. Try the club called Joy Eslava, near Puerta del Sol in the central area.
◆ Joy Eslava, Arenal, 11, 091 366 3284.

Sacristan, situated between Puerta del Sol and Plaza Mayor, is a small, quaint shop appointed in dark wood and antiques and specializing in good-quality pens. Although the staff does not speak English well, they do know their merchandise and are very helpful.
◆ Sacristan, 27 High Street, 091 366 5886.

Try Manchego, a hard, white goat cheese, after dinner, with some grapes and other fruit and a good port. This excellent cheese is worth a trip to Madrid!

Neptuno, a jewelry shop in the Hotel Husa Princesa, sells beautiful Majorcan pearls and mantilla-style shawls, as well as other jewelry, purses, wallets, and shoes. A standard-size necklace with a small pearl and an Austrian crystal will cost you between $25 and $30. The shawls are handmade and cost $100 to $150. Marissa, the owner, will ship things to you, but if you're going to be in Madrid for a week or so, she can have your order done before you leave. Although she does not speak English, she understands broken Spanish.
◆ Neptuno, Hotel Husa Princesa, Princesa, 40, 091 541 2606.

Lácrima Baccus Reserva is a kind of champagne (cava) that I've found only in Spain, but it's worth looking for.
◆ Available at Bodega de Los Reyes, c/ de Los Reyes, 6, 091 547 9213.

MILAN

My first trip to Milan was a by-product of bad airline scheduling. If you want to go from Los Angeles to Rome, you must change in Milan. And I'm glad I did. One of the flight attendants asked me where I was staying, and I told her at the Grand. "Oooh," she sighed, "that's a very romantic hotel." Sadly, I had to admit I was alone. "But you're in luck," she said. I was beginning to imagine great things, and I think she saw my expression change.

"No, not *that*. This is about my other love . . . food." She told me about this wonderful deli three blocks from the hotel, a little shop that would fulfill my, uh, oral needs. And she was right.

It was indeed small, but inside was a fantasyland of every kind of salami, cheese, and bread imaginable. In one corner was the most incredible, creamy, stinky gorgonzola I had ever tasted. I had the owner slice me about a pound of hard salami, very thin, and about two pounds of the gorgonzola. I bought some great bread, bread sticks, some olives (three different kinds), and walked at a much faster pace back to the hotel. Some folks come to Milan just to see da Vinci's *Last Supper*. But at the end of my meetings each day, I was there to enjoy my continuing feast.

It was either that or shopping. Milan is dangerous territory. Many flight attendants I know scout the new styles in Milan and buy elsewhere. But every once in a while, there are bargains with style. Not surprisingly, all the big Italian designers are here: Armani, Valentino, Versace, Krizia, and Missoni, to name a few.

The Armani store is nothing short of staggering in dimension (and price of goods). Trussardi has built a multifunctional space, with art, shopping, and food. Want to see some serious Milanese ladies who lunch? This is the place.

I always manage to find my way to the Piazza del Duomo, one of the biggest and liveliest squares in all of Europe, and, of course, the rather over-the-top Gothic cathedral. But my favorite stop, thanks to an Alitalia pilot who fancied himself a novice inventor, is the Science Museum. One gallery in particular is where you'll find a tribute to Leonardo da Vinci as inventor, displayed as models constructed from his notebooks. This is very cool stuff—da Vinci's airplane, his helicopter, a machine for making screws, a timber cutter, and—catch this—a system of mapmaking by aerial views, invented long before any aircraft ever flew.

Speaking of aircraft, there's Malpensa, the airport. Not one of my favorites, and besides, who in their right mind would ever name an airport Malpensa? (The Italian translation—and I'm not kidding—means "bad thought.") I've had more than my share of delayed flights out of Milan and, instead of complaining, I now make one additional stop on the way to the airport. You guessed it: that deli near the Grand Hotel, to stock up on salami and gorgonzola.

CITY TIPS

We never take the taxis because there's excellent and convenient public transportation by bus or subway. You can buy the tickets at a newspaper or tobacco stand; they cost 1,500 lire (about 75¢). Most of them have a posted time of ninety minutes per ride, and it's based on the honor system. Ninety minutes is plenty of time to get around—you can go a long distance. Sometimes the police will come on board and check to make sure everyone does have a ticket; the fine is substantial. At some stops, there are flashing lights indicating how many minutes it will be until the next departure.

If you want real hard Italian salami and the most creamy gorgonzola cheese, go to Esselunga. It has great prices, too!

◆ Esselunga, Via Amoretti 4, 002 3558 302.

Even if you want high-end clothing, you can find deals in Milan. I bought my husband some Ermenegildo Zegna suits, which cost about $2,500 each in the United States and about $1,000 at Zegna in Milan. He then had them tailored at the Houston Zegna store, which didn't charge him a nickel for the service.

◆ Ermenegildo Zegna, Via Verri #3, 002 76006437, www.zegna.com/homefla.htm.

There's no need to go to Bergdorf's in New York when you can buy king-size sheets for much less at the Pratesi store in Milan. I know $1,000 is still a lot of money for sheets, but it's much cheaper than comparable items in the States. If you fax them your order, Pratesi will send the merchandise directly to you in the United States.

◆ Pratesi, Via Montenapolene #27 E, 002 76012755.

At Il Salvagente you can find designer clothes at deep-discount, outlet-level prices, because the clothes are from a past season, they are in sample sizes, or they are ready for liquidation. The shop sells men's and women's clothing, including shoes. It also has high-fashion evening gowns by famous Italian designers such as Bruno Cavali, Ferragamo, and Gucci. A dress that originally cost $1,500 might be marked down to $300 or $400. On my last visit, I saw a coat that looked like it had been discarded in the wrong section. As I tried it on, women gathered around me, trying to buy it right off my back. It was a $900 coat, but I got it for $150—and I had to practically run out of the store to keep those women from snatching it when I took it off my shoulders.

◆ Il Salvagente, Via Fratelli Bronzetti 16, 002 76110328.

MUNICH

Munich has always been a city of secrets to me, but also a city of luxury. I was there the first time for the 1972 Olympics, and two years later for *Newsweek,* to watch them shoot a movie called *Rollerball.*

My father flew over to join me, and one afternoon, we drove around. It is the only town I've been to where you can order a beer with your Big Mac. Then my father surprised me by asking to see Dachau, the former concentration camp.

In 1974 Dachau was not listed on any road map, and everyone we stopped claimed they had no idea where it was. It was clear no one wanted us to find the place. Eventually we came across three nuns and asked them if they knew where Dachau was. "You're in it," they smiled.

It was already 4:30 in the afternoon and the sun was setting. They let us in, with the warning that the camp would be closing in half an hour. It was, to say the least, a moving experience. At precisely 5 P.M., we heard the bell ringing at the Protestant chapel, then at the Catholic chapel and at the small Jewish house of worship. The priest, the minister, and the rabbi, almost in synchrony, emerged from their buildings and escorted us slowly toward the entrance. We all walked in silence. There was nothing to be said. But we all knew why we were there.

I went back a few years later with friends—and insisted we go late in the afternoon. We repeated the experience, only this time the directions were more forthcoming. Dachau had a distinguished place on the maps.

When we returned to Munich we discussed that amazing juxtaposition of experience—Dachau, a terrible but essential reminder of the past, and Munich, a symbol of a sophisticated future embracing reconciliation.

It's a young city, perhaps because it has such a large student population. Bavaria has BMWs and Mad King Ludwig, horse-drawn carriages and one of the best airports in the world. Another benefit is that you can use Munich as a train hub to the Czech Republic. Of course, you could also buy a new BMW, drive it around Germany for two weeks, and then have it shipped back to the States. Flight crew may not be there to buy cars, but they know to go to the museums on Sundays (when they are free).

You have to love the Munich airport. With 23.6 million passengers, it is now the eighth-busiest airport in Europe. A number of people arrive in Munich to head out to Füssen—not just to see Mad King Ludwig's castle, but to attend the special musical as well as the theater built to honor him. Legend has it that one night Ludwig simply walked out onto the lake near the castle and disappeared. Leave it to German engineering to design a theater that re-creates that moment—filling the stage with ninety tons of water in two minutes and then, just as quickly, making it disappear.

CITY TIPS

The Underground takes you to the center of town in twenty minutes, and trains run every twenty minutes. It costs $9, but a cab would cost you $60. Follow the green signs with an "S" and pay at the machine before you get on the train. The machines don't take coins—bills only.

You can get a partner day card for the railroad and travel for one day in Munich for DM14. It's a very good deal, although not widely known. One card is good for up to five people, and you can travel from 6 A.M. until evening. You can also take your bicycle everywhere on the subway, but you have to pay extra for it.

Take the S6 subway to Starnberg and visit the lake, Starnberger See. When you emerge from the train station, you are right at the lake. If you turn left from the station and walk for fifteen minutes, there's an all-grass, very clean beach where you can swim. You can also take a boat ride to a cute little place called Tutzing.

Wirtshaus serves traditional Bavarian food in the heart of Munich. Order the Schweinbraten (pork on the spit), which is about $7 and comes with dumplings, cabbage, or sauerkraut. Wash it down with a Paulaner, the beer served here. Try to sit somewhere in the middle, so you can absorb the atmosphere fully. Be sure to make a reservation.
◆ Wirtshaus, Lilienstrasse 51, 089 448 1400. Hours 5 P.M. to
1 A.M., Monday through Friday; 10 A.M. to 1 A.M., Saturday,
Sunday, and holidays.

Dampfnudeln is a type of traditional Bavarian food that you can find at Hundskugel. It looks very much like one of those white Chinese buns, but not as sticky—it's fluffier and lighter and is served mostly as a dessert.
◆ Hundskugel, Hotterstrasse 18, 089 264272.

Milerb makes a concentrated herb paste from basilisa, basil, garlic, parsley, peanut oil, and other seasonal ingredients. It comes in a tiny glass jar, and you mix a small amount with a bit more oil, some vinegar, and salt and pepper to make a delicious salad dressing. You can find this herb paste in Hit, a supermarket across the street from the Hilton Hotel.
◆ Hit, 30 Rosenheimerstrasse, 089 4808860.

Ski clothes are cheaper in Germany than in the United States, and in February everything goes on sale. Sport Scheck is a good place to look for bargains.

◆ Sport Scheck, Sendlinger Strasse 6, 089 21660.

The Reformhaus, the German version of a health food store, sells all-natural products, lotions, organic fruit, and my favorite line of skin care products by Dr. Hauschka. Sample kits sell for only DM8 (about $6) and come in a metal box containing their whole line of products. You can try different travel-size bottles to see whether you like them.

◆ Reformhaus, Hauptbahnhof, S-Bahn station, First Floor, 089 593873.

PARIS

My first trip to Europe was with my family when I was twelve years old. On the approach to Orly, there was a delay at the airport, and the captain used the extra time to fly us over the city and around the Eiffel Tower. I was so excited that I threw up. A very understanding Pan Am stewardess helped my mother clean up my mess.

I've long since conquered airsickness, but not the excitement of flying to Paris. In my four decades of travel to the City of Light, I can honestly say I have never had a bad experience. For me, the stereotype of Parisians as rude and inconsiderate is about as far from the truth as one can get. "To understand Paris is like understanding a woman," one pilot told me. "You must surrender to her first, and then you can love her."

My surrender came years ago, and my love affair continues today. Paris remains one of the great cities for people watching in the world. Even if you're alone, you derive a certain sense of unexpected emotional fulfillment just by watching other people in love.

There's an inevitability to Paris—you can't avoid being in love with it. You don't just become enthused by the city, you become *infused* with it.

"If I can't fly into Paris at least once every ten days," a flight attendant once told me, "then my life isn't complete." Indeed, I don't care what the weather is in Paris as long as I can indulge in its pleasures. And thanks to my flight attendant friends, I have a sort of routine now when I arrive. Steak tartare at the café at the

Plaza Athénée, or a late afternoon lunch of a signature lobster sandwich at the Prince de Galles. Drinks at the small, charming bar at the Hotel Raphael. And dinner? Where to start? Where to finish?

I people-watch at Le Café Marly or at Brasserie Pittsburg. I'm drawn to the power hotels of the right bank, and I religiously return to the George V. But don't count out the Meurice Hotel. It's not just a sensational piece of art, but it has an incredible bookstore right next door. If money is no object, check out the Presidential Suite at the Hotel Royal Monceau, which has a bed that is said to be the biggest in Europe.

Also, the world's biggest flea market—on the outskirts of the city—is worth a visit. When you visit the Marché aux Puces Clignancourt on Saturdays, Sundays, or Mondays, you're not just looking—with two thousand vendors along twenty-three blocks, you *will* buy something.

Paris is also a hub for travel. Take the train from the Gare du Nord out to the Loire Valley for a balloon ride. Or rent a car and drive three hours out of the city to the medieval town of Troyes. Nearby, in the Champagne region, is the small Drappier champagne house, to which I go at least once a year—usually in September, to watch and sometimes participate in the annual grape harvest.

But I always return to Paris—frequently with a magnum or two of champagne. Not champagne to pack, mind you. Champagne to share.

AIRPORT TIPS

It is fairly convenient to get into the city. You can take either the RER train, which takes you to the center of the city, or Air France buses to designated points. A round-trip by bus costs about $12, and you can buy tickets outside the terminals where the buses stop or from the bus drivers. The Paris Métro system is very easy to use, even if you don't speak French. Every line is color-coded and number-coded, and maps are readily available. A taxi ride into Paris will cost you around $50, depending on where you are going, and most taxi drivers can find an address if it's written down. Taxi drivers in Paris seem be nicer these days.

The rapid RER train serves the airport. Line B runs from the TGV station at Terminal 2 to the Gare du Nord, Châtelet-les-Halles, St.-Michel, and Denfert-Rochereau, with connections for the Métro. Air France coaches depart from all terminals to Place Charles de Gaulle, Paris-Montparnasse, rue du Commandant Mouchotte, Gare de Lyon, and boulevard Diderot.

CITY TIPS

If you ever thought the French were rude and unfriendly, the Café du Commerce will change your mind. It is four stories high and built around an atrium. As you enter in the summer, you walk past cases of fresh seafood, where you are greeted by a tuxedo-clad maître d'. Immediately after being seated, a server brings you fresh bread right out of the oven, with butter. You also get the house wine, or you can order one of your choosing. If you are not familiar with the wines, the maître d' will be happy to help you pick one. In the summer, they open the old-fashioned wrought-iron roof to the sky. In the winter, the specialty is a stew delivered to your table in a black cast-iron pot with legs and a handle. The stew consists of a whole potato, a whole carrot, a whole onion, and a large piece of beef cooked in a delicious broth. A starter, dinner, and dessert will cost you only about 20 euros. The dishes are hearty, country-style French food. This is definitely not the spot for a romantic dinner be-

cause it's loud and busy. People at a nearby table may start a conversation with you, and before you know it they are sitting with you at your table. And don't worry if you do not speak French—an English menu is available.
◆ Café du Commerce, 51 rue du Commerce, 01 45750327, www.lecafeducommerce.com.

The Hotel Beaugrenelle is very small, but it's in a great location near the Eiffel Tower. There are many bakeries, grocery stores, and restaurants nearby, and it's only a few minutes from where you pick up the boats to cruise on the Seine. It's also just one block from a Métro station. Mr. Nasser, the hotel's owner, is warm and friendly, and has a wonderfully helpful front desk staff. There is a charming bar in the lobby of the hotel, which is open only to guests. Included with the price of a room is a French breakfast of cheese and sausages, fresh baguettes, and hot chocolate or coffee, which is served in the lobby.
◆ Hotel Beaugrenelle, 82, rue St.-Charles, 01 45786163, www. hotelbeaugralize.com.

Cristal Vendôme in the Place Vendôme, near the Louvre and the Hotel Intercontinental, is a wonderful place to go for fine crystal. Their prices are excellent.
◆ Cristal Vendôme, 1 rue de Castiglione, 01 49270960.

Levasseur is a magnificent art gallery, which represents some of the best local Parisian artists in a variety of media, including oil paintings, watercolors, and etchings.
◆ Levasseur, 232 rue de Rivoli, 01 42607759.

L'Épi Dupin in St.-Germain is one of the best-kept secrets in Paris. Every dish I've had there has been fabulous. It's not the most inexpensive restaurant—dinner will cost about $28, without wine—but it's worth it. If you are a chocaholic, be sure to try

the unbelievable tiny oval-shaped chocolate pastry, covered in chocolate sauce and filled with liquid chocolate.
◆ L'Épi Dupin, 11 rue Dupin, 01 42226456.

Ernest Hemingway used to hang out at Les Deux Magots, probably the best place in Paris for sitting, gossiping, and people watching. Their hot chocolate and wines are very good, though a bit pricey. You can sit outdoors year-round because they heat their outdoor seating.
◆ Les Deux Magots, 6 Place, 170 boulevard St.-Germain-des-Prés, 01 45 485525.

If you like cookies, then don't miss Ladue's. They make pista-chio, chocolate, lemon, and vanilla macaroons that are so fresh they have to be eaten within forty-eight hours. The tearoom and the coffee room are painted beautifully, and you are served with silver and china. Everything is gorgeous!
◆ Ladue's, 75 avenue des Champs Élysées, 01 40750875.

People go to Angelina's year-round to have their magnificent hot chocolate served in real china with chantilly—whipped cream cut with ice water because it is so rich. This treat costs $7 to $10, but it's well worth it! Angelina's was a favorite of Coco Chanel's. The seats by the window are the best.
◆ Angelina's, 226 rue de Rivoli, 01 42608200.

Sagil is where we go for tax-free and duty-free items. They have a good selection of makeup, perfume, scarves, Gucci sunglasses, and high-end watches at a huge savings.
◆ Sagil, 242 rue de Rivoli, 01 32607181.

Most Americans have no idea that they can bring back more than one or two bottles of wine. So find good, sturdy luggage and get a Styrofoam wine carrier from any upscale liquor store in the United States, which will allow you to safely check bottles of wine with your baggage. When you hit Paris, head for Les Domaines Qui Montent. In the St.-Germain shop, ask for Cyrille Pesquet, who speaks fluent English and gives great recommendations for wine.

◆ Les Domaines Qui Montent, 22 rue L'Abbé Gregoire, 01 45487340; 22 rue Cardinet, 01 42276396; 136 boulevard Voltaire, 01 43568915.

Nicholas's is a chain of very small stores in Paris, specializing mostly in wine. These stores are among the best places to buy wine in the city. The prices are nowhere near what we pay in the States. You can find a good bottle of red wine in France for $15 to $20. You might spend $150 for a comparable bottle in the States.

◆ Nicholas's, 31 place Madeleine, 01 49240852.

Monoprix is like a Target store, but with a grocery section and wines. I recommend a burgundy that you can find there called Brouilly, which should be served a bit chilled. They also stock a nice selection of Bordeaux.

◆ Monoprix, 21 avenue de l'Opéra, 01 42617808.

When it comes to romance, the bar at the Hôtel Coste takes the prize. This is one of the most exclusive old Parisian hotels, with extraordinary rooms, views, and decor.

◆ Hôtel Coste, 239 rue St.-Honoré, 01 42445000.

The Jardin du Luxembourg is a runner's paradise. The gardens are huge and beautiful, with statues and ponds and a pony ride for children. There's a château in the middle of it. It's all so . . . Parisian. It's also a wonderful place to go for a picnic with a bottle of wine. We sit and watch the painters near the pond. It's one of my favorite things to do, and there's no admission fee.

◆ Jardin du Luxembourg, located near the Sorbonne and just south of the Latin Quarter.

Peter Gage, a tiny salon within walking distance of the Hôtel de Ville, is a little intimidating because the stylists wear studded black leather and have that biker look, but people swear by the haircuts. Peter Gage, the owner, does not speak English, so there really isn't any consulting involved—you just go in there and let him do his thing. Cuts cost about 65 euros and take about two hours. The shop is very small—only one chair—so you have to make an appointment two weeks in advance.
◆ Peter Gage, 23 rue du Bourg, 01 42787972.

If you see a lot of flight attendants on their knees at the Church of the Miraculous Medal, don't worry about impending air disaster. They are simply joining the people who come here to pray to St. Catherine because of the inscription at the altar promising that those who pray here will have their prayers answered. Many people will attest to the validity of the claim. The church is near the Sedres/Babylon Métro stop, and right across from the Bon Marché, a nice department store.
◆ Church of the Miraculous Medal, 140 rue du Bac, 75340 Cedex 7, 01 49547888.

If you need to buy children's clothing, wait till you get to Paris. The clothing at the Du Pareil au Meme stores is made entirely of natural fabrics. They are very cute and reasonably priced. They carry sizes from infant to fourteen years.
◆ Du Pareil au Meme, 27 rue du Commerce, 01 45759340, www.dpam.com.

You can't go wrong with most of the selections on the menu at Le Bistrot de Breteuil, located in the very upscale 7th Arrondissemont overlooking the Place de Breteuil, a pretty square with a large statue near Les Invalides and the Tour Eiffel. Try the salad with goat cheese to start, and end with a crème brûlée for dessert. The portions are good-sized, and the main course comes with a vegetable. You also get a bottle of wine and coffee with your meal. It's a good idea to make a reservation for a good table. In summer you can dine outside, which can be a relief from the smokers inside.

◆ Le Bistrot de Breteuil, 3 place de Breteuil, 01 45670727.

The sepia-toned decor at Brasserie Flo will make you feel as if you have dropped in on a movie set from the 1930s. These restaurants generally occupy historical sites where the people watching tends to be most interesting. The food is good, and they usually offer a prix fixe menu that is midpriced by Parisian standards. Although you "own" the table for the evening in most French restaurants, you will find the service here very well or-chestrated. Don't forget that coffee always comes after dessert in France, so you don't look like an American tourist by expecting it when the dessert is served.

◆ Brasserie Flo, 7 cour de Petites-Ecuries, 01 47701359.

Un Peu restaurant is a little place on a tiny, hard-to-find street, but it has a reasonably priced menu and great food. You can enjoy an appetizer and a main course for 50 euros and order a nice house wine. The wait staff is very friendly, and they all speak En-glish. Start with a goat-cheese-topped lettuce salad, then try the rack of lamb, which is small but comes with a delicious honey-and-teriyaki sauce with a burning thyme branch to set it off.

◆ Un Peu, 1 rue Christine, 01 40517164.

Nestled between the Champ de Mars (the park leading to the Eiffel Tower) and Les Invalides, Le Bistrot du 7 offers surpris-ingly good food at an affordable price. The menu is extensive. Start with a Greek mushroom salad, and try the chèvre (goat cheese) for dessert. A demi carafe of a light, dry Rhône wine will make this memorable.

◆ Le Bistrot du 7, 56 boulevard Latour-Mauburg, 01 45519308.

Le Méridien Montparnasse is an expensive, but lovely, hotel. The rooms are slightly on the small side, but that's not uncommon in Europe. A typical French breakfast buffet consisting of an assortment of cheeses, meats, and rolls comes with the room. The staff is young, speaks English, and is very helpful. (You know what they say about the French being rude? It's not true.) Across the street is a major long-distance train station, convenient for regional travel.

◆ Le Méridien Montparnasse, 19 rue du Commandant Mouchotte, 01 44364436, www.lemeridien-montparnasse.com.

At La Maison du Miel you will find honey unlike any other you've had in the world. This shop is dedicated entirely to honey and honey-based products, such as soap and oil. Try the lavender honey!

◆ La Maison du Miel, 24 rue de Vignon, 01 47422670, www.maison-du-miel.com.

Maybe it just tastes good because you're eating it in Paris, but Berthillon, on the Ile St.-Louis, seems to have the best ice cream in the world—worth waiting in line for. When was the last time you had caramel ice cream or chocolate nougat? They also have a staggering variety of sorbets in flavors like apricot, cocoa, cherry, anise, green citron, and assorted berries. Be sure to try the fraise des bois—these berries look like miniature strawberries and have the most exquisite flavor.

◆ Berthillon, 31 rue St.-Louis en l'Ile, 01 43543161.

We had one of the best meals of our lives at Maison de Campagne. My friend raved about the duck. I had pork stuffed with prunes, and it was so good that it was embarrassing because I wanted to lick the plate! One tempting dessert was like molten chocolate. Dinner was $30 to $40 per person, with wine.

◆ Maison de Campagne, 18 bis, rue Pierre Demours, 01 45722851.

The first time we stumbled on La Relais de Venise, we thought we had made a terrible mistake. It was August and it was ninety degrees outside when we decided we wanted to eat steak. First, the waitress brings you a salad with a lovely vinaigrette dressing. If you finish it, she brings you more salad. Then she brings out the steak, which comes with a wonderful garlicky sauce and a big pile of pomme frites on the side. If you finish that off, she brings you more, and she'll bring you more pomme frites. And she keeps bringing them until you say no! They have fraise de bois and cream for dessert, if you still have room for it. The entire meal, with wine, was only 15 euros.

◆ La Relais de Venise, 271 boulevard Pereire, 014 5742797.

Many places in Paris are closed during August, but Bistrot St.-Ferdinand, near the Arc de Triomphe, is one place that remains open during the holiday month. They offer a prix fixe meal, which includes a kir royale, appetizer, entrée, dessert, and half a bottle of wine, for 29 euros.

◆ Bistrot St.-Ferdinand, 175 boulevard Perairearis, 01 45743332.

The American Hospital in Paris will treat any American who walks in the door. This is where flight crew members go whenever we have a medical problem in Paris.

◆ American Hospital, 63 boulevard Victor Hugo, 92200 Neuillu-sur-Seine, 01 46412525.

École de Ritz Escoffier is a cooking school at the Ritz Hotel. They mainly do cooking demonstrations, but you can also take classes there just by showing up. For $30, we spent about three hours learning how to prepare seafood. The interpreter was quite charming, with a good sense of humor, so we felt free to ask questions. The equipment and lighting were excellent, and they even gave us the recipes. Best of all, when the cooking was all done, we were allowed to sample it!

◆ École de Ritz Escoffier, place Vendôme, 75041 Cedex 01, 0143163050.

The real reason to go to Paris is to sample the cuisine. One of our favorite restaurants is Auberge de la Reine Blanche, which means "guest house of the white queen." This is a seventeenth-century house owned by Patrick Gentry, on Ile St.-Louis, one of the two islands right in the center of the city, surrounded by the Seine. It's a casual place—very cozy—but you should make reservations. The food is not only good, it's plentiful—almost too much. I advise you to be very hungry and be prepared to spend a few hours eating. In the winter the French onion soup is a good starter. I also recommend the coq au vin. They always have wonderful special dishes, and their fish is delicious.

◆ Auberge de la Reine Blanche, 30 rue St.-Louis en l'Ile, 01 46330787.

Au nom de la Rose, on the Rue du Bac in the St.-Germaine area, lives up to its name. The shop sells rose soaps, dried roses, rose pictures and prints, and every decorative rose-themed item you could think of. Their lovely soaps are very delicate, like rose petals.

◆ Au nom de la Rose, 46 rue du Bac, 01 42222212, www.aunomdelarose.fr.

If you find Julia Child inspiring, take a one-day course (called a "demonstration") at the Cordon Bleu cooking school. Contact the school directly to find out what they have scheduled. They usually offer two- or three-hour demonstrations in the mornings, afternoons, and evenings, during which they show professional techniques for making sauces, food preparation, and proper equipment use. You can watch them prepare something, and then you get to taste it afterward.

◆ Cordon Bleu, 8 rue Léon Delhomme, 01 53682250, paris@cordonbleu.net.

Although E. Dehillerin caters to professional chefs, anyone can shop there. They carry all types of very high quality cooking utensils and pots and pans, but they are especially recommended for their copper pots. Tax on cookware is really high—about eighteen percent—so show your receipts at the airport upon departing in order to get reimbursed.

◆ E. Dehillerin, 18 rue Coquillière, 1st Arrondissement, 01 42365313.

You must have a sense of humor to eat at Le Refuge du Passe. The owner was once an actor, and all the waiters are in show business in some way. They love to tease and joke around with customers—in fact, at times they can be downright insulting. It is much more fun if you are with someone who speaks and understands French so you can participate in the badinage. The restaurant is very cozy and small, and seating is almost family-style since the tables are so close together. The menu is in French, but most of the staff speak enough English that you should be able to order. Reservations are recommended.

◆ Le Refuge du Passe, 32 rue du Fer à Moulins, 01 47072991.

Although they serve chili later in the evening, you definitely don't come to the Rosebud Bar for the food—it's more of what you might call a watering hole. Hemingway and a lot of other writers used to spend time there. Neither large nor fancy, it's nevertheless a very busy (and smoky) place, and the conversation is always interesting around the tables and the large bar.

◆ Rosebud Bar, 11 bis rue Delambre, 14th Arrondissement, 01 43204413.

ROME

Since I was twelve, Rome has been, for me, a city of late afternoon shadows and golden magic light. Whether they are of standing on the Spanish Steps, being at the Vatican, or relaxing on the rooftop bar of the Eden Hotel (Fellini's old haunt), my memories of Rome are bathed in the special light that defines the Eternal City.

"I am never bored in Rome," one flight attendant told me. "But I get this feeling that with twenty-five hundred years of history, Rome is bored with me!"

I am often overwhelmed by the city, but not intimidated by it.

Yes, there's the Vatican, the Trevi Fountain (you really must toss in a coin for good luck), the Spanish Steps, and the other must-sees, but for me, Rome is a city to be experienced in slow motion. You walk slowly. You eat slowly. You take it all in slowly.

You have to love a city where most folks don't eat breakfast. Instead, they go to a local bar or café for "elevensas." (Eleven is when most of the bars/cafés open!)

Rome does not possess just one past, but an amazing collection of pasts. Pick the one you want and focus: Caesar or Goethe, Mussolini or Michelangelo. They're all still there, in one form or another. You discover the past in a nonlinear way. You never go anywhere directly in Rome. You simply drift, meander, and stray. Except, of course, in August, when everyone flees the city for the sea or the mountains.

But even in August, Rome can be enjoyed. Italy produces more different kinds of wine than any other country in the world.

And many of their finest wines are not well known beyond their region, so it's not surprising that flight crews love this country.

Prices are cheapest if you follow the Italian example and drink standing up at the bar. As soon as you sit down, the cost of your order goes up.

AIRPORT TIPS

Tazza d'Oro, at the Fiumicino Airport, is a famous coffee shop that serves really good sandwiches and coffee. They also will grind the coffee beans and pack them, so you can take them with you. Try the Greco sandwich—two pieces of pizzalike bread with spinach and provolone in between. A decaf cappuccino costs about $1.50, and the Greco sandwich runs about $2.
◆ Tazza d'Oro, Terminal A, Departure Hall, 06 65010646.

The easiest way to go through Customs seems to be to exit the airport to the left, although not many people know about it. (This is at the American Airlines desk.) It's not always open, but it's worth a try.

The quality of the food and beverages in hotels and airports in Europe seems much higher and more reasonably priced than in the United States. And if I'm ever stuck in an airport, I'd want it to be in Rome. The smell of espresso when you walk around just makes you feel good!

In Italy, the taxis are much smaller than the American ones, so keep this in mind when you use the World Traveler's bags (the big bags on wheels).

My favorite airport is Rome's Leonardo da Vinci because the duty-free shopping there is extraordinary—the best I've ever seen! You can get a bottle of Chianti for $8. They have fresh pastas, balsamic vinegars, and olive oils with herbs, garlic, and any flavor combination you can imagine. You can buy fabulous Italian mushrooms, fresh or dried.

◆ Departures Terminal, Airport General Information Line, 06 390665951.

CITY TIPS

Claudio Tacchi Marcello is a wonderful goldsmith and sculptor who runs a shop near the Spanish Steps at Via della Mercede. I take pictures of earrings and bracelets that I like from Neiman Marcus or Bergdorf Goodman, and he can replicate them for a fraction of what it would cost in the States. If you spend over a certain amount, then your tax is refunded. And he's reliable and fair. Because he works for himself, it's a good idea to call first to make sure he will be in his shop.

◆ Claudio Tacchi Marcello, Via della Mercede, 12/A, 06 6787546.

Girarrosto Fiorentino's serves good food—especially fish—at reasonable prices. It's not in the guidebooks, but Meryl Streep has been spotted here. The place is similar to an authentic trattoria, but some of the staff speak English and they are accustomed to dealing with Americans. Also, the place is air-conditioned, which is rare in Italy.

◆ Girarrosto Fiorentino's, 46 Via Sicilia, 06 42880660.

Once when I had food poisoning, the airline called Dr. Gianfranco Stoppani, who not only spoke English but had interned at one of the hospitals in New York City. He shared some important advice for people who travel: if you get sick to your stomach and vomit, it's probably something you ate within the past twelve hours. Sadly, Dr. Stoppani has passed away, but his wife still works at the office and Dr. Dominique Van Dorne, a former col-

league of Dr. Stoppani, has taken over his practice. So if you are in need of a doctor in Rome, she is attentive and thorough.
◆ Dr. Dominique Van Dorne, Piazza Jacini 26A, 06 3291795.

When I travel, I pack lots of shoes. The minute I land, I head for the shoemaker—there seems to be one near almost every hotel. Not only can the shoemakers in Rome fix any shoe, they are reasonable and they use materials that can withstand almost any abuse.

Graduating from just a warehouse, Lora Donna and her husband have opened a leather goods store called Grandi Firme, very near the Vatican. Although they specialize in bags, they also sell shoes, accessories, belts, gloves, and other leather goods.
◆ Grandi Firme, Via Aurelia 456 a+b, phone and fax 06 39723169.

Antico Caffé Greco is a famous café once frequented by politicians and movie stars and still retaining some of that old-time charm. But the place to go these days is Franco's, on the Via dei Gracchi near the Jolly Hotel. One day we looked over, and there was Marcello Mastroianni, with a coat flung over his shoulders.
◆ Antico Caffé Greco, Via de Condotti 86, 06 6791700.
Bar Franco, corner of Via Marcontonio Collona and Via dei Gracchi, 06 3216210.

Lots of Americans go to Rome to buy scarves, but they almost always overpay. They'll walk down Via Condutti and pay more than retail. We buy ours from the African and Pakistani vendors on the street. For the best deals, head over to the little kiosks on the Ponte Sant' Angelo. Scarves should cost under $10.

The Theater of Pompeii is now in ruins, but if you go downstairs, below the theater, you will find Pancrazio, a restaurant. The prices are moderate, and the food is excellent.
◆ Pancrazio, Piazza Biscione 92, 06 6861246.

In Europe the sales are in January and July, which is when you'll find dirt-cheap prices. Golf & Golf carries well-made, relatively inexpensive cotton shirts. They also sell sweaters, jeans, and dressier pants.

◆ Golf & Golf, Via del Campo Marzio 26, 06 6871507.

A friend asked me to buy him a wallet to give to his wife. I went to Prada, Gucci, and Fendi in London, but their wallets were in the $200 range and I didn't want to spend that much money. At Volterra in Rome, I was able to find a Valentino wallet for $80.

◆ Volterra, 48 Via del Pantheon, 06 6872582.

Most people wouldn't give Mr. Wine a second look because they have no idea what's downstairs in this wine shop—a huge and impressive wine cellar. Upstairs they have aperitifs, such as limoncello. If you ask, they will deliver to your hotel.

◆ Mr. Wine, Piazza del Parlamento 7, 06 68134141.

Ida Castellani, across from the Hotel Metropol, by the train station, sells the best gloves in Rome, and the most reasonably priced. A pair of cashmere-lined gloves costs about $28. She also sells scarves, wallets, and ties.

◆ Ida Castellani, Via Principe Amadeo, 06 4774895.

After I admired the stunning designer outfit that one of the flight attendants wore one evening, she divulged her secret and took us to Vantagio. This little place has wonderful second-hand designer clothes, such as the beautiful Burberry silk pants I found for $25 or the Malo cashmere sweater that was about $40.

◆ Vantagio, Via Vantagio, Number 1.

At L'Eau Vive, a restaurant run by Palatine nuns, the workers are all young missionaries from the Immaculate Conception convent. They serve a French continental menu with wonderful dishes including crepes, scallops with vodka sauce, pâté, coconut shrimp, salmon and a variety of baked fish, and delicious fresh vegetables and salads. Their à la carte or prix fixe menus range from about L15,000 (about $7.50 U.S.) to L50,000 (about $25), including everything except wine. The service is very elegant and attentive. This relaxing restaurant has two levels, with seating for two hundred. The second floor is decorated with beautiful, Renaissance-style frescoes and vaulted ceilings. Upstairs there are two large rooms and a smaller private dining room.

On my first flight to Europe after the events of September 11, four of us from the flight went to L'Eau Vive for a wonderful dinner and a very uplifting experience. We joined a group from Britain and the BBC, and witnessed the special performance in which the nuns danced and sang.

◆ L'Eau Vive, Via Monterone 85, 06 68802101.

SEOUL

My first flight to Seoul was in 1978 on board a large, bright orange Braniff 747. Earlier that year, with airline deregulation in full force in the United States, the management of Braniff decided they would fly every possible route not only in the United States, but in the world as well.

Braniff was trying to fly so many new routes that the airline literally ran out of aircraft. The Braniff logo was painted on the outside of our 747, but the inside was Lufthansa, and all the signage was in German.

The 747 had a passenger capacity of about 375 people. But on board that inaugural flight, including the flight crew of 14, there were just 32 people.

Our flight was a turnaround flight, meaning that the next flight from Los Angeles—our return flight—was not until five days later.

One of the flight attendants knew an American woman who was acting as curator for the Korean National Museum. We hooked up with her, and within a day she had taken us inside the back rooms of the galleries and shops on the Itaewon. She took us where the tourists were never invited.

As a result, I was able to purchase some antique wooden stacking chests from the Yi dynasty, some Korean wooden cooking tables, and an armoire built in Korea during the Japanese occupation.

While we were doing our shopping with the flight attendants, the Braniff cockpit crew was doing its part to improve

Korea's foreign exchange rate. The captain actually purchased a brand-new Hyundai—a make then unheard of in the United States—and had it loaded into the cargo hold of the 747, along with my furniture!

Not surprisingly, with such low passenger loads, Braniff stopped flying to Korea shortly thereafter, and the pleasure of a five-day layover became only a memory.

Today, virtually every major airline flies to Seoul, and South Korea boasts a vibrant economy that could easily become the strongest in Asia.

While most of the stuff on sale on the Itaewon is reproductions, you can still go there for the entertainment. Remember, the U.S. Army still has a major presence here, so check out the clubs. Or head to the Namdaemun market—an open-air market where you can find some of the best deals. And downstairs from the Namdaemun is the Namraemun, two floors of black-market goods.

CITY TIPS

All the brochures will tell you to shop on the Itaewon—that's because all the unsuspecting foreign visitors shop there. You won't find many bargains, and almost all the antiques are actually medium-to-good reproductions. Most of the good pieces are either in the museums or have already been taken out of the country.

After an exhausting day of shopping, treat yourself to a great American meal at the Nashville Bar, about a five-minute walk from the main gate of Itaewon. Here you can find hamburgers, popcorn, and pool tables while American movies and music play.

◆ Nashville Bar, 148 Jongro 4ga Jonggroku, 82 2 2273 4957.

If you crave more local cuisine, try Sanchon. Here you can find buddhist-vegetarian fare with a set menu in English. The meal consists of many small courses, with noodles, rice, and soup. The atmosphere is comfortable, with pillows on the floor.

◆ Sanchon, 14 Kwanhoondong Jongroku, 82 2 735 0312.

You can get everything from shirts to shoes at Manchester Tailors. They make nice clothing that's inexpensive. I've bought custom-tailored suits and shirts with French cuffs. They'll make ostrich and snakeskin shoes, but be careful—although they'll make you things from any kind of animal hide, it may be illegal to bring them into the United States. The man to see is Cookie, who speaks excellent English. He'll pull out a book from which you can pick out the style you want—and it's done for you in a day!

◆ Manchester Tailors, #58-5 Itaewon-Dong, Yongsan-KU, 02 790 5285.

We like to use the gym at the Grand Hyatt Hotel. You have to be a hotel guest, but the facilities are modern and well maintained, and the staff is helpful. There are outdoor and indoor pools, an aerobics area, a cardio area, and lots of weights. It's open early in the morning, which is convenient.

◆ Grand Hyatt Hotel, 747-7 Hannam-Dong Yongsan-Ku, 02 797 1234, info@grandhyattseoul.com.

SHANGHAI

In 1984, I sailed into Shanghai for the first time. As soon as I got off the ship, the *Ocean Pearl,* which was to remain in the harbor for two days during our tour, a Chinese man rode up to me on his bicycle. "You from the ship?" he asked in perfect English. I nodded. He held out his hand to shake mine. "Joe Cheng," he offered. "Great to meet you."

I asked if he lived in Shanghai. "All my life," he beamed. "Your first time here?" he asked. Yes, I told him.

He looked to be about forty. He was actually seventy-eight. And he was in great shape. Cheng proceeded to tell me his story. He was raised in a poor family in Shanghai, the only one in his family selected to learn English because they could only afford to send one child to school. Later, during World War II, his English came in handy, and he was brought on to be one of the aides to an American admiral on the U.S.S. *Missouri.*

In 1948 and again in 1949, the admiral urged him to come work for him back in Hawaii. "I always told him I would come later." Cheng remembered watching the *Missouri* sail out of Shanghai for the last time. Then came the Chinese Civil War, led by Mao Zedong—and "later" never came for Joe Cheng.

Because he spoke English, Cheng was considered a traitor and was banished to dig air raid shelters in the countryside when Richard Nixon visited China in 1971. But by the time I encountered him, things had changed; he was now back living in Shanghai and eager to show me the city.

We spent almost the entire next forty-eight hours together,

visiting the Shanghai of his past and experiencing the new city as well. We strolled the Bund, where we could still make out some of the old, faded logos of the Western companies that once had a large presence here—Shell Oil, British American Tobacco. "If you look hard enough," Joe suggested, "you just might see the ghosts of the American MPs rounding up the drunken sailors."

Joe made money by teaching English—a language once banned—to locals in Shanghai. Many of his students had moved to the United States. "I hope to get there one day," he said, "but they won't give me a visa." At one point, I was crossing a bridge across the appropriately named Huang Pu River (yes, it stinks) and had the distinct impression that I was being followed—not just by one person, but by a number of people. And so, when I summoned the courage to turn around, imagine my surprise to find myself surrounded by about thirty Chinese people who found my Western dress and beard curious. They were following me hoping that I would turn around so they could practice their English!

Over at the old Cathay Hotel, renamed the Peace Hotel by the Chinese communists, a large, broken, four-sided electric clock in the art deco lobby displayed the time in the world's leading cities—Beijing, Moscow, Bucharest, and Prague. And at night, the world's oldest jazz band (average age eighty) attempted to play Duke Ellington and Benny Goodman.

China was indeed changing, and nowhere was that change felt more than in Shanghai. Fourteen million people were getting their confidence back and celebrating the birthplace of Chinese capitalism, home of Asia's biggest stock exchange, and its biggest city. New hotels. World-class restaurants.

I'll always remember my second trip to Shanghai, just a year later. The same jazz band was struggling at the Peace Hotel, but right across the street they had opened the Peace Café. I went in for lunch—and ordered a bacon, lettuce, and tomato sandwich.

Anita Baker was singing on the loudspeakers. And the manager had permed his hair. As I paid the check and got up to leave, the manager walked over to me. "Enjoy your lunch?" he asked. "Absolutely," I responded. "OK, see you later, alligator," he said, and I waved in return. "*No!*" he yelled, running after me. "You're supposed to say, "In a while, crocodile!"

Before you think Shanghai has become totally westernized, do not despair. Just go to the flower and bird market or the long bar (what's left of it) on the Bund, or try dinner at Lei Long Zhen, one of Shanghai's oldest and finest restaurants. And you can still buy some mementos of the Cultural Revolution any place in town.

Just three years after I first met Joe, I came back and brought friends. I tried to reach him, and a relative told me he no longer lived in Shanghai. He had moved—to Manhattan!

CITY TIPS

You are guaranteed an unusual experience at Hong Zi Ji (the Red Chicken), a flight crew favorite. All the servers wear roller skates as they follow diners to the seafood tanks, where you point to what you want and they write it down. Next you select shellfish, snake (really!), or eel from their respective tanks, and any delectables you might desire from the tidal pool. At the end of the line, everything is weighed (you are charged by weight for these items) and taken to the kitchen to be prepared for you. Then you and your waiter proceed to the other side of the line, where you point to the vegetables, pork, duck, chicken, soup, and rice (regular or fried) that you would like. In addition to all this food, you get a floor show consisting of a dozen women who dance and sing and go through a number of costume changes, as well as two sisters who perform tricks on their roller skates. (They are surprisingly good.) As in many Asian countries, there is no tipping here. Our bill for three people, with beer and wine, came to about $40. Reservations are recommended, and unless you arrive with someone who speaks Chinese, it is wise to make sure the restaurant captain, Feng Tao, is working that night.

◆ Hong Zi Ji, 188 Aomen Road, 021 62661188.

A must-stop for me after a long flight to Shanghai is a spa called Sea Cloud Bathing House, located in a six-story building about five blocks from the Holiday Inn Crown Plaza. There are separate ladies' and men's levels for the baths, which include aloe baths, lucidian baths, and steam baths. You are required to remove your clothing for these, so if you are very modest, you might want to bring your own towel because the ones they give you are too small to cover you completely. If you go only for the baths, the cost is $5. However, you can also get a full body scrub, reflexology treatment, and wonderful Chinese accupressure massages that focus on different body parts or all over. (The massage area is coed, but you wear pajamas for this.) You can also receive a special treatment that uses heated glass balls that are placed on your back to remove the bad *chi* (energy). The building includes a billiard room as well as a very nice teahouse.

◆ Sea Cloud Bathing House, 888 Fanyu Lu, 021 64070011.

Eddy Tam's Gallery does professional art and picture framing. They have a wide selection of frames and they will package everything for delivery to your hotel room or for you to take back. Ask for Kitty, who will handle everything for you. They do very creative work, such as the baby outfit of mine that they framed in a unique shadowbox arrangement. Including the matting, most framing work will cost under $20, and they are very reliable.

◆ Eddy Tam's Gallery, 15 and 20 Maoming Nan Road, 021 62536715, e-mail eddytam@eastday.com.

Need something tailored quickly, or even a new suit? In Shanghai, we always go to Danni Design Company. Qiumin Lu, the proprietor, is fast, cheap, and fantastic. She can do alterations as well as create new garments based on a design that you like. Everything is very inexpensive, and the quality of the work is dependable.

◆ Danni Design Company, #99 Fahua Zheng Road, 021 62820925.

SINGAPORE

I remember when Singapore was Asia's party town. Flight crews loved it because it was a living, breathing amusement park without artificial rides. This was a time when the bum boats were on the water, the hawkers and the satay stands flourished, and the transvestites would pose on Bugis Street. I remember the "peddlers"—the old men in incredibly good physical shape who would run you around town on tricycles built for three. As you rode around the old Arab Street, you'd look over and on the next tricycle there'd be a Pan Am crew having just as much fun as you were. We were all headed for the Long Bar at the old Raffles, serving the positively overrated and borderline-disgusting Singapore sling.

Today, some people call Singapore boring—and to a certain extent, it is. The government of Lee Kuan Yew did its best to sterilize the place. Where else is chewing gum (or even possessing it) illegal? The bum boats and the rhythm of Bugis Street are long gone. But the food is better than ever, though you'll have a hard time finding it on the streets anymore. These days, virtually everything is located in indoor food courts, but once inside you're in for a treat: everything from noodles to soups and Indian curries awaits.

Then there's Chinatown (and the massive Chinatown complex), with restaurants like the Jolly Yummy (try the chicken rice) or Joe Pork and Fish Porridge (don't let the name scare you), where you can sample the soup. (It's stand number 02-069 if you get lost.)

If you don't go to Singapore to shop or eat, go for the gardens and the parks. It's a small island state that has ten thousand acres of parklands—not to mention a pretty amazing bird park. Even the terminals at Changi International are botanical wonders—passengers get to see exotic species at the well-managed hangar.

Raffles is still there—it's been redone and the hotel upgraded. But let me warn you: enjoy a drink there, or two. But the Singapore sling is still one of the most thoroughly pathetic drinks ever invented.

AIRPORT TIPS

I like to buy live orchids in the airport and take them home for friends. The shop is about twenty meters from Customs—you can't miss it because it attracts a crowd. Twenty-five stems will cost about $7 U.S. There are no seeds, which is why you can bring them on board. There are many different colors and types available, and they last for a couple of weeks.
◆ Galactic Flower Shop, Terminal 2 Departure Transit Central, Terminal 2 Departure Check-In North, +65 5425766.

The airport has an outdoor pool that costs $10.30 for admission, including towels and showers. In addition to the pool, there's a Jacuzzi, bamboo garden, and cactus garden in Terminal 1, and a garden terrace in Terminal 2.

The Singapore Airport is crowded, but it's also spacious and airy, with high ceilings and a lot of light coming in. Although there are lots of people around, you feel like you have space and it's less pressured than other airports.

CITY TIPS

In the Little India area on Seragoon Road there are shops selling a variety of fresh and exotic spices. You can also get curries
in different varieties and mixtures than you will find at home.
They come packaged in little plastic bags for easy transport.
Your hotel can give you maps and directions; you can take the
bus there and the shops stay open late.
◆ Little India, Seragoon Road.

The Night Safari at the Singapore Zoo is a great opportunity to
see all the nocturnal animals in action. The zoo provides a tram
to take you around, and gives you background information on all
the animals. You can also get quite near them through the plastic glass—you can stare straight into the eyes of a hyena, for example. You can take a train, bus, or cab to the zoo, and they
allow you to walk around after the tour.
◆ Night Safari, Singapore Zoo, +65 2741322, www.zoo.com.sg.
Animal shows at 8 and 9 P.M. daily.

Star Cruise ships have casinos on board and local people use
them for gambling on the weekends, so during the week the
company offers cruises to try to fill the ships. These cruises are
very casual and, compared to other cruises, very cheap. The ship
makes its way up the Straits of Malacca along the Malaysian
coast to Puget and then turns back, so you get to see a lot of the
countryside. There is a different destination each day except the
last day, which is spent on the return trip. You can book your
ticket directly through Star Cruises, and you have a choice of
rooms: standard, a room with big windows, or one with a balcony. This is a nice change from Singapore if you have five days
to spare for an inexpensive cruise, and the passengers are not
only old people—there are families and single people as well.
The program includes a wide variety of things to do—theater,
modern rock bands, and more.

◆ Star Cruises, reservations +65 60331011313,
www.starcruises.com.

Nothing beats Sentosa Beach for a jog. It's my favorite running beach. It's on an island and is open only for limited hours, so go early (it opens at 6 A.M.) and beat the heat. You can take the ferry there for about $1. The Dragon Trail, which is for kids, has all sizes and shapes of model dragons.
◆ Sentosa Beach, Ferry Terminal, located directly opposite the World Trade Centre, www.newasia-singapore.gen.in/attractions/isles/getting.html (four-minute ride from mainland to Sentosa).

Go to Fisherman's Village for lunch or dinner and sit at tables right on the beach. This place is so far out of the city that mostly only local people go there, and it's very cheap. They show you live fish, and you point out which one you want. They grill all the fish there and serve them on huge palm leaves. A one-pound fish will cost you $5 to $6 U.S. In the evening, the place is wonderful because it's not too humid. Most people there don't speak fluent English, so you point and smile a lot. It's about one hour from the city, and public transportation is available.
◆ Fisherman's Village, 167 Pasir Iris Road, +65 2769595, +65 5851211.

At Wing Seong Fatty's Restaurant you'll pay less than $20 U.S. for a full stomach and two or three Tsingtao or Tiger beers. This is a fun place for people watching, and the food is good, too. (Try the garlic green beans.) It doesn't stay open late because it's a bit far from town, so get there by 7 or 8 P.M. Located between the harbor and Orchard Road, which is famous for its nightlife and shopping centers, you can get to it by taxi from downtown or take the subway.
◆ Wing Seong Fatty's Restaurant, Bencoolen Street 175m, +65 3381087.

When I'm not flying, I'm an actor, so I'm always looking for fabrics for costumes. In Singapore, Arab Street is my favorite place to buy fabrics because of the wide variety. It's a row of about twenty shops along a two-hundred-meter-long street. You can find lots of silks and organzas, and I've also bought a lot of stuff with sequins. Prices range from S$1.50 to S$10 per meter, about a third of what you'd normally pay.

If you need to relax after a long flight, visit Origin Foot Massage. This treatment is based on Egyptian reflexology, which starts with the pressure points on your foot, each of which corresponds to a different part of your body. The forty-five minute treatment will run the gamut from pain to pleasure, but afterward you will feel like you are walking on air!
◆ Origin Foot Massage, 7 Raffles Boulevard, +65 3362802.

I regard my flights to Singapore as clothing shuttles—I bring either my own clothes or outfits from friends and have them copied superbly at Prince Tailors. This is not a typical shopping mall—you're encouraged to bargain, which can cut the prices in half. (Never accept the first price.) Last time I was there, I ordered a tux and suit in the afternoon. They were ready that evening and were even delivered to my hotel room. I paid around $600 for both, and they threw in two monogrammed shirts and some silk ties for free. These are high-quality, custom-tailored garments. The cost in the United States would be over $1,100. If they do not finish an order in time for your departure, they can ship it as dry cleaning so no duty is paid. Ask for Sam.
◆ Prince Tailors, 400 Orchard Road, 01-26 Orchard Towers, +65 7351989, e-mail princetailors@lycos.com.

Orchard Road is not the best area for shopping. I learned that when a crew member took me to an area called Little India, a high-rise shopping center where all the stores specialize in electronics. Tourists tend not to find Little India because it's not very close to the big hotels. Go to Sim Lim Towers and Sim Lim Square. I looked at a Panasonic Home Theater with a DVD player and sound system that at home (New Zealand) would normally cost about $1,700 N.Z., but in Little India was S$900 ($1,100 N.Z.). The best thing to do is to compare prices and bargain.

◆ Sim Lim Towers and Sim Lim Square, Rochor Canal Road. Visit SLS Computer Components Pricelist Page at
web.singnet.com.sg/ ~ maxxum/price.html.

SOUTH AMERICA

To most Americans, South America remains an enigma that is just beginning to be discovered by the masses.

Honestly, Lima is not my favorite layover city. But it does have a purpose. While Lima is the industrial, political, and commercial center of Peru, most flight crews will tell you it's really the way station en route to Cuzco and Machu Picchu. Lima is a city of chaos, pollution, and guerrilla street shopping. You can't go anywhere without confronting the *ambulantes*—the street sellers. In fact, if you can't find it on the streets, then you just can't find it.

Rio is, well, wild. It's an extremely busy port, with an even busier airport. The more than 5.5 million Cariocas who live there sure know how to party. Although Rio is not Brazil's largest city, it certainly acts that way. One or two blocks off the main beach streets, you'll discover that the city is one of the most troubled in the world. About twenty percent of the people who live in Rio merely *exist* in the favelas, which blanket the slopes of surrounding hillsides. The slums are dangerous, unemployment is high, and crime is a problem.

The good news about Rio is that with a little common sense, you can survive and even enjoy it. Starting with the food, try the mashed beans with roasted pork loin, cabbage, and rice, and my favorite, *churrasco*, the wide variety of great barbequed meats.

São Paolo (the largest city) may be the industrial and financial center of Brazil, but it's a flight crew secret for shopping and eating. With more than one million Japanese living in São

Paolo, it is the largest Japanese city outside of Tokyo. It has great sushi. And with three million Italians living there, it has great pasta, too.

Buenos Aires is complex, conflicted, and always frenetic. It never sleeps, and no one ever eats early there. It is also one of the more seductive cities in the world. The flight crews turned me on to the outdoor cafés and the weekend markets, and steered me clear of the touristy tango shows. We rented boats and cruised the Río de la Plata, did day trips to Uruguay, and hopped planes for the short ride up to Iguazu and the Devil's Gorge. On longer trips we motored out into the countryside for overnights at the romantic and elegant *estancias,* and I even tried to ride horses that I was convinced were determined to kill me.

B.A. is perhaps the most elegant, European-styled city in South America, where Italian and German names outnumber Spanish. Argentina just happens to be the world's eighth-largest country in the world.

My favorite South American country is Chile. The first time there, I wasn't expecting much, and was I misinformed! Not only did a B.A. flight attendant show me how badly misinformed I was, but she met a local man, married him, and now lives in Santiago. Consider this: this little string bean of land has it all—the Pacific Ocean, the Andes, more lakes than you ever thought possible, and Patagonia, with fjords and glaciers. In Santiago you are thirty miles from ski slopes and sixty miles from beaches. I haven't even mentioned the seafood and wine in the Bellavista district, the elegant bars of the General Holley district, and the amazing Thai seafood restaurant out by the pool at the Hyatt. But the best part is that Santiago has one of the highest standards and lowest costs of living in South America. The clincher is that the country has one of the most advanced, sophisticated telecommunications networks I've ever experienced. For an e-mail junkie like me, Chile is a dream come true. I wouldn't be surprised if, within the next few years,

I ended up buying a place on the coast, near a nineteenth-century former fishing village named La Serena.

AIRPORT TIPS

São Paolo

São Paolo's Guarulhos Airport is a nice, big international airport with a McDonald's. Order a *guarana*, a delicious soda made from the guava fruit. It tastes almost like ginger ale.

◆ McDonald's, Terminal 2, Floor 1.

If you miss a flight, stay at the excellent Hotel Deville Guarulhos, with easy transportation to and from the airport as well as to points downtown.

◆ Hotel Deville Guarulhos, Avenido Monteiro Lobato S/N, CeCap-Cumbica, Guarhulhos 07190-000, (011) 6468-0400.

CITY TIPS

Buenos Aires

Buenos Aires is a city in turmoil, but its energy is very attractive. Grant's, on the street level in the Recoleta area, is a crew favorite for dinner because the food is delicious and affordable. Their huge dinner buffet includes sushi, Chinese food, grilled meat, lamb, and a large assortment of appetizers, all for $10.

◆ Grant's, Las Heras 1925, 011 4801 9099.

As in Spain, nothing here really starts till after 10 P.M., but then Milion, a hip tapas bar, is a fun place to go. It's located in an old three-story mansion. In the courtyard, there's a small garage where they show black-and-white movies. Upstairs, you sit among the columns at little tables with white table-cloths and candles. It's a very medieval and dramatic-looking place.

◆ Milion, Parana 1048 Capital, 011 4815 9925, milion@sion.com.

Chilean wines may be lighter and more popular, but people like me who enjoy a full-bodied cabernet or merlot prefer the Argentine wines, from the Mendoza region. Fond de Cave and Trapiche are two good varieties to try.

The famous San Telmo Market is held on Sundays and attracts lots of people, including many tourists. We go at eight in the morning, when the vendors are setting up, or at five in the evening, when they are packing up. You can find wonderful antique brass fixtures, even mailboxes and doorbells. We also look for antique pewter seltzer bottles, with beautiful old-style green glass. Other collectibles found here include the very old Bakelite telephones; although they're not wired for the United States, the conversion is easy.

◆ San Telmo Market, Main Square, Plaza Dorrego.

Take the train down to Le Tigre, an Argentine version of Cape Cod, about a forty-minute ride from town. For about $5, you can ride on the charming, old-style train. The train station itself is in a beautiful building.

◆ Tren de la Costa, Estación Delta, Le Tigre, 011 47326300X0; Estación Maipu, Olivios, 011 43174400 (Olivios is a neighborhood in Buenos Aires).

You can get great custom-made leather goods, such as pants, skirts, and vests, from Silvia Chocron.

◆ Silvia Chocron, Marcelo T. de Alvear 550, 1058 Capital Federal, 011 3131788.

Lima

Check out the Indian Market in a nice area of the city called Mira Flores. You will find crafts and items like sweaters and llama blankets that are as soft as cashmere. Everything is very cheap, but be sure to bargain. It's easy and safe to walk to this area.

◆ Mira Flores, 6th and 10th blocks of Avenue La Marina, Pueblo Libre, Petit Thouars, blocks 51–54.

In the little park in front of the Catholic church in Mira Flores, there is live music on Sundays. Local artists sell paintings of the cathedral for very cheap. Then we head for the Museo del Oro del Peru (Museum of Gold), to see the Indian artifacts made of gold.

◆ San Francisco Church, 3rd Block of Ancash Street.
Museo del Oro del Peru, Alonso de Molina 1100 Monterrico, 01 4352917.

Montevideo

Whenever we're in Uruguay, we head for the Leather Factory in Plaza de Independencia, which is across the square from the crew hotel. The factory is located above a restaurant, and when you walk up the stairs you will see patches from all the different air force crews that have visited the factory over the last thirty years. These same military flight crew members come back today as commercial airline pilots to buy leather goods and look for their military patches from twenty years ago. This place can custom-tailor any leather garment, and the prices are excellent. A leather jacket might go for around $60. Look for a guy named Walter—he is there religiously, seven days a week.

◆ Leather Factory, 832, Montevideo, 02 901 6226.

Rio de Janeiro

I love going to the hippie fair, on the border between Copacabana and Ipanema, right on the water. It's similar to a flea market. This is a great place to find handbags—I bought six for under $100.

Dining out in Brazil is good and so cheap. A lot of crew members go to Barra Grill, for the typically South American *churrascaria*. You serve yourself from a buffet that includes sushi, salads, and desserts. Servers also walk around offering meat on a stick, which has been marinated and cooked over an open grill until it is very flavorful and so tender that you can eat it with a fork. (The thing to remember is that they always bring around the cheaper cuts of meat first, so you have to pace yourself.) The salmon is particularly good, but you have to request it because it doesn't appear on the menu. Be sure to try their cheese bread and excellent pastries, too. A meal, including appetizers, main course, wine, and coffee, will cost around $18. Dress is business casual, so I wouldn't go in jeans—locals tend to dress a little more formally. The inside is quite large, and the service is really good. Since South Americans tend to eat late, you should have no problem if you go at 7 P.M., but if you go around 9 P.M., which is family hour, it will really be packed. Give yourself plenty of time to eat.
◆ Barra Grill, 314 Ministro Ivan Lins Avenue, Barra da Tijuca, 021 4934003.

LeBoy, a gay dance club in LeBlon, is a big place with multiple levels and guys dancing in cages. They play house music and technopop, and they also have a drag-queen show. It's a young and trendy place, mostly for people under thirty, but it's not as snotty as a similar place would be in the States. Celebrities such as Brazilian supermodel Giselle Bundchen have been spotted here.
◆ LeBoy, Rua Raul Pompeia, 102 Copacabana, 021 5134993.

We like to go hang-gliding with Paolo Celani at Just Fly, south of Copacabana. You're harnessed tandem-style to another person, who takes pictures of you with a camera mounted to the

wing. Your first jump costs around $65, but the price goes down for your next jump. Flights last about a half hour and always depend on the weather. Cash payment is preferred.
◆ Just Fly, 021 22680565 tel/fax, 021 99857540 mobile, justfly@justfly.com.br.

They dump sewage right into the bay, so the ocean is very polluted in Rio and I would avoid swimming there. However, there's good surfing for medium-to-experienced surfers at Barra, a beach about forty minutes north of Rio. For about $25 you can take a cab to Barra, and the driver will wait for you if you negotiate this beforehand. You can rent boards on the beach at Barra for about $3 for two hours or so. You don't need a wetsuit, because the climate is equatorial—the temperature remains in the mid- to high 70s year-round. It's a good idea to have a waterproof wallet, so that you can keep all your money on you. (I don't trust the combination safes in the hotels.) Don't end up on the beach at night. If you leave by 3 P.M., you will miss the traffic heading back into Rio.
◆ Barra beach, Avenue Sernambetiba.

Marius is a fantastic buffet-style restaurant serving different kinds of salads and a wide array of seafood, including clams, mussels, and calamari. At your table, ask the waiter for *picanha*, which is more flavorful than filet mignon. The buffet costs about $14, and the service here is excellent. Located in the Leme area on the Copacabana Beach, this place is an interesting and eclectic mix of styles, from the contemporary, multicolored roof to the glossy wood floors and the vaguely nautical decor.
◆ Marius, Avenida Atlantica 290, 021 5422393.

Santiago

Providencia, near the Sheraton Hotel, is a popular area of bars, hotels, and clubs. Entre Negros on General Holly Street is a youth-oriented local hangout, where they play a lot of American music, with a Chilean song or two mixed in. Overall, the prices are pretty reasonable.

◆ Sheraton Hotel, Avenue Santa Maria 1742, 02 2335000; Avenue Suecia 0186, 02 3342094.

You can get anything you want to eat in Santiago. Chilean-Thai? No problem at the Hyatt Regency. Want French food? Go to Kilometre, the best French restaurant in Santiago, famous for its wines and cheeses.

◆ Hyatt Regency, Kennedy Avenue 4601, 02 2181234.
Kilometre, Dardignac 0145, Providencia Santiago, 02 7770410.

Como Agua Para el Chocolate is a very good seafood restaurant in the old section of town.

◆ Como Agua Para el Chocolate, Constitucion 88, 02 7778740.

Carmencita's is a reliable place to get all kinds of clothes altered, at very reasonable prices. Your garments can be ready the next day if you ask, or you can pick them up on your next trip.

◆ Carmencita's Portugal 56, Local 7, Alto FTE, Torre #6, 02 665-2867.

São Paolo and Campinas

The best way to travel within Brazil is by some form of mass transit because the traffic is horrendous. Instead of driving, take the Capparelli bus, which will cost $12 to $15 round trip to get wherever you need to go. These buses are more comfortable than touring Greyhound buses, with seats that recline, TVs that are operational, and headrests that have linen on them.

◆ Capparelli Bus, 011 2218940.

At the tables in Brazilian churrascarias, you use a green token to indicate to the waiter that you want more food, and a red token to mean "Slow down, I'm too full right now." They keep bringing you delicious filet mignon–like meats called *picanha*, which are so flavorful and tender that they just slice it off the spit onto your plate. Twenty seconds after the first serving, another waiter comes over with roast pork. This continues until you indicate "no more." There's also a bountiful buffet of vegetables and accompaniments.

Nine West shoes are made in South America, and at Banana Price, you can get them for around $20 a pair.
◆ Banana Price, Alameda Lorena #1604, 011 30813460.

Gepedra and his son, who run a mom-and-pop jewelry shop, will repair, copy, or design anything you want in 18-karat gold. For example, they created an alligator out of green emeralds for a friend. They can redo the settings of antique rings. And Gepedra will sit with you and discuss your needs.
◆ Gepedra's, Rua Haddock Lobo, Suite 137, ph/f 011 8539204 and 30632763, www.gepedras.com.br.

About an hour and a half by bus outside of São Paolo there's a town called Campinas that's noted for its university. The best hotel there is the Royal Palm Plaza Hotel & Racquet Club, which is upscale, but worth it for the wonderful pool and great buffets. A lovely lunch for two will cost about $35.
◆ Royal Palm Plaza Hotel Resort, Avenue Royal Palm Plaza #277, Jardim Plaza, Nova California, 019 37388000.

If you're a dancer, then Brazil is the place to go. Americans dance with their shoulders, but Brazilians dance with their hips. You can't avoid the nightlife in Campinas, where you will find a lot of places to put your dancing skills to the test.

If you want to get around in Brazil, you can rent a simple car that runs on propane or alcohol, because regular gas is way too expensive there. The alcohol-burning cars are generally pretty small—typically, Fiats and some small Fords such as the Fiesta. You can get rental information from Localiza Rent A Car.

◆ Localiza Rent A Car, 031 32477100, www.localiza.com.br.

If you rent a car, make the trip to a beach called Uba Tuba, about a three-hour drive from São Paolo. It's in a nice residential area, and it attracts lots of young people—and lots of middle-aged people acting younger! Although it's a bit touristy, there are a couple of nice restaurants and hotels.

The São Paulo area is a great place for antiquing and thrift shopping, with prices generally much lower than in the United States. Almost every city in Brazil has what they call a hippie fair, which is basically a swap meet where all the merchandise is handcrafted. In Belo Horizonte, the fair is on Alfonso Pena, next to the city park, where the trees are large and the foliage is just beautiful. At the fair, you pay in cash and barter for everything. In smaller cities like Belo, the people are friendlier and you can bargain more easily than in Rio, where they are used to tourists. Since the fair is located in the mining area, you can find good deals on topaz, aquamarine, and other precious and semi-precious stone jewelry.

SYDNEY AND MELBOURNE

On my first flight into Australia, right after the Qantas captain announced we were starting our approach into Sydney, a woman sitting in the row in front of me rang her flight attendant call button. When the purser approached, she asked him, "What's the best side of the plane to see the city from?" Without hesitation, he deadpanned, "That would be from the inside, Madam."

Everyone howled with laughter. Minutes later, we were in Sydney and I was in for quite an adventure, thanks to that same purser.

He told me about the secret tours of the Opera House that you can arrange if you call ahead, places in the city to avoid (Kings Cross), and what not to miss (Rose Bay and the seaplane flight to a wild restaurant named Pete's Bite). He explained that tipping wasn't expected. And he told me to wear plenty of sunscreen.

I had already made one mistake: a reservation at the Hotel Rex—a despicable place, and, thankfully, one that's no longer with us. I made my second mistake by driving; how I managed not to kill anyone is still a mystery to me. But I made it across the Harbour Bridge to the beach in Manly, where I made my third mistake—underestimating the intensity of the sun. I got so burned that I spent the next two nights sleeping in the half-full bathtub in my hotel room.

Once I recovered from that, I was ready to experience the real Sydney. Following the purser's advice, I headed to Rose Bay and the flight out to Pete's Bite, accessible only by seaplane or boat. Its owners are real characters. He cooked, she sang, and their dog, a Doberman mix named Caesar, howled. It was quite entertaining. (Caesar is gone now, but the experience is still worth it.)

Afterward, I boarded the Indian Pacific—one of the more amazing trains I have ever taken. It's the longest piece of straight railroad track in the world, running between Perth and Sydney. After my visit to Perth, I had to convince my friends that I didn't use any filters on my cameras. The color of the Indian Ocean is really that shade of intense green.

In Adelaide, I ate my first (and last) kangaroo dish and visited the Barossa Valley, where I spent a week touring some very sophisticated vineyards.

But Sydney remained the hub. In recent years, I've made the pleasant discovery of the Hunter Valley (another wine mecca), and a return visit to Melbourne confirmed reports by flight attendants that it has now become hotter than Sydney. The restaurant scene in St. Kilda's (the Stokehouse, in particular), is popular, as is the wine region of the Yarra Valley. (I ballooned over it, then went to the Healdsburg Animal Sanctuary, where they actually bring the animals to you.)

In Melbourne, some friends took me on a late-night walk over to Celestial Place and a Chinese restaurant called the Supper Inn, where at 1 A.M. on a typical night there's a long line outside to get in. I hate lines, but this one was worth it. We didn't eat till close to 2 A.M., but no one complained.

The 2000 Olympics in Sydney may not have helped the Australian economy—as was the case with all other Olympic venues, the city built too many hotel rooms. That's to your benefit now. The Olympics also improved the airport, so they've minimized the schlep factor.

Financially, Sydney is a tourist's dream. With the strong power of the U.S. dollar, it's an incredibly affordable—and uncrowded—city. Using Sydney as a hub, you can fly north to

Brisbane and see the Great Barrier Reef. Or using Melbourne as a hub, you can fly south to Hobart in Tasmania. When you put all of this into perspective, with old-world values and new-world technology, your biggest challenge will not be in getting there, but in leaving.

AIRPORT TIPS

I've been all around the world, and the cheapest duty-free shop is Downtown Duty Free, inside the Sydney airport. This is a great place to buy perfume because it can be twenty to forty percent cheaper in Sydney than anywhere else. For example, Angel perfume is $100 in the United States, but it's only around $60 in Sydney.
◆ Downtown Duty Free, 02 9317 4822.

CITY TIPS

Sydney

The Royal Botanic Gardens, near the Opera House, is a green park area that's quite nice for running. (Sydney is very safe.) The gardens are not big, but the view is superb.
◆ Royal Botanic Gardens, Mrs. Macquarie's Road, 02 9231 8125.

At Tharen's, the walls are covered with hats that you are welcome to try on while you eat. A glass or two of wine is about all it takes for people to start trying them all on and assuming a personality to match the type of hat they're wearing. The menu here is equally varied and includes rack of lamb diablo and roast duck with bok choy. Prices for main courses range from $18 to $24 AU. There is also a three-course prix fixe dinner for $47.20 AU, which includes a choice of six entrées. Enjoy a glass of port after your meal. In the early evening they play dinner music, but later it changes to Sixties and Seventies music and people get up to dance. The place gets busy, so be sure to make a booking (reservation).

◆ Tharen's, 13-15 Kellett Way in Kings Cross, 02 9326 9510.

At the Strand College of Beauty Therapy, about a block and a half from the Queen Victoria Building, you can get a one-hour massage and a facial for $50 AU, which is just perfect after a long flight. They take appointments on Monday, Tuesday, Thursday, and Friday. Tipping is not allowed because they're all students.

◆ Strand College of Beauty Therapy, 383 George Street, Fifth Level, 02 9299 1737, www.strandcollege.com.au.

Since flights to Australia are such a long haul, knowing a good chiropractor can come in handy. Dr. Steven Crome is very professional and knowledgeable, and will make you feel comfortable.

◆ Dr. Steven Crome, King George Clinic, Suite 417, 375 George Street, 02 9290 3800.

The Rocks is a charming area of Sydney near the the ferryboats of Circular Quay (pronounced "key"). It is also a cornucopia of great restaurants, art galleries, trendy boutiques, and a huge DFS Galleries Duty Free Store. A favorite among the crews is the Crystal Gallery. Owner Biannca Bace has filled the store with wonderful scents, books on relaxation techniques, meditation information, healing crystals, and other merchandise designed for calming and soothing. Biannca also does numerology and can read your personality using colors. You will feel energized just by entering the store!

◆ Crystal Gallery, The Rocks, 14-16 Nurse's Walk, 02 9247 8663, www.therocks.com.au/shops/crystal/gallery.htm.

The tour of Old Sydney Town functions as a basic primer of Australian history, representing the city as it was two hundred years ago. Street actors speaking the King's English portray the convicts, Royal Marines, and Redcoats who once inhabited the city. They interact with visitors and are convincingly rough and tough. This is a fun way to learn a bit of history.

◆ Old Sydney Town, Pacific Highway, Somersby (near Gosford), 02 4340 1104, www.oldsydneytown.com.au.

I love browsing through all the shops in the Queen Victoria Building. The QVB, as it is referred to in Sydney, is a large building on George Street downtown. The basement leads to the subway and also has restaurants and shops. On the second floor, Nelson Leong has his clothing design studio. Nelson, a native Chinese but now an Australian citizen, designs evening-wear and suits for women. His designs are haute couture, elegant, and innovative without being gaudy; they are quite well known in Australia and have recently been receiving recognition in Paris. He also designs wedding dresses and will do custom work. He uses lots of silk, brocades, and antique lace. Prices start in the mid-hundreds, but in Australian dollars this is a good value for a garment that is very different from what you'd find at a department store. Last time I was there I looked at a beautiful floor-length evening gown of pink antique French lace with a cashmere top that was $2,700 AU. Custom items can also be made. If you must have a particular outfit, but can't quite afford it at that moment, you can put your item on lay-by (layaway); they will ship it to you when you pay off your balance. Alterations are available if something doesn't fit quite right, and they are happy to ship your purchase for you. Jaime, Nelson's brother, is the shop manager and Ursula is the charming salesperson.

◆ Nelson Leong, Queen Victoria Building, No. 7-9, Gallery One, 02 9265 6869, www.qvb.com.au.

Mohr's Seafood is a tiny hole in the wall with five tables and no atmosphere, but the fish is absolutely delicious and the combinations imaginative. The menu is written on a blackboard on the back wall, but they also give you a daily handwritten menu. They do not serve crab or lobster, but only the freshest local fish. Be sure to try the mussels, which are out of this world. Main courses come with a vegetable and potatoes or rice, and average $25 AU; you can purchase additional side orders, plus coffee, soft drinks, and dessert. They do not have a liquor license, but the pub across the alley will sell and cork a bottle of wine for you to take to the restaurant. Mohr's gets busy after 6 P.M. and they don't take reservations, so you can have a drink in the pub while waiting for your table. Insider tip: do not order Foster's beer when you are in Australia—you will be laughed at. Instead, order the Victoria Bitter.

◆ Mohr's Seafood, 202 Devonshire Street, Surry Hills, 02 9318 1326.

Madame Korner in the Sydney Hilton Arcade is the place to go for hot wax treatments. Call ahead and they can usually get you in right away. The staff is very professional, and the price is affordable. Tip the staff about ten percent.

◆ Madame Korner, 484 George Street in the Sydney Hilton Arcade, 02 9264 1241, www.korner.com.au.

I won't leave Australia without a package of Tim-Tams, which are only available there. These are yummy chocolate-coated cookies that are similar to a biscuit. They also come in double chocolate. You can get them anywhere in Sydney, but Woolworth's is a convenient place to buy them.

◆ Woolworth's, St. Ives Shopping Village, 166 Mona Vale Road, St. Ives N.S.W., 02 9144 7014.

The Ginseng Bathhouse, part of the Crest Hotel in the Kings Cross area, is a Korean-style bathhouse, where many women crew members go. You can get body scrubs and all sorts of pampering.

◆ Ginseng Bathhouse, 111 Darlinghurst Road, 02 9358 2755.

I fly all over the world, but the only place I go jogging is in Sydney. If you're a runner, you must try jogging through Centennial Gardens, right on the harbor beach. Mornings are best, when it's least crowded and most peaceful. It's right in the center of the city but sufficiently out of the way to be relaxing. In the garden, there's a flowerbed area, a tropical hothouse, and a palm area. I start at the Opera House and follow the edge of the harbor, which is the most scenic route. One word of caution: the gates shut at sundown.

◆ Centennial Parkland, between Oxford Street and Allison Road, 02 9339 6699.

On weekends go to Paddy's Market, near Chinatown, at the end of George Street. If you are looking for sheepskin rugs, slippers, or even car seat covers, this is the place to go. You can always get a good deal, but they only take cash.

◆ Paddy's Market, Haymarket, opposite the Entertainment Centre, general enquiries 02 9325 6200, www.sydneymarkets.com.au.

Thirty-six hours in Sydney on a layover is plenty of time to get a stylish haircut at Carl Azzi. A really expensive haircut in Australia seems normally priced to Americans (about $77 AU). Carl is very hip and will make you look beautiful. His shop is located in the Piccadilly shopping center right behind the Sydney Hilton. Call for appointments.

◆ Carl Azzi, 310 Pitt Street, 02 9264 4066, www.carlazzi.com.

Anzac Biscuits are granola cookies that the Australian army used to fortify soldiers during World War II. (Anzac is the acronym for the Australia–New Zealand Alliance.) You can find them at any grocery store in Sydney. They contain wattle seeds (whatever they are), but I sure do like them!

Head to the Fish on the Rocks for lunch and get the *barramundi*—a local Australian fish. If you are looking for a little history, the Lord Nelson Brewery Hotel is the oldest pub in Sydney. After eating at the Fish on the Rocks, the Lord Nelson Brewery Hotel is a great place to stop for a pint since it is only one block away. Three other great bars are Establishment, the Slip Inn, and Hotel CBD. The Marble Bar at the Sydney Hilton is also a nice place to start an elegant evening on the town. The whole bar is made of marble, and the place has live music nightly. Go to the Rocks Market on George Street—a free, open market where you can find all sorts of unique items, such as arts and crafts and handmade chocolates, as well as live music from local bands.

◆ Fish on the Rocks, 29 Kent Street, 9252 4614.

Lord Nelson Brewery, 19 Kent Street, 02 9251 4044.

Establishment, 252 George Street, 02 9240 3000.

Slip Inn, 111 Sussex Street, 02 9299 4777.

Hotel CBD, 75 York Street, 02 9299 8911.

Marble Bar, 259 Pitt Street, 02 9266 2000.

One of my favorite day trips is to Black Wattle Bay and the Sydney Fish Market. You can find fresh seafood cooked just the way you like it. You can also get wine, and there are bakeries and picnic tables, where you can sit down and eat. And the best part is that you don't need to spend more than $10. Locals will tell you to try the "Bugs" mini steamed lobsters.

◆ Sydney Fish Market, corner of Pyrmont Bridge Road and Bank Street.

Invariably, after arriving in Australia, you will wake up in the middle of the night as a result of the time change. When you do, go to Coles grocery store for the muesli, fruit, and yogurt mixtures made by Bircher. They're fabulous! My personal favorite is the mixed berry.

◆ Available at many Coles locations throughout Australia, (800) 061 562, www.coles.com/au.

If you are looking to meet a cute Aussie surfer during your stay, check out the Steyne Hotel–Manly on Manly Beach. All the Manly men (get it?) hang out there. The sunsets are also beautiful, if you can bear to look away from the great male scenery.

◆ Steyne Hotel–Manly, 75; Corso Manly, 02 9977 4977.

Melbourne

Seeing a movie at Gold Class, the very plush part of the Greater Union movie houses, is a bit more expensive—$18 AU as opposed to $12 AU for a regular movie ticket—but it's worth the difference. There are only thirty-six seats, and each one is an overstuffed recliner with a table next to it. There is a full bar plus tables and chairs where you can have a drink before you go in. After you have purchased your ticket, you order what you would like to eat and specify the time at which you would like it served, based on a time line of the movie. The food is delivered directly to your seat at the specified time during the movie. The seats are arranged so the waiter does not have to reach over more than one person to deliver it. I started with wine, and then I had Thai meatballs and grilled vegetables delivered soon after the start of the movie. A while after that, I had more wine, and about forty-five minutes before the end, dessert and a cappuccino. By the time I was done, I had spent around $40 AU, including the movie ticket. Sounds like a lot, but it's actually just over $20 U.S. We usually go on weekdays, when it's less crowded.

◆ Village Century City Walk, 285 Springvale Road, Glen Waverly, 03 9550 8666, www.melbournemovies.com.au/theatres.html.

Chelsea Fashions, a wonderful boutique-type women's clothing store, designs and makes all its own clothes. The designs are very original without being faddish, and women of all ages can usually find something they like. I bought a fabulous coat that is perfect for mid-temperature days. In fact, one of my flying partners liked it so much that she asked me to get her one on my next trip. When shopping Down Under, remember that the seasons are reversed, so you can get things on sale at the beginning of our summer, which is the end of theirs. Three locations.

◆ Chelsea Fashions, 269 Kensington Road, Kensington Park, 08 8431 2225.

Initially, I fell in love with the showerheads at the Grand Hyatt in Melbourne (the hotel will actually sell you one). But then I discovered its workout facilities. Don't miss the spinning class, conducted by Max, an excellent instructor (and the owner of the hotel). He is very demanding and will help you concentrate on your technique. Be sure to bring your own headphones, because each bike has its own plug to receive music and instructions from Max. (You can purchase them at the fitness center if you forget.) If you have never done spinning and would like to learn the basics—or if you simply want a less intensive workout—you can opt for the "training wheels" class a couple of times a week.

◆ Grand Hyatt Hotel, 123 Collins Street, 03 9657 1234.

TOKYO

I've flown to Tokyo on dozens of airlines, and I've always found the city a puzzle that refuses to be solved. And yet I always find myself coming back. Perhaps it's the challenge of trying to make sense out of twenty-six separate cities, twenty-three wards, seven towns, and eight villages.

I've taken the advice of countless flight crews. Some advice was simple to follow: never take a cab from the airport unless someone else is paying, and never order Kobe beef unless someone else is paying. Other advice I wish I had taken was learned the hard way: there's a reason they call it the bullet train, and don't stand up in a karaoke bar or you're the next act.

Tokyo is a city that masters you, and not vice versa. You are a witness, not a participant, and are just along for the ride. This pertains to nearly everything in the city. But it's a great, exciting ride, with lots of surprises.

I remember my first visit to the Park Hyatt Tokyo. A Northwest flight attendant told me I'd love the hotel, especially the bathroom. I asked her to explain, but she would only smile.

The Park Hyatt is a beautiful hotel, with wonderfully designed rooms and spacious bathrooms. This was unlike any toilet I had ever seen. It came with lights and a control panel. I pushed one button and heard a fan. Pushed another and heard a hum (it was a heated seat). Then, while leaning over the toilet, I pushed the third button, and an electric, hydraulic bidet suddenly appeared, and the jet nozzle covered my trousers with a large circle of water.

The embarrassment lasted only a moment and was then replaced by amazement at this technological feat. An hour later I was in the general manager's office, asking how I might be able to purchase one. And two months later, one was installed in my house. It's the only toilet I've ever purchased that comes with an owner's manual!

Although most avoid Tokyo because it's too expensive (so the tips in this chapter are mostly for Narita), it was a flight crew that took me on my first visit to the early morning Tsukiji fish market in Tokyo, followed by sushi at 5:30 in the morning. They also took me to the Fiesta, a karaoke bar in the Roppongi district— six thousand British and U.S. songs in stock—and made me get up and sing "Twist and Shout." I'll never forgive them.

They've also taken me to both the Akasaka and Shinjuku parts of the city, where I've had some memorable dinners, as well as to the Imperial Gardens. Isseido and Ohya Shobo are bookstores where I've found exquisite art books, as well as somewhat rare woodblock-printed books and individual prints.

But Tokyo is also the hub for discovering other parts of Japan—such as Kyoto, my favorite Japanese city. And Nagasaki, where I learned firsthand from an A-bomb survivor what it was like and what I needed to know to try to understand their experience.

And one more word about the bullet train: pack light. Once the doors open at a stop, they don't stay open for long!

AIRPORT TIPS

The airport in Narita is awful. It costs $500 to get into the city by taxi. A cheaper way to get there is by train, which will cost you $25 to $30. The train takes forty-five minutes to an hour, and it's pretty crowded—but not as crowded as the subways in Tokyo.

At the World Plaza across from Gate 26 in the Narita Airport, you can take a thirty-minute shower for ¥300. You can also get a single day room for one hour for ¥500, and a twin day room for ¥800.

◆ Shower rooms and day rooms, Central Building, Third Floor.

Narita Airport has only one large runway for the entire operation, which means that if there's a problem on the runway, the airport is, in effect, closed. They're building a second one, but it won't be open until 2003. The inside of the airport is fairly congested, but they're expanding the airport all the time. There are some long walks to gates, however, as a result of the construction.

CITY TIPS

No matter what time we've landed in Tokyo, we invariably wake up at four the next morning. Our bodies just won't let us sleep. This used to be a problem for me until one of the pilots discovered an effective and fun method of dealing with it. At 5 A.M. we all met at the central fish market, which was busting with activity at this time of day and crammed full of some of the most amazing fish we'd ever seen (and some we'd *never* seen). It's amazing how clean this market is considering all that goes on here. We watched as the very serious fish buyers came in. They would take their small knives and make a small incision at the tail of a large tuna to examine its fat content and determine how much they would bid on the fish at auction—some of those fish go for a lot of money! At about 6 A.M., with the market closing for the day, it was time for breakfast. About one hundred yards from the market was a row of sushi bars—all open for business and crowded with fishermen from the market. I've never had better sushi. After a breakfast of eel, yellowtail, and, of course, tuna, we no longer suffered any jet lag effects at all, and we flew home refreshed. Now we repeat this ritual every time we are in Tokyo.

Nagamini, in downtown Narita, is a driving range close to all the crew hotels. It's unusual because it's electronic and there are no attendants to pick up the balls. Once the green is full, the flags act as a broom that sweeps all the balls back into a funnel where they are redistributed into the pickup area. During the winter, the place is heated, but during the summer—best of luck.
◆ Nagamini, Narita-shi, Yamanosa-ku 415, 0476 352211.

After a long trip, a facial and a leg massage at the Se Rejouir Salon on the top floor of the Rihga Royal Hotel hits the spot. You can get other treatments here as well, such as eyelash curling, hand massage, or foot care. Following your treatment, you are offered an herbal drink that tastes like vinegar but is supposed to be medicinal, with benefits for your skin—although some people claim it also acts as an aphrodisiac. The staff is friendly, although their English is minimal. It's a good idea to make an appointment ahead of time.
◆ Se Rejouir Salon, Rihga Royal Hotel Narita, 456 Kosuge, Narita-shi, Chiba 286-0127, 0476 331121.

The food at Takumi is simple, country-style cooking, and it's fresh and flavorful. In the winter, you can get *nabe,* a meal of rice, vegetables, fish, and oysters, cooked in one big pot. The seaweed salad with citrus-shoyu dressing is delicious. Westerners are not accustomed to eating seaweed, but it's actually very good with cabbage and tomatoes. I recommend the fish fry, but the *saba,* which is grilled macro, and the deep-fried oysters are also great. You can get a whole meal here for under $15, including a beer.
◆ Takumi, 1221 Hiyoshidai, Tomisato City, 0476 939825.

Tokyo can be way out of a flight attendant's budget, but a few of us have discovered the secret to eating free in Japan. The Jusco department store has incredible food displays featuring samples to try—beef, vegetables, melon, fish. I used to think that the displays were outstanding in the food halls at Harrods in London, but Japan clearly has the Brits beat. The trick is to come prepared with toothpicks. We walk around the store and eat very well. No one seems upset with us, because the samples really are there to be sampled.

◆ Jusco, Narita-shi, Hanasakicho 839, 0476 202711.

Department stores in Narita, such as Jusco, often have a 100-yen section in which you can buy things like household products, picture frames, vases, wrapping paper, lingerie bags, cookies, and stationery. You can gradually furnish your home this way, trip by trip. We'll go in there with $20, and come out with three sacks of things.

◆ ¥100 Shop, near JR Train Station, Narita-shi, Hanasakicho 839, 0476 202711.

Kyoumasu is the place to shop for dolls for your children. Prices range from $25 to $600, and the dolls range in size from a few inches to about three feet tall. I've seen them sell for much more elsewhere. The owner gives us ten percent off if we pay cash. The shop name is in Japanese on the front of the building, but you'll see "Dollshop" in English on the side.

◆ Kyoumasu, 497 Kamicho Narita-shi, Chiba, 0476 220847.

I'm always looking for the best tote bags to use as carry-ons. I looked all over Taipei, but I couldn't find any good ones. However, Hinoya Cosmetics, in Narita, has really good tote bags for about ¥10,000 that are durable and the right size for a carry-on.

◆ Hinoya Cosmetics, 557 Kamimachi, Narita-shi, 0476 220117.

Imari caters to flight crews. When it was the only restaurant available to us, he would pick us up at our hotel and drive us to his house to feed us. He is an excellent chef and his business grew, so he moved the restaurant to its current location in Narita. The whole place consists of a U-shaped grill around which patrons sit, and, although you end up smelling like the grill, the food is worth it. You can get six or seven of his delicious *gyozas* (pot stickers or dumplings) for about ¥400. A salmon or pork tenderloin dinner, which comes with miso soup, salad, rice, vegetables, and beer, is about ¥2,000. But most meals cost around ¥1,000. Imari also makes great pepper steak, and since he once worked for Air France catering service, he has western-ized some of his dishes. Beverage choices include water, beer, sake, or Coke. The menu is a little picture book, as in many places in Japan, so you can simply point to what you want.

◆ Imari, 649-603 Nanae, Narita-shi, 0476 928121.

The Barge Inn is owned by Richard Branson of Virgin Atlantic. They serve breakfast and dinner and have live music. The joke is that he named it the Barge Inn because that's how the Japanese pronounce "Virgin."

◆ Barge Inn, 538 Omote Sando, 0476 232546, www.naritabargeinn.com.

Narita is famous for eel, and at the end of September, they have an eel day. Eel is a soft fish, and it's pretty mild. Hikataya, a store on the main street of Narita (Omote Sando), bakes eel in *shoyu* (soy sauce), cooking it in full view of the customers. An eel bento (eel boxed lunch) costs ¥1,000.

◆ Hikataya, Narita-shi, Hanasakicho 5-3-8, 0476 220622.

Atyran Karaoke is where the local people go. The prices are rea-sonable, although after 8 P.M. the cost goes up about fifty per-cent. There are rooms of various sizes for groups of one to fourteen people, in addition to a party room. A five-person room costs ¥500 per hour before 8 P.M. A book with both Japanese and English songs is supplied, and you can get drinks in your room. It's near Omote Sando.

◆ Atyran Karaoke, 853-7 Hanadaki Town, 0476 232339.

Many of us go to the Western Beggar in Narita for stir-fries. It's on a side alley off of Green Street, which goes through the historic part of Narita. It's a little sit-down restaurant that holds about forty-five people. Just walk in; you don't need reservations. It's very reasonably priced for Japan—about $10 for a typical meal.

◆ Western Beggar, Narita-shi, Hanasakicho 5-3-1, 476 243907.

Aoi (which means "blue") is a karaoke place that consists of two stationary trailers, across from the ANA Hotel. It doesn't open until 11 P.M. and it closes at 3:30 A.M., and it gets crazy! You can get to Aoi either by taxi or by bus; one bus will pick you up in front of another karaoke bar called the Cage. You can take the bus from one karaoke bar to the next, and everyone sings, drinks, and has a good time.

◆ Aoi, Komaeno 152, 0476 321845.

The Cage, 374-141 Tokura Tomisato, Chiba, 0476 929102.

VENICE

I love flying into Venice purely for the thrill of taking the boat taxi right to my hotel. Short of sailing into Venice (the overnight ferry from Dubrovnik across the Adriatic is romantic enough), the taxi ride into Venice is incomparable.

"I love Venice for the footsteps," an Air France flight attendant once told me. "It is one of the last remaining cities where you can actually hear your own footsteps when you walk down the streets."

Together we walked over to San Marco Square at 1 A.M. All the cafés and stores had long since closed. Not even the notorious pigeons were around. We walked over to one of the cafés and carried chairs to the center of the square. "Listen," she said. "Nothing. It is all ours." Just then the clock struck half past one, the sound of the bells echoing all around us, and then . . . nothing.

Frequent travelers—especially flight crews—have the city down to a system, and I'm no exception. I avoid Venice entirely in June, July, and August. It's crowded, and it smells. I think I've taken only one gondola ride—they're too touristy. I prefer the number 14 public boat, which goes to the islands of Burano and Torcello. Harry's Bar is a must-stop for first-timers. Order a Bellini and take the obligatory souvenir photo—just to say you did it.

February, May, and September are Carnaval months, when you go to Florian's in San Marco. In a city defined by its bridges, 116 separate islands, and 150 canals, I cross as many as I can, preferably early in the morning. I have breakfast on the roof at the Danieli, lunch (in season) at the Excelsior out on the Lido, and dinner at the Cipriani or at Alle Testiere. Or I succumb to the temptation of the risotto at Ristorante da Ivo.

Then there's my special place. In the daytime, if the front desk clerk of the Hotel Europa and Regina is in the right mood, I ask to be shown the room where Monet lived. I head straight for the window and open it. The feeling is intense every time. As the window opens, I see what Monet saw—and painted. At night, after dinner, I head back to the Europa and Regina, to their small bar and dock, right on the water. Over drinks and the sound of water slapping against stone, I see the exact same priceless view across the canal.

CITY TIPS

If you're shopping for a mask, buy one that really captures your imagination. A typical mask, depending on the size, might cost about $40. The vendors know you're a tourist and will pay the high prices. But you can bargain if you're going to buy two or three. If you're in a group and buy five or six, you can try to get more of a discount. The bigger stores have the prices premarked, so you know what you're dealing with. I got my favorite mask, which is hand-painted and intended for decoration only, at Zago e Molin, near the gambling casino on the Grand Canal. This is a fantastic place with a huge selection. The average-size mask here will cost about $70.

◆ Zago e Molin, Strada Nuova 2363, 041 718979.

Murano is an island that is historically renowned for glassmaking. The key to booking an affordable trip to Murano is to go in a group, which will cost about $40 a person for the boat ride, plus tip. Once you get there, be sure to visit Mazzuccato International, a co-op for a particular group of artists who do unique, although rather expensive, glass work.

◆ Fondamenta Manin, #1, Murano, 041 739534.

If you are looking for a short-term apartment rental in Venice or Sicily, Rossana is the woman to contact. She fixed us up in a clean apartment with a kitchenette and beds made with fresh linens for $160 for two nights. No deposit was required; however, the rental must be confirmed by e-mail and payment must be in cash. She also gave us tips about places to see and how to get there, as well as good advice about parking in Venice (*don't* park in Venice—it's too expensive; park in the neighboring town of Mestre and take the train into Venice). She is easily accessible by phone if you have questions about or problems with your visit.

◆ Rossana, phone/fax 041 5349783, cell phone 034 79109231, e-mail info@veneziaboom.com.

We use our trips to Venice as wine-purchasing excursions. Our favorites are wines from the Veneto region, especially Valpolicella, a very light, affordable table wine. You can buy it at almost any of the many small supermarkets within the city, and even at the gas stations. You can also find it at Panorama, a supermarket similar to the ones you find in the United States.

◆ Via Orsato 13, 041 12584211.

In addition to wine, Italy is also famous for a drink called limoncello, a lemon-based liqueur that comes from the province of Naples, south of Rome. You can buy limoncello for $5 to $10, depending on the brand.

Bellini, a drink unique to Venice, was created in Harry's Bar many years ago. Named after the famous family of painters, it's made with white peaches and bubbly wine. People still go to

Harry's Bar to have a Bellini, and it's a treat—but you go only once. They cost about $12 there, and for $8 to $12 more you can buy the glass as a souvenir. However, you can get Bellinis everywhere in Venice, and it's cheaper to buy these drinks in the bigger supermarkets such as Panorama.

◆ Harry's Bar, San Marco 1323, 041 5285777.

In the spring and especially in the summer, Venice is overflowing with tourists. Take a water taxi with friends (and negotiate the price up front) to the Lido and spend the afternoon over a long lunch at the Westin Excelsior Hotel. The beach is crowded, but the hotel sits above it with a great view.

◆ Westin Excelsior Hotel, Lungomare Marconi 41, Venice Lido, 041 5260201.

The Veneto region produces a fantastic coffee called florian. Only two or three bars sell this coffee. You can buy the beans yourself, for $6 or $7 a pound, or ask them to grind them for you. A good place to get it is Caffe Florian.

◆ Caffe Florian, San Marco, 041 5224409.

Try the little bread sticks called grissini, similar to those made by Stella D'Oro that are available in the United States. They are very thin and crisp, and a box costs only about $1.80. You can get them at any Panorama in Venice.

HONORABLE MENTIONS

There are dozens of cities—from Moscow to Minneapolis, from Philadelphia to Vienna—where flight crews lay over, either by design or by delay, but where their time on the ground is not scheduled to be great. I'm not talking about the cities in which flight attendants are based (as in Minneapolis) but true layover cities. In a few cases, there are somewhat longer layovers, and for these cities we present the following flight crew secrets.

DOMESTIC

Milwaukee

Imagine a bookstore selling rare and used books at an airport! Renaissance Bookstore at Milwaukee's Mitchell Field is the place. It has every type of book you can imagine, and if you can't find it in the store, they'll track it down for you. The prices can be as low as $3 and as high as $85, and there are always several first editions and signed books as well. Some of the old books on transportation information are incredibly interesting. They also carry original *Time* and *Life* magazines from the fifties. I spotted a book on the sinking of the *Titanic,* called *A Night to Remember;* the same book on eBay was going for $1,000. I now make a point of bidding my schedules to go to Milwaukee at least once a month. Even if I don't lay over, I usually have enough time to run over to the old terminal (the Northwest Airlines terminal) and shop for books. They will ship the books to you very inexpensively so that you don't have to schlep tons of books around.

◆ Renaissance Bookstore, Northwest Terminal, Mitchell Field, (414) 747-4526.

Minneapolis/St. Paul

If you love to shop, the clean and comfortable Minneapolis/St. Paul airport is the place for you. They recently spent millions of dollars building new stores, so that it's like a shopping mall. (And there's no clothing tax in Minnesota.) The airport also runs free shuttles every fifteen minutes to the Mall of America, which is right across the street. They drop you off by the Northwest ticket counter at the Mall of America, where all of the screens with departure times are displayed, so you can shop and still keep track of your flight.

◆ Mall of America, (952) 883-8800.

Get a cup of Caribou coffee at the Minneapolis/St. Paul airport. Caribou is a local coffeehouse chain, which competes directly with Starbucks. The prices are about the same, but where Starbucks is stiff and corporate, Caribou is much more laid-back. If you order incorrectly, Caribou won't make you feel like you're stupid. Caribou is woodsy, but still trendy. Try the hot mocha coffee.

◆ Caribou Coffee, (612) 338-3814.

The main terminal at the Minneapolis airport is like a small shopping center—there is a Wilson's Leather, the Museum Company, Liz Claiborne, and Bath and Body Works, to name a few of the stores. When I want to regroup and relax for a few minutes, I go to the Starbucks in the C Concourse. Although the tables there look out on the parking lot, it is very quiet, and since you are not looking at airplanes, it is almost as if you were somewhere else. The terminal also has a bookstore and some good restaurants, and it is not nearly as crowded as others. If you don't want to take your luggage outside the airport, there are lockers throughout the terminal. One drawback of this airport is that it can be difficult to find your way around, so follow the signs carefully.

◆ Airport information line (952) 726-5500.

Philadelphia

Eat breakfast at Joe's on the B Concourse at the Philadelphia airport. It's open at 6:30 A.M., and you can get pancakes, eggs, and bacon for $4.99, which is a good price for an airport. The pancakes are huge—at least eight inches across. They cook the two eggs any way you like them, and they're fresh. The service is pretty quick.

◆ Joe's, (215) 937-5141.

If you need your shoes shined, see Won, an elderly Asian man who likes to joke around with his customers. He charges $3 for shoes and $5 for boots. His stand is set up in Terminal D, by the security checkpoint.

◆ Airport information line, (215) 937-6937.

Henry and David own Halloween, a great jewelry shop that looks more like a museum inside because there is so much unique and beautiful jewelry. They carry both vintage and modern jewelry, displayed in a very artistic manner in glass cases.

◆ Halloween, 1329 Pine Street, (215) 732-7711.

Continental Cleaners is a nice little neighborhood place. Sun, the owner, is friendly and very accommodating. If you need something done quickly, she can usually help out. She is also a seamstress and can do all kinds of alterations. Prices are reasonable—for example, a pair of pants is about $3.95.

◆ Continental Cleaners, corner of 2nd and Catherine, in Queens Village, (215) 389-8444.

I admired a passenger's haircut, and she told me about Red, Red, Red in Old City. Ross, the stylist, does modern cuts, but he makes the style suit his client. I made an appointment with him and have been getting my hair cut there ever since. A cut is only $30, which is quite reasonable.

◆ Red, Red, Red, 222 Church Street, (215) 923-4042.

Check out the lovely spa at the Loews Hotel, where you will be surrounded by soft music and peaceful waterfall sounds. While you're there, Paulina can give you a lip and bikini wax for only $45.

◆ Loews Hotel, 1200 Market Street, (215) 627-3560.

The Fork, a popular place with local people, is my favorite place for Sunday brunch. The food is absolutely fabulous—especially the eggs Benedict and quiches. They also have quite a good dinner. You definitely need to make a reservation, but if you don't, you can sit at the beautiful bar, which is also a great place to sit if you are eating alone. There is a different menu every Sunday. Brunch for two costs about $50.

◆ The Fork, 306 Market Street, (215) 625-9425.

The Blue in Green, a great place for breakfast, is funky, noisy, and fun—and none of the furniture matches. They are known for their fantastic pancakes, but their omelets are also wonderful, and made with unusual combinations of ingredients. However, this place is not for finicky eaters; they do not allow you to substitute. If you like Bloody Marys, be sure to try them here. For two people, breakfast will run about $30. If you go on a weekday before 11 A.M., you can get your entire meal for under $5. A word of caution: they only accept cash, and they do not accept reservations.

◆ Blue in Green, 7 N. 3rd Street, (215) 928-5880.

The Arden Theatre Company stages wonderful, original, out-of-the-ordinary plays. They have new plays about once a month.

This is a relatively new theater, and there are two stages within it. Both venues are small, so no matter where you sit you have a good (and comfortable!) seat. Lobbies for both venues are big and very modern.

◆ Arden Theatre Company, 40 N. 2nd Street, (215) 922-1122.

Dmitri's, a wonderful Greek restaurant, opens at 5:30 P.M., and there is always a line of people waiting to get in. It's a very small place, and they don't take reservations. Most people put their name on the list and then go to the bar across the street for a drink. When your name is up, they will come over to the bar and look for you. I recommend ordering the *talapia*, a fillet of mild whitefish in lemon and garlic, which comes with a delicious side dish of rice and steamed green vegetables. They also have great sautéed mussels. You have to bring your own liquor if you want, but there is no corkage fee.

◆ Dmitri's, 795 3rd Street, (215) 625-0556.

Pennsylvania does not sell alcohol in grocery stores. The only place you can get liquor is in the state stores, many of which close at 9 P.M. Another drawback is that often they do not have a great selection, and they are usually pretty expensive.

◆ Wine and Spirit Shop, 1628 JFK Boulevard, (215) 560-5702.

Philadelphia Restaurant and Bar Supply sells a terrific selection of cooking utensils and pots and pans at wholesale prices. They have all industry-quality products here.

◆ Philadelphia Restaurant and Bar Supply, 4th and Bainbridge Streets, (215) 925-7649.

San Jose

Whenever I'm in the San Jose airport, I go to a deli called Max's, in the American concourse area, inside security at Gates 14 and 15. They have really good homemade breads, like sourdough and wheat, and real roasted turkey and ham. A sandwich with everything on it, a pickle, and a choice of coleslaw or potato salad goes for about $6.50.

◆ Max's, (408) 938-8921.

Savannah

In Savannah, a quaint and lovely town, we like to go to a restaurant called Mrs. Wilkes for the family-style home cooking. You pay a very inexpensive fixed price for all you can eat. It's in an old house right in downtown Savannah, and you sit with whomever you're in line with. The food is delicious, but there's a wait.

◆ Mrs. Wilkes, 107 W. John, (912) 232-5997.

OVERSEAS

Acapulco

We go to Barra Vieja for their beautiful red snapper. The place has sand floors and picnic tables. It's located at the end of Barra Vieja, past the big restaurants that face the ocean, just before you get to the narrow bridge.

◆ Barra Vieja, Costera M. Aleman #1230, 0744 484 3389.

Bombay

Ravi, at Panmonde, calls himself "The Leatherman." Show him a picture of a jacket or whatever garment you want, and twenty-four hours later he will have made it for you. He can even make modifications in designs. The quality is excellent, and the prices are right. The best part is that if you don't like what he's made, you don't have to buy it.

◆ Panmonde, Seaside Hotel, next door to Sun and Sand Hotel, A.B Nair Road, 022 6202290.

Brussels

Brussels is sometimes considered the ugly stepsister of Europe, but it's improving quite a bit and is currently rather underrated.

Within the next twenty years, it should really come into its own. The European Parliament is there, and the European Economic Community (EEC), and the new buildings are assets. Brussels has become a fascinating city in which to walk around. The neighborhoods are full of lovely town houses, many of which are in art deco style.

If you order a cappuccino in Brussels, it will come with real whipped cream floating on the top and a piece of chocolate or a cookie on the side.

Although it's hard to single out a particular favorite restaurant in Belgium, some of the national dishes deserve special mention in themselves. One good dish is carbonara, which is similar to beef stew, but with no vegetables in it—it's basically beef chopped up in a dark gravy, but it's delicious. Another savory favorite is *stumph,* which is mashed potatoes with turkey and sausage. Most traditional restaurants in Belgium will serve these dishes. Belgian french fries, which you can buy at the stands on the street, are also renowned.

There are also some sweet indulgences to be found in Brussels. Belgian waffles are to die for! You can buy them on the street, and since they cook them right there, you get them while they're still warm. Although Switzerland is known for its chocolate, Belgium has even *better* chocolate. Its chocolatiers are true artists. If you are a chocoholic, this is where you want to be.

Although the atmosphere and architecture are interesting in downtown Brussels, the best place for *moules* (mussels) is the small and simple restaurant Au Vieux Bruxelles, on the corner of rue St.-Boniface and rue Franckart, uptown near Porte de Namur/Chaussee d'Ixelles. They don't take reservations and are open only when the chef is in the mood. Second-best, I have to say, is Chez Henri, which also specializes in caviar and is located at the corner of rue de Flandre and rue d'Ophem downtown, not far from St.-Catherine. Avoid the Grand Place and all the tourist traps at all costs if you want a decent meal.

◆ Au Vieux Bruxelles, 35, rue St.-Boniface, 02 5033111.
Chez Henri, rue de Flandre 113, 02 2196415.

Brugge is about forty-five minutes from Brussels and is often overlooked, but it's an adorable place—the Venice of the North. A group of little churches and restaurants surround the main square, and you use little boats to go up and down the canals, as in Holland. Trains leave for Brugge from the Central Train Station in Brussels every half hour. It costs about $16, round trip.

The atmosphere at Marieke van Brugghe, a wonderful restaurant in Brugge, is charming and inviting, accented with blond wood and candlelight, and often decorated for the season. The food is terrific and reasonably priced. There's a pleasant outdoor seating area for warm-weather dining.

◆ Marieke van Brugghe, Mariastaat 17, Brugge 8000, 050 343366), www.mvb.be.

Luxembourg

Doing business with the Bank of Luxembourg is a brush with history. The bank's vaults are part of an underground cave system that people used in World War II to hide from the German forces.

◆ Bank of Luxembourg, 80 Place of the Station, +352 499241.

Luxembourg is home to a number of castles, and the back of the largest one has been converted into two separate and very popular nightclubs, Prime Time and Yesterdays. These clubs have actually been carved out of caves in the basement of the castle, so they are naturally dark and cozy. There's no cover charge, and on weekends they're so packed with local people that dancing becomes a sort of group activity. If you rub elbows with some of the locals (which, under the circumstances, you can't help but do), they might introduce you to the private, after-hours clubs. Drink prices in Luxembourg are reasonable.

◆ Prime Time, 6 rue de la Loga, +352 223657.

Yesterdays, 46 rue de la Loga, +352 223657.

You will not regret a stay at the Hotel Intercontinental. The concierge remembers everything and everyone. For about $120, the hotel will arrange for you to rent a Harley motorcycle for a day and drive it into France or all over Germany. The Varanda Bar at the hotel is exceptional, and there is a terrific pianist who performs there and occasionally invites a few members of the audience onstage to sing with him. He has a huge repertoire of popular music, ranging from Elton John to French and Spanish songs. (He is multilingual.)

The hotel also has an excellent gym downstairs and an outdoor pool that overlooks the cliffs. It's a perfect setting, and it's not too far from downtown. The hotel employs a masseuse of the highest caliber, who also does pedicures and manicures. Ask for Im Soo Lee, at +352 26511224.

◆ Hotel Intercontinental Luxembourg, Bp. 1313, +352 43781.

Luxembourg is known for its local breweries. But the food in these places is also worth sampling. Even if you don't eat pork, you will salivate at the sight of the pork roasted so that it literally falls of the bone. The pork is served with sauerkraut and other typical German fare.

◆ Brasserie de Redange (brew pub), Grand rue 61, L-8150 Redange, +352 629311.

Brasserie Simon (microbrewery), 14, rue Joseph Simon.

Brasserie de Wiltz, L-9550 Wiltz, +352 958015.

One local beer in Luxembourg is called Mosel, after the brewery it comes from. There's also a restaurant in the brewery, which is one of the great eateries in Luxembourg. Prices are comparable to those of a nice sports-bar-type restaurant in the States. A unique feature of the cuisine is that they put eggs in almost everything—for instance, if you order chicken or a veal cutlet, it will be served with an egg on top.

Manila

The Manila Hotel is both beautiful and historic. This is where General Douglas MacArthur signed the treaty with Japan to end World War II. The elegant ambience is evident as you enter the lobby, where musicians are playing the piano and the violin. The Champagne Room at the Manila Hotel is equally elegant as befits one of the top restaurants in the Philippines. The Filipino waiters wear their traditional attire as they serve you. The cuisine is continental, with entrées such as filet mignon, but don't overlook the Filipino specialty *mapu mapu*, a very mild fish. The restaurant also affords a wonderful view of the gardens. This is not casual dining, and jackets are required for men.

◆ Champagne Room, Manila Hotel, 1 Rizal Park, 02 5270111.

At the Bay Club at the Manila Hotel, you can get a great massage for about $8 for half an hour. You can also get manicures and pedicures for about $9, and facials for about $8.

◆ Bay Club, Manila Hotel.

If you ask the bellman at any hotel in Manila about motorcycle clubs, the next thing you know, the whole club will show up at the hotel, with an extra cycle for whoever needs one. They will take you on a wild ride through the streets of metropolitan Manila. These clubs consist mostly of students, and usually they won't accept payment for the ride, but it's a good idea to buy everyone lunch or dinner. (By the way, this also works on Palawan or Legaspi.)

◆ Motorcycles and Scooters Inc., contact Jovy Villar, 02 834 2288.

Mexico City

The Chapultapec area of Presedente, near Polanco, is a great place to buy pewter. Prices are about fifty percent lower here than elsewhere. People always used to bring tequila back from Mexico, but it became much more expensive after the cactus fields burned down a few years ago. However, Bacardi is still a good buy, as are Kahlua, Bailey's Irish Cream, and Amaretto. This is also a good place to find bargains on vanilla.

Moscow

Moscow's outdoor flea market, Vernisazh Ismailova, is enormous—just the place for great shopping. You can find all kinds of Russian handicrafts, lacquerware, amber, military memorabilia, antiques, fur hats, oriental carpets, tapes and CDs, books, dolls, costumes, jewelry, and more. I found some hats that were worn by Soviet troops in Afghanistan, which are perfect to wear for summer hiking. I've also found gorgeous Russian scarves with fringes and unique teacups painted with big, gaudy gold and purple flowers. You must be prepared to bargain; vendors will accept dollars or rubles, but they do not take credit cards or checks. On weekends the market is very busy, especially during nice weather. Moscow has an excellent metro system with a stop (Ismailova) very near the market, or you can take a taxi.

◆ Vernisazh Ismailova (Moscow flea market), Ismailovsky Park.

Nagoya

If you get to Nagoya, be sure to eat at a restaurant called Ohsho, where you can get a great meal for less than $7. Try the

stir-fried veggies, and don't overlook the wonderful *gyoza*—
Japanese-style dumplings or pot stickers. The Japanese eat
gyoza only on the weekends because there's so much garlic in
them and they don't want to have garlic breath during the week
when they work.

◆ Ohsho, Sakea 43, 052 241 9801.

New Delhi

The New Delhi Sheraton is an oasis in the middle of this im-
poverished land. This hotel is a first-class surprise. It doesn't
look so special on the outside, but it's just beautiful inside, and
the staff are very professional, classy, and proper. The food here
is excellent and safe, and the tap water is potable, but be careful
not to swallow water in the shower because of the possibility of
parasites.

There's also a driving room out by the pool, where you smack
a golf ball off a tee and into a fairway projected onto a screen. An
electronic device measures the force of the impact, converts it to
a distance in yards, and thus tells you how far the ball went. It's
pretty cool.

◆ Maurya Sheraton Hotel & Towers, Diplomatic Enclave,
011 611 2233.

One night, the flight crew got in to the Sheraton around 2 A.M.
and heard music. We asked the bellman about it and he told us
about the club downstairs. We headed in that direction and
found a line of people all the way up the two flights of stairs—
and they were dressed to kill, like in a New York City disco.
When the bouncer found out I was an American, he ushered me
in, to the strains of KC and the Sunshine Band. The place was
really kicking—'70s tunes peppered with Indian songs. India
may lack public transportation, clean water, and food, but
they've got a great disco in this place.

◆ Arish Pub, Sheraton Hotel, 011 611 2233.

Prague

At the crystal place called Erpet you will find true European old-world craftsmanship and fabulous colored-glass genuine Czech crystal. This is unique merchandise that you won't find anywhere else. Prices are moderate to expensive.

◆ Erpet, Old Town Square #27, 02 2422 9755, www.erpet.cz.

La Provence, a restaurant with a comfortable ambience, attracts a nice mixed crowd. The restaurant is in the basement, and there's a bar upstairs. Prices are reasonable, a selection of wine is available, and the food is good. I recommend the chicken with lots of garlic. Reservations are necessary.

◆ La Provence, Stupartska #9, Prague 1, 02 5733 5050.

Puerto Vallarta

Beverly and Willow are a married coupled who perform in Nuevo Vallarta, a fast-growing resort development twenty minutes north of PV and home to the Seashore Restaurant. They have recorded a CD in Nashville, which they sell at their gigs, and they have a huge local following. There's no cover charge for their shows.

◆ Seashore Restaurant, Nuevo Vallarta.

Another fun spot is Aria, a piano bar on the south side of town (an area with lots of clubs) that started out as a gay bar but now attracts straight singles and couples as well. One of the club's owners, a Canadian named Darryl, entertains most nights, playing and singing a huge repertoire of show tunes and the like. This is a funky place, with comfortable chairs, nice curtains on always-open windows, and a small balcony rimming the place. Drink prices are reasonable.

◆ Aria Piano Lounge, Pino Suarez 210.

There are two things I shop for in Puerto Vallarta. The first is a skin cream called Tortuga, or turtle lotion—although I don't think it's really made out of turtles because that would be illegal. You can buy it at any pharmacy, and it's quite inexpensive. The second item, of course, is tequila. You don't find any real bargains on this, so I search for the more unusual brands, such as Centinario, for about $7 a bottle.

Santo Domingo

My feet are always a mess because I'm a runner. The best pedicure I ever had was at Jaragua, a hotel in Santo Domingo. Although the pedicurist didn't speak much English and I don't speak much Spanish, we managed to communicate, and when she was done my feet looked great! Hotel services also include manicures and massages.

◆ Hotel Jaragua, 367 Avenue, George Washington, (809) 221-2222.

Taipei

Usually we get to Taipei only when there are intense headwinds and we can't make Hong Kong or if we have to divert to Taipei for fuel. On such an occasion we discovered the Jade Market. They also sell coral, as well as flowers here—and the merchandise is much cheaper than buying at the stores because you can bargain.

◆ Jade Market, Chien Kuo North Road. Open Saturdays and Sundays.

A lot of mountain bikes are made in Taipei, and there are at least three giant bike shops in which to find them. You can save as much as $300 to $600 on a bike, although you will have to pay to ship it back. Still, it's well worth buying it there. The store will box your bike for you and ship it to your hotel. Most of the clerks speak English and are very helpful.

◆ Seventh Park Bike Store, #159, Sec. 2, Chen Guo South Road, 2701 1591, 2701 1595.

THE CONTRIBUTORS

Here, in alphabetical order, are the people who directly made this book possible. They are pilots and flight attendants from more than thirty U.S. and foreign airlines. They fly for commuter airlines, major airlines, and cargo carriers. Their tenure ranges from just six months to nearly forty years, and a few billion miles in between. But what they all have in common is a continuing love affair with their layover cities. In some cases, the city in which a pilot or flight attendant is officially based is not where he or she lives. Many are commuters themselves. But they certainly know what to do, whom to see, and where to go as soon as they land—here, there, and just about everywhere.

Aguirre, Arturo, flight attendant 2 years with National, based in Las Vegas

Aguirre, Nancy, flight attendant 15 years with United, based in Chicago

Albeche, Karen, flight attendant 7 years with Swissair, based in Zurich

Allen, Jo, flight attendant 32 years with Continental, based in Newark

Amaral, Bev, flight attendant 15 years with America West, based in Phoenix

Anderson, Cheryl, flight attendant 18 years with American, based in Los Angeles

Anderson, Rita, flight attendant 32 years with Pan Am/Delta, based in Auckland

Arabak, Bill, pilot 24 years with Raytheon Travel Air, based in Portland

Aucone, Randy, flight attendant 6 months with Frontier, based in Denver

Axelsson, Linda, flight attendant 37 years with US Airways, based in Philadelphia

Babbitt, Marnie, flight attendant 3 years with America West, based in Phoenix

Balbach, Stewart, flight attendant 25 years with Northwest, based in Chicago

Ballew, Marcia, flight attendant 36 years with American, based in Dallas

Bassi, Maria, flight attendant 2½ years with Delta, based in New York

Bauer, Tamara, flight attendant 32 years with Continental, based in Houston

Beltv, Mary, flight attendant 2½ years with National, based in Las Vegas

Benally, Nick, flight attendant 4 years with Delta, based in New York

Bierg, Keely, flight attendant 8 years with Air New Zealand, based in Auckland

Blake, Alva, flight attendant 20 years with Western/Delta, based in Atlanta

Blumensaadt, Ann, flight attendant 32 years with Pan Am/Delta, based in New York

Boe, Susan, flight attendant 35 years with American, based in Los Angeles

Boettcher, Pete, pilot 11 years with American, based in New York

Bombace, Valeria, flight attendant 5 years with Alitalia, based in Milan

Bottome, Rick, flight attendant 23 years with American, based in Los Angeles

Bowens, Robin, flight attendant 11 years with United, based in Chicago

Brandt, Vicki, flight attendant 25 years with Delta, based in Fort Lauderdale

Braxton, Scott, flight attendant 4^1/$_2$ years with Northwest, based in Detroit

Brennan, Nancy, flight attendant 19 years with American, based in Los Angeles

Breslin, Chuck, pilot 20 years with Big Sky, based in Billings

Broski, Mickel, flight attendant 6 years with Lufthansa, based in Frankfurt

Brown, David, pilot 9 years with Delta, based in Dallas

Brown, Jovanna, flight attendant 38^1/$_2$ years with TWA/American, based in St. Louis

Burdette, Elaine, flight attendant 13 years with US Airways, based in Philadelphia

Burger, Peter, pilot 32 years with Swissair, based in Zurich

Burke, Elsie, flight attendant 4 years with TWA, based in New York

Cajuste, Tammy, flight attendant 11 years with American, based in San Francisco

Caridi, Claudia, flight attendant 34 years with Pan Am/United, based in Washington, D.C.

Casa, Margaret, flight attendant 31 years with Pan Am/Delta, based in New York

Ceragioli, Katrien, flight attendant 1^1/$_2$ years with Jet Blue, based in New York

Champion, Bruce, flight attendant 18 years with American, based in San Francisco

Charmforoosh, Farhad, pilot 12 years with United, based in Chicago

Chisholm, Georgeanna, flight attendant for Pan Am/Delta for 33 years, based in New York

Cicciari, David, pilot 3 years with Northwest, based in Detroit

Clark, Nakachi, flight attendant 2^1/$_2$ years with National, based in Las Vegas

Close, Jim, flight attendant 24 years with Delta, based in Cincinnati

Coburn, Sherri, flight attendant 22 years with American, based in Miami

Coman, Christy, flight attendant 12 years with American, based in Dallas

Combs, Dee, flight attendant 33 years with Continental, based in Houston

Combs, Leanne, flight attendant with Northwest, based in Memphis

Condon, Becky, pilot 15 years with Delta, based in Atlanta

Constable, Tom, pilot 18 years with American, based in San Francisco

Copps, Chandler, pilot 17 years with Midwest Express, based in Milwaukee

Courtney, Lynda, flight attendant 28 years with American, based in Los Angeles

Crooke, Jan, flight attendant 29 years with American, based in Chicago, Dallas, Los Angeles, and New York

Crowell, Terri, flight attendant 37 years with United, based in Los Angeles

Cullen, Bonnie, flight attendant 1½ years with United, based in Chicago and Washington, D.C.

Cumnock, Paula, flight attendant 14 years with United, based in Chicago

D'Amico-Dolio, Mecca, flight attendant 23 years with TWA, based in Chicago

D'Angelo, Gary, pilot 2½ years with Atlas/Atlas Air Freighters, based in Fort Lauderdale

Davis, Paula, flight attendant 12 years with Southwest, based in Phoenix

Delameter, Pat, flight attendant 34 years with American, based in Los Angeles

Donahue, Jack, pilot 22 years with Midway/United, based in San Francisco

Dougherty, Barbara, flight attendant 30 years with Delta, based in Salt Lake City

Duvall, Sara, flight attendant 12 years with United, based in Washington, D.C.

Eisenlauer, Barbara, flight attendant 28 years with Delta, based in New York

Ellis, Melody, flight attendant 9 months with Frontier, based in Denver

Emciso, Omar, flight attendant 3 years with United, based in San Francisco

Emery, Pamela, flight attendant 12 years with United, based in Chicago and Washington, D.C.

Emmert, Jennifer, flight attendant 11 years with United, based in Chicago

Epps, Heidi, flight attendant 12 years with Delta, based in New Orleans

Erl, Leanna, flight attendant 2 years with United, based in San Francisco

Erl, Lorenz, pilot 11 years with American, based in San Francisco

Evans, Cheryl, flight attendant 36 years with American, based in San Francisco

Evans, Cynthia, flight attendant 30 years with United, based in Los Angeles

Ewers, LeLand, pilot 12 years with Atlantic Coast, based in Washington, D.C.

Ewers, Mary Jo, flight attendant 7 years with United and 3 years with United Express, based in Washington, D.C.

Fabro, Henry, flight attendant 16 years with Hawaiian, based in Los Angeles

Farber, Richard "Scoop," pilot 6 years with United, based in Chicago

Fariello, Gina, flight attendant 30 years with TWA, based in Los Angeles, New York, San Francisco, and St. Louis

Fariello, Richard, retired pilot 33 1/2 years with TWA, based in Los Angeles, New York, San Francisco, and St. Louis

Feeney, Mike, pilot 12 years with Aloha, based in Honolulu

Figueroa, Margaret Mary Blossom, flight attendant 17 years with American, based in Dallas

Finbow, Richard, flight attendant 2 years with Frontier, based in Denver

Fischer, John, flight attendant 2 years with Frontier, based in Denver

Flapps, Nigel, flight attendant 16 years with British Airways, based in London

Fletcher, Claudia, flight attendant 11 years with United, based in San Francisco

Ford, Karen, flight attendant 30 years with American, based in Los Angeles

Frank, Lorraine, flight attendant 7 months with Southwest, based in Oakland

Gado, Maria, flight attendant 6 years with Continental, based in Newark

Garton, Mary, flight attendant 8 years with United, based in Chicago and San Francisco

Geopfarth, Roger, pilot 33 years with United/PSA/US Airways, based in Philadelphia

Gilman, Sandy, pilot 36 years with DHL, based in Cincinnati

Goode, Jennifer, flight attendant 7 years with United, based in Chicago

Goodhue, Nancy, flight attendant 30 years with Delta, based in New York

Gorrell, Jane, flight attendant 21 years with American, based in Chicago

Granara, Fabiola, flight attendant 4 years with Alitalia, based in Milan

Graves, Sharon, flight attendant 32 years with TWA, based in New York

Griffiths, David, pilot 21 years with Northwest, based in Minneapolis

Grigg, Peggy, flight attendant 10 years with United and 15 years with Eastern, based in Chicago, Newark, and New York

Gwynn, Cathy, flight attendant 11 years with Alaska, based in Portland

Hagan, Bill, pilot 23 years with United, based in New York

Hartley, Pamela, flight attendant 2½ years with Southwest, based in Baltimore

Hassett, Margaret, flight attendant 24 years with Delta, based in New York

Hatchett, Terri, flight attendant 22 years with American, based in Los Angeles

Herrera, Irene, flight attendant 16 years with American, based in San Jose

Hester, Jean, flight attendant 24 years with Delta, based in Atlanta

Hill, Marilyn, flight attendant 37 years with Northwest, based in Minneapolis

Hogan, Leslie, flight attendant 33 years with Pan Am/Delta, based in New York

Holman, Anne, flight attendant 31 years with Pan Am/Delta, based in New York

Holmes, Kim, flight attendant 13½ years with Delta, based in Atlanta

Hoover, Nicolas, flight attendant 3 years with Mesa (America West, US Airways), based in Columbus

Howard, Lee, pilot 35 years with Big Sky, based in Billings

Jackson, Joan, flight attendant 31 years with Pan Am/Delta, based in New York

Jacobs, Dan, pilot, based in Las Vegas

Jacobs, Pat, flight attendant 35 years with American, based in San Jose

Jarman, Julie-Ann, flight attendant 18 years with American, based in Miami

Jenkins, Valerie, flight attendant 2 years with Jet Blue, based in New York

Jewett, Bob, pilot 32½ years with Delta, based in Dallas

Kharjudparn, "A" Warayut, flight attendant 1 year with Qantas, based in Bangkok

Kisfaludy, Johanna, flight attendant 14 years with Continental, based in Pittsburgh

Kopps, Katrina, flight attendant 16 years with United, based in Chicago

Koster, Eileen, flight attendant 31 years with Pan Am/Delta, based in Los Angeles

Kracke, Bettina, flight attendant 6 years with Lufthansa, based in Frankfurt

Kucera, Jan, flight attendant 15 years with Delta, based in New York

Kulback, Stacie, flight attendant 12 years with United, based in San Francisco

Kullick, Linda, flight attendant 10 years with United, based in Chicago, Los Angeles, Newark, and San Francisco

Ladewig, Sandy, flight attendant 24 years with Continental, based in Houston

Lagle, Gina, flight attendant 2 1/2 years with National, based in Las Vegas

Lam-Genova, Cindy, flight attendant 27 years with Hawaiian, based in Los Angeles

Lampel, Mark, flight attendant 25 years with Pan Am/Delta, based in New York

Lawson, Tammi, flight attendant 13 years with American, based in New York

Leber, Jerry, pilot 6 years with United, based in Chicago

Li, Dokeng, flight attendant 4 years with United, based in Miami

Lin, Henry, flight attendant 11 years with United, based in New York

Linder, Kristine, flight attendant 10 years with American, based in San Jose

Linder, Manuela, flight attendant 3 1/2 years with Swissair, based in Zurich

Lipinski, Greg, pilot 6 years with United, based in Chicago

Liu, Harry, flight attendant 21 years with Pan Am/Delta, based in Portland

Logan, Shannon, flight attendant 30 years with Pan Am/Delta, based in New York

Lozada, Roberto, flight attendant 10 years with Delta, based in New York

Lui-Kwan, Alex, flight attendant 17 years with Hawaiian, based in Honolulu

Lukasik, Steve, flight attendant 8 years with United, based in San Francisco

Mackey, Anita, flight attendant 38 years with TWA, based in New York

Macmillan, Gean, flight attendant 8 years with British Airways, based in London

Malone, Chase, flight attendant 36 years with United, based in Chicago

Marston, Kathy, flight attendant 18 years with TWA, based in Los Angeles

Martinez, Marty, flight attendant 13 years with American, based in Chicago

Martisius, Eric, retired pilot, 22 years with Eastern, 2 years with Evergreen International, and 8 years with EVA, based in Los Angeles

Martisius, Janice, flight attendant with American, based in Los Angeles

May, Joyce, pilot, 20 years with American, based in New York

Mazerolles, Marie Helene, flight attendant 25 years with Air France, based in Paris

McCartney, Robert, pilot with Continental and former flight attendant 5 years with Jet America and Alaska, based in Newark

McClenghan, Marci, flight attendant 32 years with United, based in Los Angeles

McDermott, Diane, flight attendant 11 years with United, based in San Francisco

McDonough, Kathleen, flight attendant 30 years with Pan Am/ Delta, based in New York

McKeon, John, pilot 3 years with National, based in Las Vegas

McKeon, Mary, flight attendant 19 years with America West, based in Phoenix

McLynn, Mavis, flight attendant 15 years with US Airways, based in Philadelphia

Meese, Grant, flight attendant 8 years with Air New Zealand, based in Auckland

Michael, Marsha, flight attendant 30 years with Pan Am/Delta, based in New York

Miller, Judith, flight attendant 6 years with Frontier, based in Denver

Mitchell, Linda, flight attendant 35 years with Pan Am/United, based in Los Angeles

Mitchell, Mike, pilot 6 1/2 years with United, based in Chicago

Miyadate, Masaki, flight attendant 14 years with American, based in San Francisco

Montiel, Maria, flight attendant 39 years with Pan Am/Delta, based in New York

Moraitis, Alexandra, flight attendant 4 years with Delta, based in New York

Moreno, Adalberto "Bert," flight attendant 15 years with Continental, based in Houston

Morgan, James, flight attendant 2 1/2 years with National, based in Las Vegas

Mudaliar, Sharda, flight attendant with Air Pacific, based in Suva

Muehlmann, Frank, pilot 11 years with Crossair/Swissair, based in Zurich

Nehlsen, Rebecca, flight attendant 13 years with United, based in Las Vegas

Nielson, Elizabeth, flight attendant 9 1/2 years with United, based in Chicago

Norton, Keely, flight attendant 5 years with American, based in Dallas

Norton, Laurie, flight attendant 24 years with Northwest, based in Detroit

Orchard, Sandra, flight attendant 41 years with American, based in Los Angeles

O'Sullivan, Eleanor, flight attendant 1 year with TWA, based in New York

Ozawa, Debbie, flight attendant 27 years with Aloha, based in Honolulu

Pearsall, John, pilot 21 years with National, based in Las Vegas

Perez, Edward, flight attendant 14 years with Pan Am/Delta, based in Atlanta

Peterson, Brad, pilot $2\frac{1}{2}$ years with Big Sky, based in Billings

Phillips, June, flight attendant 22 years with Eastern, based in Atlanta, Miami, and New Orleans

Piccolo, Denise, flight attendant $1\frac{1}{2}$ years with Jet Blue, based in New York

Pretorius, Karen, flight attendant 5 years with South African Airways, based in Johannesburg

Proffitt, Vince, pilot $2\frac{1}{2}$ years with Comair, based in Cincinnati

Psyk, Sue, flight attendant 37 years with Northwest, based in Minneapolis

Pulskamp, Bonnie, flight attendant 37 years with American, based in Los Angeles

Ramey, Kim, flight attendant 16 years with American, based in Los Angeles

Ramirez, Jaime, flight attendant 1 year with Jet Blue, based in New York

Reid, Connie, flight attendant 19 years with Northwest, based in Minneapolis

Renon, Marc, flight attendant 13 years with Air France, based in Paris

Renwick, Peggy, flight attendant 23 years with Northwest, based in Detroit

Robbins, Mark, pilot 35 years with United, based in Los Angeles

Roberts, Chris, pilot 12 years with American, based in Los Angeles

Robinson, Carrie, flight attendant 10 years with United, based in Los Angeles

Robinson, Dwight, flight attendant 3 years with Delta, based in New York

Robinson, Penny, flight attendant 33 years with United, based in Los Angeles

Roman-Matos, Migdalia, flight attendant 13 years with Delta, based in New York

Rutili-Lemer, Emily, flight attendant 36 years with TWA, based in New York

Sanders, Billy, flight attendant 4 years with United, based in Oakland

Sapone, Ken, flight attendant 10 years with United, based in San Francisco

Scarborough, Gay, flight attendant with American, based in Los Angeles

Schamburger, Sharon, flight attendant 8 years with United, based in Los Angeles

Schlatter, Renee, flight attendant 16 years with Delta, based in Los Angeles

Schraner, Manuela, flight attendant 7 years with Swissair, based in Zurich

Scott, Sandy, flight attendant 41 years with American, based in Los Angeles

Serralta, Ann Marie, flight attendant 32 years with Pan Am/Delta, based in New York

Shahruri, Rima, flight attendant 1¹/₂ years with Royal Jordanian, based in Amman

Sheriff, Mary Beth, flight attendant 8 years with Continental, based in Newark

Sherk, Carolina, flight attendant 34 years with TWA, based in Los Angeles

Sinclair, Bill, flight attendant 1¹/₂ years with America West, based in Phoenix

Smith, Sandra, flight attendant 35 years with Pan Am/United, based in Los Angeles

Snyder, Scott, pilot 13 years with Northwest, based in Detroit

Solomon, Scott, pilot 1¹/₂ years with American Eagle/Atlantic Southeast, based in Dallas

Sommer, Patricia, flight attendant 22 years with Pan Am/Delta, based in New York

Spencer, Patricia, flight attendant 25 years with American, based in New York

Spies, Mindy, flight attendant 11 years with United, based in Chicago

Stanfield, Marni, fight attendant 32 years with Pan Am/United, based in Los Angeles

Stanley, Steven, flight attendant 21 years with Delta, based in New Orleans

Steinberg, Paul, pilot 12 years with American, based in Los Angeles

Steocklin, Eric, flight attendant 10 years with Swissair, based in Zurich

Stephenson, Walter, flight attendant 18 years with American, based in Miami

Strahm, Terry, flight attendant 3 years with Frontier, based in Denver

Sullivan, Peggy, flight attendant 25 years with American, based in Los Angeles

Tamura, Colleen, flight attendant 17 years with American, based in Honolulu

Teresi, Gwynn, flight attendant 6 years with American, based in Dallas

Thampidoksutti, Natchai "Kat," flight attendant 2 years with JAL, based in Bangkok

Thompson, Lissa, flight attendant 25 years with American, based in Los Angeles

Thompson, Nikki, flight attendant 6 years with American, based in Dallas

Travaillour, Andre, flight attendant 7 years with Swissair, based in Zurich

Travaillour, Jasmin, flight attendant 6 years with Swissair, based in Zurich

Uribe, Kathy, flight attendant 37 years with Continental, based in Houston

Vaquilar, Eileen, flight attendant 23 years with American, based in New York

Vascellaro, Angela, pilot 16 years with Continental, based in Houston

Vaughan, Cindy, flight attendant 20 years with American, based in Chicago

Watkins, Woody, flight attendant 33 years with American, based in Chicago

Wilkinson, Mark, pilot 2½ years with United, based in Los Angeles

Williams, Ailsa, flight attendant 28 years with Pan Am/Delta, based in New York

Williams, Monica, flight attendant 2 years with Jet Blue, based in New York

Willis, Linne, flight attendant 17 years with Hawaiian, based in Los Angeles

Withaeger, Rosemary, flight attendant 20 years with Northwest, based in Detroit

Worley, Ali, flight attendant 12 years with British Airways, based in London

Wredenfors, Eva, flight attendant 34 years with Pan Am/Delta, based in New York

Yamamoto, Randy, flight attendant 17 years with Northwest, based in Toronto

Yoosik, Ni, flight attendant 2 years with JAL, based in Bangkok

Young, Bob, pilot 25 years with Continental, based in Newark

INDEX

ABOUT THE AUTHOR

Peter Greenberg is the travel editor of NBC's *Today* show and the author of *The Travel Detective*. He is also the chief correspondent for the Discovery Network's Travel Channel, and editor at large for *National Geographic Traveler* magazine. He appears regularly on *Oprah*.

ABOUT THE TYPE

This book was set in Caslon, a typeface first designed in 1722 by William Caslon. Its widespread use by most English printers in the early eighteenth century soon supplanted the Dutch typefaces that had formerly prevailed. The roman is considered a "workhorse" typeface due to its pleasant, open appearance, while the italic is exceedingly decorative.